HIS OWN MAN
The Life of Neville Cardus

His Own Man

THE LIFE OF
NEVILLE CARDUS

Christopher Brookes

METHUEN

To
my family and J.D.P.

First published in Great Britain 1985
by Methuen London Ltd
11 New Fetter Lane, London EC4P 4EE
Copyright © 1985 Christopher Brookes
Reproduced, printed and bound in Great Britain by
Hazell Watson & Viney Limited,
Member of the BPCC Group,
Aylesbury, Bucks

British Library Cataloguing in Publication Data
Brookes, Christopher
  His own man: the life of Neville Cardus.
  1. Cardus, Neville 2. Journalists——Great
Britain——Biography
  I. Title
  780'.8'50924   PN5123.C28
  ISBN 0-413-50940-0

CONTENTS

ILLUSTRATIONS

Acknowledgments and thanks are due to Else Mayer-Lismann for plates 1a, 1b, 3c, 5c, 6a, 6b, 7a; to Margaret Hughes for plates 2b, 3a; to Marjorie Robinson for plates 4a, 4b, 5b; to Angus McLachlan for plate 5a; to Shrewsbury School for plate 2a; to the *Daily Express* for plate 7b; to the *Guardian* for plates 3c, 8; to Fox Photos for plate 4c and to Manchester Central Library for plate 1c.

ACKNOWLEDGMENTS

In the course of preparing this book I have met, or have spoken to, many of Sir Neville's oldest friends and closest associates. Not only was their advice invaluable and unhesitatingly given, but their company was always a source of great personal pleasure. Space prevents me from recording all their names, but I would like to take this opportunity to acknowledge my debt to the following: Professor Peter Daniel, Alfred Francis, Peter Cotes, Marjorie Robinson and Peter Cory, Sir Donald Bradman, Harold and Gladys Priestley, Ronald Weitzman, Sir Clifford Curzon, Michael Kennedy, Angus McLachlan, Sir Rupert Hart-Davis, Muriel Cohen, J. L. Holmes, Sir James Colyer-Fergusson, Desmond Shawe-Taylor and Lindsey Browne.

I have also been greatly helped by advice on musical matters from Dr Derrick Wright and John Coblenz; by the assistance of Mark Jones of the BBC Sound Archives Library; and by the encouragement and practical support of my family.

I would like to record my particular gratitude to Else Mayer-Lismann and Margaret Hughes. The support they have given to me over the past five years is an eloquent statement of their enduring love for Sir Neville.

Lastly I would like to express my sincere thanks to Christopher Falkus, whose idea the book was, and without whose unfailing understanding it would not have been completed.

Prologue

[I]

Walking down Baker Street in the general direction of Portman Square, the chances are that most people wouldn't notice a small, unprepossessing restaurant on the left. Provided their senses have not been irreparably dulled by the tedium of office life or the mesmeric properties of the nearby Planetarium, they will be searching subconsciously for a master detective and his congenial companion: such is the legend of this particular thoroughfare. Yet sandwiched between a betting shop and an establishment specialising in the sale of Mary Quant tights, and apparently eschewing any association with *haute cuisine*, is the London Steak House. One of hundreds spawned during the 1960s, and unlikely ever to grace the pages of Michelin, this eating place seems entirely content with its station in life, its very existence testifying to the enduring appeal of solid, unpretentious food for a population of whom the majority rarely, if ever, stray above the foothills of epicurean adventure.

Unlikely though it may seem, there is one respect in which this restaurant is totally unique. Not long ago a worthy citizen of Manchester, Mr Harold Priestley, suggested to its proprietor that an effort should be made to honour the memory of a loyal customer who had recently died. What Mr Priestley had in mind, and was willing to provide, was a framed photograph of the person in question, to be hung on the wall above his favourite table. The suggestion was gratefully accepted and a suitable photograph duly framed, presented and hung.

The subject of this unlikely honour was Sir Neville Cardus, long-time music critic and cricket correspondent of the *Manchester Guardian*,* writer, broadcaster and raconteur *par excellence*. But a short step from the flat – 22, Bickenhall Mansions – where he spent the last seven years of his life, the London Steak House had become a favourite rendezvous as old age took its toll of Sir Neville's energies. Looking back, it also represented a final staging-post in an odyssey which had begun in Manchester some eighty or so years before. Like an ageing warrior recalling past campaigns, Sir Neville looked upon those evenings at the Steak House as an ideal opportunity to take his friends back on a guided tour through the outstanding memories of his career, imbuing each with that restless, romantic enthusiasm which had propelled this lad from Rusholme through the music and cricket capitals of the world before finally coming to rest in London.

Sir Neville Cardus died on Friday, 28 February 1975, at the Nuffield Hospital to which he had been moved, much against his wishes, a few days earlier after suffering what was variously described as a 'collapse', 'stroke' and 'fall' at his flat the previous weekend.

As it happened, Sir Neville was unusually well acquainted with the prospect of death. Glancing through an edition of a Buckinghamshire paper some years earlier, he had been slightly taken aback to read an account of his own demise. When asked to comment, he responded in characteristic vein, 'I have no wish to challenge the authority of the press. They must know something.'

And indeed the press reacted swiftly to the announcement of Sir Neville's death. First into the field (or graveyard), the *Manchester Evening News* devoted front, middle and back-page columns to Sir Neville as its reporters strove to capture the significance of his

* Though Sir Neville always thought of himself as a *Manchester Guardian* man, his career spanned a period of great change in the identity and format of the paper. By the time he died, the *M.G.* had a new name, a much-altered lay-out, and was published in a different place. In his excellent *Guardian: Biography of a Newspaper* (London, 1971), David Ayerst recounted how Laurence Scott's post-war programme for change incorporated three major innovations: (i) news on the front page (first introduced on 29 September 1952); (ii) dropping 'Manchester' from the title (24 August 1959) and (iii) printing in London (from 11 September 1960).

achievements. It is a measure of their success that readers that night were left in no doubt about the importance of Cardus's contribution to the world of music criticism, though establishing his rightful hierarchical status within that world proved to be more difficult. 'Cardus, King of Critics' was the verdict of a staff reporter, whilst for John Kay he was a mere 'knight of the pen'. Be that as it may, John Robert-Blum spoke for everyone when he concluded that Cardus 'had become one of the world's great critics' and, as such, 'an inspiration to millions'.

Of course music was only one of the spheres in which Sir Neville had excelled. Many would argue that his reporting of cricket matches was of even greater significance. For Geoffrey Mather, for example, Cardus was simply 'the man who made cricket his own', while for John Beaven, writing in that most popular of tabloids, the *Daily Mirror*, he was 'the greatest cricket writer and most enchanting music critic of his time'.

In public as well as in private, Sir Neville was inclined to belittle his achievements. To be paid to watch cricket at Lord's in the afternoon and hear Lotte Lehmann as Strauss's Marschallin in the evening, he used to say, was nothing less than an act of Providence. Whatever the explanation, his admirers were quick to point out that Cardus's writing added a new dimension to such occasions. Like a good brandy, he helped audiences digest the past and savour the future. It was left to J. W. Lambert to pinpoint the quintessential Cardus. Offering the *Sunday Times's* tribute, he wrote of Sir Neville that

> he treated his cricket and his music, his pleasure in wine and beautiful women, as a civilised man should: they were vital elements in a full life, never the subject of bleak adjudication in a void.

The most balanced assessment of Cardus's career was provided by Michael Kennedy in the *Daily Telegraph*. A fellow music critic and writer, Kennedy began his obituary by acknowledging his old friend's achievement in raising 'sports reporting to the status of an art form', and went on to record the following tribute:

> His descriptions of cricket and cricketers rank among the most distinguished examples of the English essay. His flair for the

telling phrase which caught the fleeting moment and gave it a permanence never deserted him.

Had Neville done no more than report cricket matches his place in history would have been secure. But, as Kennedy went on to explain, cricket was but a prelude to a greater love – music. In this, the *ne plus ultra* of all art forms, his emotional and aesthetic antennae became most highly attuned, and hence his empathic understanding most profound. By developing an ability to communicate his own appreciation of Wagner, Strauss, Elgar, Delius and, above all, Mahler, he gave to British audiences an insight into the *spirit* of composition and performance such as had never previously existed.

That the *Daily Telegraph* should have carried perhaps the most thoughtful of tributes to Sir Neville was not purely coincidental nor, it has to be said, was it entirely due to Michael Kennedy's own efforts. As was his wont, Cardus was determined to have the last word – albeit posthumously. Kennedy recalls how he once told Sir Neville, when the latter was still at his prime (i.e. around 1969!), that he had been drafting his obituary. 'Please send me a proof,' Cardus requested, 'as I shan't have the pleasure of reading it when it appears.' This Kennedy did, and received by return of post a series of factual corrections.

No matter how shrewd or generous other tributes to Sir Neville may have been, it was inevitable that most of his friends and readers would turn to the *Guardian* for the final word. For many music- and cricket-lovers the world over Cardus *was* the *Manchester Guardian*; few would doubt that as 'N.C.' and 'Cricketer', he had for years been one of the paper's biggest attractions. In terms of column space, the *Guardian* certainly rose to the occasion. The formal obituary which appeared on page six under the heading 'Sir Neville Cardus – creative critic of international fame', spread over eight columns before concluding that he 'was one of the two most internationally renowned journalists the *Guardian* has produced this century'. Though the identity of the co-recipient of this accolade remains a closely guarded secret, Cardus's qualities were not as elusive. Repeating the familiar 'two strings to his bow' theme, the writer ventured the opinion that while 'a love of each of these activities (cricket and music) is not unusual . . . the ability to write about each with peculiar distinction is rare'. In a passage which must have missed appearing in 'Pseuds Corner' by only the shortest of short heads, the piece concludes that Cardus's genius derived from the fact that the conjunction of music and cricket 'satisfied a late romantic urge to respond in words to visual and aural stimuli, to match the drama of action or of music in his own words. It was a satisfying form of power, perhaps.'

A few pages later came the heart of the *Guardian*'s response. J. B. Priestley recalled the man himself; Hugo Cole discussed his place in the tradition of music criticism, and John Arlott assessed his contribution to cricket literature. Each in their own way highlighted aspects of Sir Neville's mystique. For Priestley,

> he was at heart a modest man, always determined to go his own way, be himself but never puffed with pride about that way and that self . . . a superb all-round writer who could write equally well about pantomime and Paderewski . . . a member of a natural élite, one who did it all himself outside the embrace of the State and the local education authorities.

But Priestley's assessment is not wholly laudatory. In an extremely perceptive aside, he recalls how on the last page of his autobiography Cardus claimed that 'it is only in the arts that I have found the only religion that is real and once found omnipresent'. 'No doubt,' rejoins Priestley,

> but while, God knows, I would not have had him waste a morning and a couple of paragraphs on party politics, he might have remembered that the arts do not exist in mid-air, that we have to give some thought to the society in which these arts flourish or wither. However deeply felt, the aesthetic creed is not enough.

Acknowledging that this was only a minor blemish, Priestley proceeds to a final statement which, for its insight and eloquence, deserves to be quoted in full.

> As few men I have known have done, he turned himself into his own man, sensitive, eloquent, golden-hearted in his shared enjoyment of every good thing that came his way, a man who brought style and nobility to his daily journalism, who has left

us in his books so much to sustain us through a bewildering menacing time. Here was – and still is – a superbly talented brave soul.

Not untypically, the *Guardian*'s compositors managed to impose their own unique stamp on his distinguished prose. In a passage in which Priestley assesses the effect of Cardus's stay in Australia, their concentration wavered – with fatal results! 'Those thousands of miles away from home brought *death* to his writing and height to his stature as a writer.' (Italics my own.)

Hugo Cole fared better. Expressing in a more understandable form part of the message of the paper's obituary, he explained how Sir Neville's 'genius in handling words and his ability to put something of his own inimitable character into all he wrote gave him the power to translate his own enjoyment and appreciation of music to large non-specialist audiences'. As possibly the last distinguished music critic never to have received any formal musical training, Cardus 'at his finest and most spontaneous . . . made us hear music through his ears and receive the message as he received it: which was not necessarily as other well brought-up listeners would have heard it'.

John Arlott, a close personal friend of Sir Neville's as well as a co-author, immediately put his finger on Cardus's contribution to the realm of cricket literature. Whereas, Arlott wrote, 'his other subjects had all been regularly treated by literature writers . . . cricket, sport in general, had not had that benefit'. He was

the first writer to evoke cricket; to create a mythology out of the folk hero players; essentially to put the feelings of ordinary cricket watchers into words. . . . There can never be a greater cricket writer than Neville Cardus. He created it. Others performed what he showed them. There is not one of his juniors who has not been affected by him, and a few who have not, shamelessly, copied him.

There remained the leader, the editor's own tribute to one of his paper's most renowned employees. At first sight, the piece seemed harmless enough. Taking consistency, clarity and breadth of vision to be the hallmarks of a great critic, the writer confirmed that there was no disputing Sir Neville's right to such an accolade. Uninspiring though this may have been, there was as yet little to which one might take exception. But the third paragraph was a different matter. Addressing itself to the theme enunciated in its title – 'The debt to Neville Cardus' – the leader ventured the opinion that 'the *Guardian* owes much to Neville Cardus' and acknowledged that 'for the paper itself his death is a sad moment'. But, it continued, 'to our benefit, and we believe to his, he had a long innings'. Whatever prompted this observation, it was to say the least ill-judged not least because the *Guardian*'s seemingly unsympathetic treatment of Cardus towards the end of his life had long been a source of dismay to many of his friends.

Barely a week had passed before Lunchtime O'Booze in *Private Eye* launched a frontal assault on both the 'miserly, non-conformist businessmen of the *Guardian*' and their 'repulsive leader'. However justified the criticism may have been, the timing and language of the article were badly misjudged. Neville himself would never have approved. Fierce criticism, even outright condemnation, was acceptable and often necessary but crude, vitriolic outbursts were not his style. *Con brio*, often and with great effect; *con clamore* never. Far from igniting the collective wrath of Cardus devotees the world over, it succeeded only in aggravating the suffering of his friends.

Distressing though the *Private Eye* episode undoubtedly was, when seen against the broad background of Sir Neville's life and work it warrants only the briefest of mentions. Whatever the truth behind the various accusations that the *Guardian* had treated him badly, the fact remains that for most of his life Cardus remained largely oblivious to arguments about 'fair pay', 'just rewards', 'adequate pensions' and the like. His relationship with the *Manchester Guardian* did not depend on such considerations: to him it was a mystical union, born of admiration and ambition; a union which transcended all worldly calculations and was thus immune to their divisive influence. 'A dear tyrant, the *M.G.*,' he once wrote, 'I have never been able to break free from it.' And he never did. The disillusionment of his later years was not brought about by a belated recognition of past injustices, no matter how iniquitous these may have been. His frustration and anger were born of a sense of loss. They were the reactions of an old man raging 'against the dying of the light'. The '*M.G.*', as he had known it, was no more. In the twilight of his career, he had to come to terms with its motley successor, the *Guardian*, whose masters he saw as betraying a great tradition, and whose pages bore the savage imprint of a new species of predatory sub-editor.

Whether by accident or design, these remained essentially private matters during Sir Neville's lifetime. Encased in volumes of gilded autobiography, the memory of the poor, short-sighted bastard from Rusholme passed into folklore, there to stand as a timely reminder of the enduring virtues of ambition, determination and self-help. And with these qualities enjoying such a spectacular revival in political circles, Sir Neville may soon become a strong candidate for early canonisation.

Death itself might have been expected to signal a major reappraisal of Sir Neville's achievements. All the ingredients for a grand debunking session were present: a larger-than-life reputation silhouetted against the back-drop of a fiercely competitive profession. What better way for a young journalist to launch a career than to indulge in a spot of irreverent character assassination? To the surprise of many of his friends and colleagues, Sir Neville's reputation has thus far survived his death without too much difficulty. There has of course been some sporadic sniping. *Telegraph* readers in Eastbourne have long complained that Cardus's descriptions of cricket matches left the reader enamoured of the spectacle but entirely ignorant of its outcome, while, in similar vein, disciples of a rival school of music criticism never tire of pointing out that though Sir Neville may have possessed a unique ability to convey the spirit of music, his grasp of the finer points of technique and composition left much to be desired. Neither criticism is without substance: each could easily be made the basis of a general critique of Cardus's work. But as yet the legions of professional iconoclasts who hover like vultures over the obituary columns of the quality press have refrained from directing their fire in his direction. And, as if to answer those who doubted the resilience of his reputation, Sir Neville is today very much in vogue. To the consternation of pipe-smoking, tweed-jacketed gentlemen from Guildford to Gravesend, even the *Daily Telegraph* recently carried a reference to 'the immortal Cardus' in its report of a particularly dreary Roses match.

To advance such a claim is doubtless to tempt fate. Yet the fact remains that a most colourful reputation, established many years ago in a very different world, has thus far stood the test of time. In part, the secret lies in the quality of the work on which it is based. Leaving aside all the arguments about the merits of his personal style of commentary and criticism, there can be little doubting his status within the English-speaking world as one of the finest exponents of that tradition. The ease and precision with which he distilled and disseminated the essence of performances on pitch and platform alike gives the lie to the élitist notion that artistic appreciation is of necessity an intellectual aptitude. Like it or not, his columns not only brought 'established' music to a wider audience than ever before, but also championed the inclusion in British concert programmes of a whole range of new works. As 'Cricketer', he alone was responsible for transforming the reporting of first-class cricket from a dull, mechanical recitation of facts and figures into a vivid literary medium. And if, at the end of his career, he tended to dwell on the great figures of his youth, the beguiling richness of his language and imagery provided ample compensation for any loss of detail thus incurred.

In this respect, Cardus may have been exceptionally fortunate in the timing, if not the circumstances, of his birth. In recent years, reactions to the Proustian flavour in his writing have subtly changed. Where once his reverence for the great figures of the past was treated as an occasionally irritating idiosyncrasy, today this same trait elicits a far more sympathetic response. Dangerous though comparisons with the past may be, looking back over his *Guardian* columns it is tempting to conclude that the performances he attended in Manchester, London, Vienna and Salzburg before the outbreak of war in 1939 were better than those on offer today. Certainly, an expensive visit to one of the all too frequently under-rehearsed and poorly conceived productions at Covent Garden does little to disprove this suspicion.

Timing apart, the circumstances of Cardus's birth could hardly have been less propitious. Born within a stone's throw of a great cultural heritage, yet separated from it, as he would have it, by the entire social span of Victorian England, he seemed destined to succumb to the stultifying rigidities of a class-bound society. All the ability in the world counts for nothing as long as circumstances conspire to deny it a means of expression. That Sir Neville managed not only to educate himself but also, against all the odds, to find an outlet for his talents is testament to more than the happy quirks of fate to which, in later years, he liked to attribute his success. In overcoming the disadvantages of his early years – the 'struggle' described in the first of his autobiographies – Cardus developed a character which embraced both exceptional sensitivity and resilience. Forged originally as a defence against the impact of 'those endless streets that stretched away in a static, lean, dreary hopelessness', this combination became for him a lifelong source of energy, ambition, enthusiasm and compassion.

[II]

The circumstances of his birth provided an ideal setting for another classic encounter between adversity and ambition, a point lost neither on Sir Neville when he came to write his autobiographies, nor on his friends when they came to review his life and work. Few of their pieces omitted some reference to his murky origins. Bill Grundy, for example, recalled 'the boy born in a Manchester slum [who] grew up in the worst area of Manchester during one of Manchester's worst times'. The standard format then included references to Cardus's non-existent father, mysterious mother and flamboyant aunt, as well as his exploits delivering laundry, selling chocolate and pushing a joiner's cart. At this point, the magic ingredients of ambition and luck are added and, lo and behold, metamorphosis – Sir Neville Cardus, music critic of international renown, journalist and cricket reporter *par excellence*. What had begun life as part of Fleet Street folklore thus attained the status of biographical fact: a legend had been authenticated by default and sanctified *in absentia*.

No one was to blame. There was no suggestion of deception, obfuscation or collusion, nor should the absence of any subsequent reassessment be taken as evidence of a conspiracy of silence. The truth of the matter was that a spell had been cast many years before when a master raconteur had begun to tell his own story. From that moment Neville Cardus became a biographer's nightmare. This may seem a harsh criticism to level at a man who had lovingly crafted three volumes of autobiography,* but a brief glance at any of these works will suffice to show that they were never conceived as reference books. Largely eschewing dates and background information,

---

* *Autobiography*, written in Sydney when he was in his fifties and published in 1947, *Second Innings* (1950) and *Full Score* (1970).

they convey the spirit rather than the anatomy of his life. Parts of *Autobiography* create the impression of a man seeking a past before it was too late. Enjoying both the exercise and the end-product, Cardus could not refrain from repeating the experience, in *Second Innings* and *Full Score*.

For all their literary merits, the full significance of his autobiographies lies elsewhere. They are biographical facts in their own right. 'A well-written life,' Thomas Carlyle once wrote, 'is almost as rare as a well-spent one.' In Sir Neville's case, not only were both conditions satisfied, but they were mutually sustaining: the quality of the one being both a cause and consequence of the other. Autobiography was for him as much a voyage of self-discovery as an exercise in historical reconstruction. He used the medium to combine, extend and burnish the collective image of 'N.C.' and 'Cricketer' and, far from being disconcerted by those who criticised his approach to autobiography as little more than unbridled self-indulgence, he positively revelled in the freedom it gave him. When, for example, his Aunt Beatrice's daughter complained that he had 'made my mother seem a prostitute', Sir Neville retorted, 'On the contrary, my dear, I've put her into great literature.'

Cardus never attempted to disguise his intentions in writing *Autobiography*, nor the audience it was intended for. Midway through the book he wrote,

> Interest in autobiography should begin at home, and though I hope to present my life and its setting attractively, my chief intent is to delight and engross myself. A modest or inhibited autobiography is written without entertainment to the writer and read with distrust by the reader. An autobiography should suggest that the writer is living his life again, day to day, year to year. . . . An autobiography is not a biography: on every page, the reader must be persuaded to think that what's to come is still unsure.[1]

By providing Cardus with the opportunity to re-explore his history, *Autobiography* became a crucial milestone in the journey it recounted. That in the course of tracing the development of his personality, Sir Neville – perhaps unwittingly – should be party to the creation of an *alter ego* was the predictable outcome of the mode of autobiographical writing he adopted. By constructing a complex identity, the elusive chemistry of which was known only to its creator, *Autobiography* both substantiated a legend and unleashed a devastating pre-emptive strike at the would-be biographer. Trollope himself could not have imagined a more dutiful adherence to the advice once offered by the admirable Doctor Thorne: 'In these days a man is nobody unless his biography is kept so far posted up that it may be ready for the national breakfast table on the morning of his demise.'

Whether Cardus conceived of his *Autobiography* in quite these terms – as a means, that is, of distilling greatness from what might otherwise have been remembered only as a source of passing pleasure – we will never know. But it was clearly no accident that the book was written twelve thousand miles from home. Sydney was in many respects the ideal setting in which to carry out the task he had set himself. Surrounded by first- and second-generation Australians whose origins as often as not were as modest as his own, Cardus succeeded in escaping the inhibiting memories of his childhood, and the occasional diffidence which was their legacy. Here he could order his past as he wished, persuading the reader at every turn that 'what's to come is still unsure' – as indeed it frequently was – yet never leaving him in any doubt as to the ultimate success of the mission. Nor was it a coincidence that, in terms of both substance and style, *Autobiography* stands head and shoulders above its sequels. Written when Cardus was at the height of his powers, the story of the 'uneducated boy who became comfortably off without once consciously working to make money' left an impression which neither *Second Innings* nor *Full Score* could match. By the time the latter appeared in 1970, the combined effects of *anno domini* and repetition had drained the original tale of much of its intrinsic fascination. It was a case of having visited the well too often. The rich seam of memory, imagination and humour was close to exhaustion: what remained seemed by comparison little more than a residue of stylistic artifice.

Autobiography is most revealing of Cardus when it is considered as a work of art. Henry Havelock Ellis made the point most succinctly when he noted that 'every artist writes his own autobiography'. Cardus used the autobiographical medium both to recount his personal history and, more importantly, to discover a fresh view of humanity. As the latter aim comes to the fore, so the text begins to stray from the conventional byways of autobiography. Instead of allowing his past to emerge as a stream of objective fact, Cardus often resorts to intuition, firstly to sustain a more vivid image of his life and times but thereafter to evoke a fleeting glimpse of a higher order of experience.

It is impossible to miss the traces of nineteenth-century central European aestheticism in all this. During the 1930s, Cardus became almost intoxicated with the likes of Kant and Goethe. Later, tucked away in a small, sweaty flat in Sydney, he seized upon the opportunity provided by *Autobiography* to apply some of their lofty aesthetic notions to his own past history. From the Olympian detachment of his role as narrator, Cardus argues that there is in effect no such thing as objective vision. Once we, the readers, have entered into his perspective, we are obliged to look at the world through his eyes. However unfamiliar and perplexing this view may be, we are persuaded that it represents more than a momentary vision: as a product of his own artistic intuition, it has become durable and permanent. It is an interpretation of reality, based not on concepts but on intuition, and generated not through cognition but through the aesthetic impulse of sensuous forms. 'Art', wrote Goethe,

> does not undertake to emulate nature in its breadth and depth. It sticks to the surface of natural phenomena; but it has its own depth, its own power; it crystallises the highest of these superficial phenomena by recognising in them the character of lawfulness, the perfection of harmonious proportion, the summit of beauty, the dignity, the height of passion.

Not to be outdone, Cardus takes the opportunity in the last paragraph of *Autobiography* to express his own version of the aesthetic creed.

> For the Kingdom of Heaven is there: it is in the arts that I have found the only religion that is real and, once found, omnipresent. . . . Without creative urge and imagination man would be less than animals. There is for me no accounting in terms of evolution or survival-value for the sense of beauty, for laughter and tears that come and go without material prompting, for the ache after the perfect form and the ineluctable vision. If I know that my Redeemer liveth it is not on the Church's testimony but because of what Handel affirms. As

Jowett put it to Margot: 'My dear child, you must believe in God in spite of what the clergy may tell you.'

Uneven is perhaps the fairest description of reactions to this metaphysical excursion. By closing on such a mystical note *Autobiography* succeeded in bemusing admirers and critics alike, neither being utterly sure what it all meant. As for the general reader, he was left merely wondering. With Cardus still at the height of his powers, there was no telling where the next volume might lead. The more cynical of his admirers may have detected a devilishly subtle marketing strategy at hand, and though it is hard to imagine Sir Neville being party to such a strategy the subsequent publication of two further volumes of autobiography testified to the continuing demand for his writings. In the event, neither *Second Innings* – Cardus's own favourite, but described by one reviewer as a 'slim volume' – nor *Full Score* succeeded in recapturing the intrinsic fascination of *Autobiography*. The weakness of these volumes left a biographical vacuum which Robin Daniels's collection of recorded conversations with Sir Neville, published after his death, did little to fill.

Eight years after his death, it would appear at first sight as if little had changed. Cardus's professional reputation remains as high as ever, whilst his public continue to know little more of the man himself than he chose to reveal. Though highly coloured and often shrouded in confusing aesthetic mist, those handpicked details so painstakingly pieced together nearly forty years ago remain the *fons et origo* of conventional wisdom. Strange though this may seem, there is at least a suggestion of a plausible explanation at hand. In the first place, only the incurable optimist or insufferable egotist would have tried to upstage a work as distinctive as *Autobiography*, particularly while its author was still alive and kicking. Secondly, to have produced a worthy alternative would have required new material which it is doubtful that Cardus himself would have been willing or able to provide.

During the twenty-eight years which elapsed between the publication of *Autobiography* and his death, Sir Neville grew very attached to the identity which he had created for himself. A full-blown biography, no matter how sympathetically handled, could not have avoided presenting certain aspects of his life in a different light. To an old man, particularly one who derived such pleasure from recounting tales from his past, such a prospect must have seemed a doubtful privilege. But however much Cardus may have baulked at the thought of biographical dissection, to the potential publisher who believed, probably correctly, that as far as most of Sir Neville's followers were concerned there were very few details of their hero's life 'worth talking about that had not already been recorded in his own volumes of autobiography', it was the cold, hard logic of supply and demand which counted most heavily against such a project. The likelihood of the resulting book commanding much of a market was sufficiently remote to dissuade even the most enthusiastic of commissioning editors

In recent years, however, the position has changed. Even before his death, the basis of Sir Neville's relationship with his public had inevitably begun to shift away from a shared background of cultural, including cricketing, experience. Since 1975 this process has continued uninterrupted to the point at which today the continuing popularity of his works derives mainly from an admiration for their intrinsic quality and a growing curiousity about the man himself. Most people who read Cardus today know little of music and cricket between the wars, let alone in Victorian Lancashire. Ranji, Rhodes, Robey and Richter are at best names plucked from a history book. Yet it was in their shadows that Sir Neville was born and grew up. They fired his imagination and fuelled his ambition. To find the source of his triumphs we must thus return to the scene of theirs.

I

Origins

'. . . but you must fear,
His greatness weigh'd, his will is not his own;
For he himself is subject to his birth.'[1]

[I]

Manchester. Shock city of the age. Landmark in world history. Nursery of the industrial revolution. Forcing house of political and economic liberalism and favourite stomping-ground of its most illustrious advocates. Fountainhead of international trade unionism and host to the first Trade Union Congress. Home of Britain's oldest symphony orchestra and the numerous emigré communities to whose enthusiasm for culture it owed so much. Home too of Lancashire cricket; of MacLaren, Spooner and Tyldesley. Scene of the classic Ashes encounter in 1896; of Victor Trumper's finest hour and poor Fred Tate's worst. Ruskin dubbed the city 'the Venice of the North', and another observer was so impressed by what he saw that he claimed for Manchester the mantle of the city states of antiquity. Though at first sight this may seem a little far-fetched, you need only dwell for a moment and recall the likes of Bright and Cobden, Hallé and Richter and the immortal Hornby and Barlow to see what he meant: unless, that is, you happen to be in the vicinity of the River Irwell and its murky vapours, in which case you'd be lucky to see nearby Ancoats, never mind ancient Rome.

An awesome heritage thus awaited the boy born to Ada Cardus early on the morning of 2 April 1889. This child, christened John Frederick Neville, was to take his mother's maiden name as his surname in adult life, thereby laying the foundation of a delightful farrago of fact and fiction which was eventually to become his legend. Whether young Neville really never knew his father or else decided at a later date to keep the latter's identity a secret remains a tantalising mystery. In *Autobiography*, the gentleman (though the title hardly seems appropriate) warrants only the briefest of mentions: he was, we are told, 'tall, saturnine of countenance and one of the first violins in an orchestra'. Evidently he had other strings to his bow, for his sudden exit from Neville's life came about as a result of a visit 'to the coast of West Africa on "business",' in the course of which 'it was subsequently arranged for him to die'. In this way, the dictates of Victorian morality were satisfied and the natural curiosity of youth stifled.

Though there must have been times, particularly as a child, when Neville found his illegitimacy an embarrassment, for most of his life it was a sin of omission from which he made enormous conversational capital. It was typical of both his humour and his reaction to illegitimacy that on more than one occasion he should have been heard to say of his father: 'In my blackest moments, I think he must have been Toscanini!' The true identity of his father may never be discovered. The more one probes, the deeper the mystery becomes. The absence of any reference to Neville's birth – at least under the name of Cardus – in the official Register is surprising, but not totally inexplicable. The omission could be explained in terms either of his family's ignorance of their legal obligations or of his mother's fear of being labelled an 'abandoned creature' (the conventional epithet for a prostitute). But the tantalising references to his origins scattered about the autobiographical volumes are much harder to make sense of.

In *Autobiography* itself, for example, whilst claiming that he 'never believed the story about my father and West Africa', Cardus implicitly suggests that his Aunt Beatrice succeeded in keeping the truth from him. However, the details recorded on his wedding certificate tell a different story. Here the faceless, tropical entrepreneur reappears in the guise of Frederick Cardus, a civil servant by profession. For the less sceptical amongst his readers who were prepared to accept that Neville's father may have shared the same name as his mother's father, the details contained in various editions of *Who's Who* must have come as a bitter shock. In 1951 Neville described himself as the son of Robert Stanislaw Cardus and Ada Newsome. Robert Cardus was the name of his maternal grandfather, though where Stanislaw came from is anyone's guess.

Ada was certainly his mother's first name, but from which of her consorts she acquired the surname is another matter.

With the issue now totally confused, and that most hallowed of institutions, the nuclear family, shaken to its semi-detached foundations, Neville evidently decided that there was little to be gained and much to be lost from encouraging further salacious speculation about his origins. Thereafter, his contributions to *Who's Who* became increasingly discreet until by the last years of his life only a few anodyne details remained. Under normal circumstances, that would have been the end of the story.

But there are inconsistencies in Cardus's account of his early years. For example, he wrote his mother Ada out of his life in the early pages of *Autobiography*, but in real life she lived until December 1954. In fact, Neville was in Sydney covering the second Australia–England Test match when he received a telegram from the Manchester Branch of Williams and Glyn's Bank, informing him of her death and seeking instructions on how to handle her estate. However rarely he may have seen his mother since the break-up of the family *circa* 1910, to disregard her through the best part of three volumes of autobiography was a strange decision and one which inevitably raises doubts about the accuracy of much of the information they contain. This is particularly true of the paternity issue. It is difficult to believe that at some point in her long life Cardus's mother did not disclose the identity of his father.

Whatever the case, with both mother and father introduced and dismissed in the space of a few pages, the way was clear for Neville to present the other characters who were to figure in his early life. His mother was one of three sisters, each of whom openly and unashamedly graced 'the oldest of professions and became an adornment to it'. As with his illegitimacy, Neville played the nocturnal behaviour of the sisters for all it was worth, with the predictable but unfortunate result that its relevance has been exaggerated and often misunderstood. In the first place, there is no way of telling how often the sisters plied their trade, though from the revelations which accompanied his aunt Beatrice's appearance in court on a breach of promise suit it seems likely that hers was more than an occasional dalliance. Secondly, even if it transpired that both mother and aunts were full-time prostitutes, their behaviour can be interpreted only by the standards of the time.

Then as now, there was a hierarchy of prostitution. The sisters seem to have occupied a status mid-way between the squalid world of the back-street whore and the pampered pleasures of the 'kept woman'. Public attitudes varied according to background, belief and bank balance. Whereas outraged moralists denounced 'abandoned creatures' as a source of corruption and decay, and the mill-owners of Macclesfield prided themselves on sacking girls who 'erred' but once, the urban poor were often obliged to look upon prostitution as one, perhaps the only, way of supplementing their meagre earnings. For the Cardus family and their like, it remained one of the 'winked-at perquisites of the poor'. Others, more mindful perhaps of the pleasures entailed, were content to pursue a policy known in Whitehall as 'principled opposition' – in other words, public condemnation and private enjoyment. Lastly, there were a few misguided souls who, to the great consternation of the Establishment, held the extraordinary opinion that a more tolerant and sympathetic attitude to prostitution and illegitimacy might yield positive social benefits. One witness went so far as to proclaim:

> I find it very generally ... the case that, where the mills and factories are nearly free from mothers of illegitimate children, there the streets are infested with prostitutes; and on the contrary, where the girls are permitted to return to their work, after giving birth to a child, there the streets are kept comparatively clear of these unhappy beings.[2]

Whether Beatrice and her sisters had been driven to prostitution as a last resort is a moot point, but, whatever the reason, Neville was conceived in a spirit of pragmatic realism. When, soon after his birth, his mother realised that pressures of work were likely to prevent her from properly discharging the basic maternal duties, she naturally turned to the other members of her family for support. The people in question were, by any standards, an unusual collection and in retrospect it is perhaps not so surprising that Neville turned out to be the exception he was. His grandfather Robert was a retired police constable who sported a lumpy, scarred cranium to remind himself (and others) of the day many years before when he had crossed truncheons with that notorious, and 'in his day, much respected', criminal, Charles Peace. By the time young Neville appeared on the scene, this loyal custodian of the peace had retired to the security and relative quiet of his own kitchen, there to devote himself to a study of those sources of infinite wisdom, the Bible, his daily newspaper and the racing cards.

Neville's grandmother Ann, like her husband, remains a shadowy figure throughout his memoirs. She was destined to outlive Robert and one of her daughters despite suffering from persistent congestion of the upper respiratory tracts, a condition for which she took creosote and received little sympathy. Cardus tells us that, on the death of his wife, Robert 'put on black clothes and gave up the *Sporting Chronicle Handicap Book* for ever'. Moving though this picture may be, it is based on a strange misconception of the order of their departure. Robert Cardus died on 16 October 1900 at 12, Claremont Street, not more than a mile from Summer Place where Neville spent his childhood. (In pronouncing the cause of death to have been apoplexy, the local doctor, John Scott M.B., was merely following the time-honoured practice in cases where little was known of the deceased except that he had developed a very red face and had lost the power of speech about three days before finally passing away.) And contrary to the impression given in *Autobiography*, Ann Cardus lived until December 1907, by which time she had reached the ripe old age of seventy-two.

Robert and Ann were an ordinary, but slightly unlucky, couple. To have been blessed with three physiologically normal children was usually an occasion for rejoicing, not complaint. But in their case, the fact that all three happened to be girls, at a time when the only work available to the great majority of women was only one step removed from slave labour, hardly augured well for the family's future prosperity. As one of his purposes in writing so much autobiography was to cement the image of distance and detachment which he loved so much, Cardus could hardly have been expected to devote much space to the rest of his family. Even so, the speed with which, in every case bar one, his closest relatives are whisked on and off stage still comes as something of a shock. Take his Aunt Jessica, for instance: the youngest of the sisters, she lived with young Neville at Summer Place, yet is mentioned only once in the space of three volumes.

Others may have been even less fortunate. Though Cardus never refers to any kin beyond his immediate family, it is at least possible that other members of the clan lived nearby. Cardus wasn't a particularly common name and the George Cardus who was listed in Slater's Street Directory as living at 4, Summer Place in 1901 could well have been a relative who moved in after Robert's death. And if this was the case, he was possibly the same George Cardus who had previously lived round the corner in Nelson Street, and who in 1889 had become the proud father of a baby girl called Beatrice. Even more intriguing is the possibility that Neville was not an only child. Though he never so much as hinted at the existence of brothers or sisters, those who knew the family when they lived at Summer Place recall that Ada also had a daughter called Esther, who later owned a dress shop in Great Western Street.

One figure stands out amidst all this mystery and confusion. To say that young Neville had a soft spot for his Aunt Beatrice would be something of an understatement. As a child, he would not have viewed the comings and goings at Number 4 in the same way as the neighbours, from behind the sanctimonious sobriety of their twitching curtains, most certainly did. Blissfully unaware of the weighty moral issues at stake, he embarked on a life-long love affair with his aunt which neither her sensational court appearance nor her early death could upset. In his eyes, she could do no wrong, even when it came to administering a well-deserved thrashing. By all accounts, Beatrice was a striking figure. Tall and blue-eyed, endowed with 'a lovely weak mouth, without lipstick' and 'the husky voice of Mrs Patrick Campbell', she was every inch the leading lady her nephew believed she could have been. It was to Beatrice that he turned for comfort and support when his mother's work took her away for long periods. (For reasons best known to herself, Ada tended to arrange more 'away fixtures' than her sister.) In the then not-so-delicate business of child-rearing, Beatrice was often all that stood between Neville and the condition which now goes by the terrifying title of 'maternal deprivation'. More important still, she gave him his first cricket bat.

How far Neville's description of his aunt corresponded with reality we will never know. The likelihood is that as he grew up and Beatrice died, aged only twenty-eight, so the image of his 'wonderful aunt' was subtly recast. By the time *Autobiography* came to be written, the simple innocence of childhood had given way to an idealised vision of what might have been. But in either form, she remained a potent inspirational force. 'One or two pieces I treasure,' he told Robin Daniels,

such as ... the portrait-in-words of my Aunt Beatrice in my

autobiography. There she is, for all time; and it is all done in about 5,000 words. I envy the Cardus who could write that. In Australia I had a vision based on the reality of this beautiful and wonderful person in my life when I was a boy. . . . I thought about my Aunt Beatrice and then she spoke, came into my being. She contributed the material; I was the medium.[3]

There were occasions in Neville's life when he revealed an almost ruthless streak which contrasts with the popular image of the naive lad who reached his 'happy isles' on the back of honest endeavour, ability and a good deal of luck. The dismissal (in *Autobiography*, though not in real life) of Beatrice is a case in point. Infatuated with his aunt though he may have been, Sir Neville was enough of a realist to know that, given the opportunity, she could steal the show. With a clinical detachment worthy of the most professional of assassins, she was summarily despatched. Cardus himself recalled the incident:

I can see it now. It was a beautiful afternoon. But I was too engrossed in my writing to go out for a walk. I had come to the description of my wonderful Aunt Beatrice and she almost took over the book. I had written 1,500 words about her when all of a sudden I exclaimed, 'This is my autobiography, Beatrice; not your biography. I'm sorry but I'm going to have to kill you.'[4]

Beatrice meanwhile, happily oblivious to the cruel fate that awaited her, continued down 'the primrose path of dalliance'. As the rest of the family sat down to the daily ritual of high tea, she would disappear upstairs to her bedroom and, if Neville is to be believed, the great luxury of a bathroom, to reappear much later clad seductively in the latest fashions.

On one memorable occasion, her entrance was so dramatic as to disturb even her usually taciturn father. 'A daughter of mine,' he thundered. 'Anybody would take you for an actress!' It was a savage rebuke. Mortified, Beatrice fled to the safety of her own room where she donned a less striking costume before daring to face the old man's wrath again. Happily for Neville, who awaited Beatrice's daily appearance at the top of the stairs with all the hushed expectation of an audience at a Parisian couturier's spring show, these outbursts were few and far between. Normally, Beatrice would parade her latest outfit in front of a spellbound nephew before disappearing in a flurry of crêpe and lace for the *demi-monde* of Manchester's Oxford Street.

[II]

It was on one of these nocturnal outings that Beatrice met her most exotic consort, Mustapha Karsa, the Turkish Consul in Manchester. While Neville refers to this episode in *Autobiography*, for once his description of events hardly compares with the coverage it received in the press. Having gone to such lengths to emphasise Beatrice's distinctive qualities and appearance, it is difficult to understand why Neville should have chosen to play down the climax of her most outrageous escapade – unless, that is, he felt that she was threatening to steal his thunder. Whatever the reason, having met each other at the Comedy Theatre where Beatrice was sometimes employed as an attendant, this unlikely couple embarked on an affair which caused eyebrows to be raised in the staid surroundings of Sale, where he lived, and chaos in Summer Place, where she was 'based'.

Shortly after their first meeting, Mustapha and Beatrice tripped their way round the 'hotspots' of Lancashire, ravaging middle-class morality wherever they went. Liverpool, New Brighton, Southport and Blackpool all benefited from his pocket and her appetite. Whether Paris was ever included in this grand tour, as Cardus suggests, is more doubtful, but wherever they went the couple certainly enjoyed themselves. When at last passion, or leastwise Mustapha's, cooled, Beatrice was left with only one recourse – the law. Nothing if not a fighter, she brought an action against her erstwhile consort for 'breach of promise', and the case duly came up before Mr Justice Wells at Manchester Assizes on 21 April 1902.

The papers had a field-day. Under the banner headline 'The Lustful Turk', the *Daily Dispatch* devoted three full-page columns, and a series of cartoon cameos of the central protagonists, to the case. Other stories paled in comparison: major headlines like 'Beef Trust Defiant' and 'Fifty Years of the Manchester Sanitary Association' went unnoticed; even an advertisement which claimed to reveal what 'Every Woman should know about the wonderful Marvel Whirling Spray' seemed strangely irrelevant. Setting the scene, the *Dispatch*'s reporter wrote:

The breach of promise case interested a large audience for several hours at Manchester Assizes yesterday, and in many respects it was remarkable. The amours of this elderly merchant – he is over 50 – with an attendant at the Comedy Theatre was found to provide a story at once sordid and in a way romantic.

The plaintiff in the breach of promise case, Miss Beatrice Cardus, is about twenty-two years of age, tall and good-looking. It was in April, 1899, that Mustapha Karsa, who was said to be entitled to be called Bey, met the plaintiff . . . there was no promise of marriage until September, 1900.

With both parties represented by K.C.s, a facility to which plaintiffs from the slums didn't normally have access, the stage was set for a battle royal. And so it proved. One by one, the Carduses took the stand as they strove to establish the authenticity of Beatrice's claims. Mrs Ann Cardus testified that Karsa had said that he was very fond of her daughter and that he proposed to marry her. He had, she claimed, '. . . talked in rather large figures, saying that he would settle £5,000 upon the plaintiff and that he had an income of ten or twelve thousand pounds.' Beatrice herself was then called to the witness box to recount her version of the events surrounding a visit to Liverpool. 'A Trip to Liverpool', the *Dispatch* announced:

In November 1900, very soon after the engagement, the plaintiff's father, who was a policeman, died, and the defendant attended the funeral in his carriage . . . when he was introduced to relatives and friends as the plaintiff's intended husband, the defendant asked her to go to Liverpool with him. . . . At Liverpool they met the Turkish Consul for that place and they all three had lunch together at the Alexandra Hotel. In the afternoon, they went to New Brighton, returning to the hotel in the evening.

The defendant had suggested that they should return by the half-past ten or eleven train but when, after supper, the plaintiff said it was time to be going, he said 'There is no train and you will have to stay in Liverpool.' The defendant persuaded her (and the learned counsel was not at all sure that he was not assisted in doing so by his friend, the Liverpool Consul). They occupied the same bedroom, and did not return to Manchester until half-past nine the next morning. The plaintiff assured her mother that she and the defendant had occupied separate rooms, and that no harm had come to her.

After some little time, she was pressed by her mother and finally told what had happened at Liverpool. Mrs Cardus spoke to the defendant, who said that he was going to marry the plaintiff within a few months and that therefore it was not necessary to say anything more about it.

Armed with this assurance and sweetened by a regular supply of gifts, like the coat 'for which the defendant paid £6.10s', Beatrice continued her relationship with Karsa. 'On several occasions afterwards,' she went away with him, each time telling her mother that she had been staying with her brother-in-law, a Mr Joseph, who lived in Timperley. At this point young Neville enters the story as it was his mother, Ada, who was living with Joseph at this time. Whether they were ever married was a point to which the defence counsel was to return, but whatever the precise status of their relationship, Neville spent several weeks with the Josephs at Timperley.

The outcome of the trial hinged upon Karsa's intentions. Answering a question from her own counsel, Beatrice told the court, who by this time were utterly engrossed in the strange tales being recounted from the dock, that Karsa had given her 'a string of beads instead of an engagement ring', claiming that this was 'the custom in Turkey'. Cross-examined about the extent of her knowledge of Karsa's circumstances, she replied that she had been introduced to a lady described as Mrs Karsa and subsequently, in company with that lady and Mrs Joseph, they had returned to the defendant's house for dinner. Mr Karsa occupied the head of the table and Mrs Karsa sat opposite.

Asked to explain her reaction to this complex and intriguing state of affairs, Beatrice replied that 'she had always understood that Mrs Karsa was the defendant's housekeeper. She thought that the eight children were by the defendant's dead wife. He told her that he wanted her to look after the children, the eldest of whom was about fourteen.'

At this point, Karsa took the stand. Described as having 'a business as a merchant and shipper in Whitworth Street' and being 'a Musselman by faith', he vigorously denied ever having suggested that the plaintiff should keep herself free to marry him when he returned from abroad. When pressed on the question of whether he had ever promised to marry Beatrice, he replied, looking directly at the jury, 'Nothing of the sort.' Defence counsel then sought to discredit Neville's mother's testimony by showing that, like Beatrice, she was little more than a prostitute. Asked about her sister's relationship with Mr Joseph, Beatrice stubbornly maintained that 'she had no reason to suppose that Mr and Mrs Joseph were not married. The ceremony took place at Southport, but neither she nor any other member of the family was present. Her sister had been previously married, but was divorced. In that case, Mr Joseph was the co-respondent.'

If Neville was in court to hear these extraordinary disclosures, he must by now have been totally confused about his ancestry. Could this Joseph, a Hebrew shipper from Sale, friend of his aunt's paramour, have included playing as first violinist in a visiting orchestra amongst his many talents? Before anyone could answer this conundrum, the defence counsel had elicited a categorical denial from Karsa that Joseph had ever married Ada Cardus.

In his concluding address, the defence counsel, Mr Taylor K.C., drew the attention of the jury to the wider implications of the verdict they must soon consider. Warning them against trying the defendant for immorality, he explained that

> the only question was whether he had made a promise to marry the plaintiff, and whether having broken that promise, damages were to be found against him. If the jury were to accept such engagements as the plaintiff had described, he did not know where such actions would stop.

From the tenor of his summing-up, it was clear that Mr Justice Wills thought little of these arguments, and even less of Mustapha Karsa.

> 'Whether the defendant be a Christian or a Musselman or anything else, he is a very bad man and the case is a very cruel one.' His lordship continued to comment strongly on the defendant whom he described as 'this lustful Turk', and who, despite his office of Consul in Manchester, visited the house of the plaintiff's father – a common policeman. The defendant

could not have married the plaintiff in this country, for if he had
he would have run the very great chance of being indicted for
bigamy. His lordship, in conclusion, expressed the opinion that
the plaintiff was entitled to very substantial damages.

It was the sort of summation which, if given today, would probably
trigger off a public outcry. But eighty years ago, no one batted an
eyelid, least of all the jury who meekly retired to their room, to return
only thirty-five minutes later with a judgement in favour of the
plaintiff and a recommendation for damages of not less than £200, a
suggestion His Lordship was only too pleased to accept.

III

From the small bay-window of 4, Summer Place, Rusholme, young
Neville Cardus first looked out on to the great metropolis which
was to be his home for nearly forty years. The childhood spent in
Summer Place is in many respects as much of a mystery as his
ancestry. The early chapters of *Autobiography* are a curious mixture
of colour, wit, insight and unsettling vagueness – curious, that is,
until they are understood as the product of a mature personality
which had deliberately and painstakingly detached itself from its
origins. In *Autobiography* Cardus explicitly acknowledged the
peculiar standpoint from which he chose to recall his youth. 'I can
write of this boy without self-consciousness. He happened so long
ago. He might have been my son.' By the time Robin Daniels came
to record the last of his *Conversations with Cardus*, the distance which
separated Sir Neville from the carefree lad who used to roam the
streets of Manchester had widened to a point at which it could no
longer be contained within a single generation. Hence the simple
but important modification of his earlier claim: 'I think of that boy.
He is so far from me that I can talk of him as though he were my
grandson. . . .'

Strange though it may seem today, the strong element of detachment in Neville's conception of autobiography was a direct consequence of the terms in which he understood his own personality.
Though it is true that his infatuation with the ideas of Kant and
Goethe on occasions resulted in outbursts of what a close friend
once described as 'German metaphysical windbaggery', this does
not mean that *Autobiography* should be dismissed as an injudicious

attempt to explain the past in terms of the language of 'pure reason'.
As the following passage from a letter he wrote in October 1949
shows, Neville's admiration for mid-European metaphysicians did
not blind him to the extent to which their thought processes differed
from his own:

> I have no talent for logical thinking, so I will abandon even a
> feeble attempt to rationalise about what is in me less a belief
> than an intuition. I have read much of metaphysics but not, I'm
> afraid, by means of abstract reasoning. The Kantian categories,
> when first my intelligence grasped them as concepts, immedi-
> ately stirred a sensation in my consciousness, and a warmth not
> to be counted a reaction of 'pure reason'. I was then aware of an
> enlargement of the capacity for living, body as well as mind –
> the whole man of me quickened, not the brain cells only. I do
> not claim to have good brains, but I do boast a good mind; and
> by mind I mean intelligence suffused with feeling, a conscious-
> ness that does not fall or flow into order by logic, but according
> to the law whereby frost on a window pane is distributed in
> patterns of seemingly inevitable equipoise.

Though it is obscured by the yards of prolixity which follow, the
reference to 'intuition' contains the key to both the passage itself,
and the autobiographical perspective it introduces. Admitting the
limitations of his capacity for rational thinking, Neville offers
instead, almost as an alternative, a mind which 'cannot separate
head from heart, grey matter from viscera', yet which holds out the
promise of a deeper insight into the nature of humanity than mere *a
priori* reasoning can provide. This type of mind, Neville argued, was
in a sense better suited to the phenomena it confronted. 'I am always
wondering', he wrote,

> at the type of mind that can think along a straight line, from
> premise to conclusion, go right ahead avoiding 'excluded
> missiles' and what not, foreseeing the end in the beginning all
> the time. Such people imagine they can plan their own lives, or
> careers, an assumption which implies a belief in the continuity
> of self or ego. It must all be very dull and uncreative, such a
> mental state, such a belief. It is . . . a narrowing view and spirit,
> a single track of logic and human conceit extending to eternity.

Having thus signalled his intentions, Neville lost little time in launching a frontal assault on conventional notions of personality, and personality development. In the very next paragraph, he asked: 'Can any of us look back on all our years and honestly see or feel a singleness of being, and continuous identity, a self which has evolved from one and the same cocoon in the same unifying "I" day-by-day?' Before the reader could assess the intellectual merits of this challenge, let alone its implications, Neville delivered the final *coup de grâce* in the form of an assertion of the essential difference between Cardus 'the boy' and Cardus 'the man'.

> I hardly 'recognise' myself when young; how should I; for as a boy I was entirely different in thought, emotion, physical constitution, psychologically and chemically. So far from having been conscious of a persistence of one ego I am today inclined to swear that more than two Souls or lives have dwelt within my shape and vessel. My batteries of consciousness have not only been recharged, but different wavelengths discovered. I have in a way – so have all of us, if we would rid ourselves of a contrary fixed idea – gone through reincarnation. (I do not 'believe' in reincarnation as a notion of which intellect approves; but more convincing evidence of it has come my way than of personal immortality.)[5]

This statement, culminating in the novel claim to 'reincarnation', is crucial to an understanding of both Neville's character and the terms in which he chose to present himself to the public. His autobiographies amount to a highly selective and polished view of his life. They provide, as Henry Adams once noted, 'a shield of protection from the grave'. In Neville's case, however, the 'shield' functioned in life as well as thereafter. The challenge is to discover what lay behind that shield, and to understand why it was erected.

Whatever other criticisms may be laid at Cardus's door, it can never be said that he lacked imagination and ingenuity. The claim that he was able to view his childhood as if through the eyes of a different, albeit related, person is advanced with sufficient conviction and panache to dissuade a reader from questioning its plausibility and purpose until the spell has been well and truly cast. A more inquisitive reader might well glimpse a different Cardus, an artist struggling to resolve a source of tension within his own personality – an emerging sense of what he was and what he would like to have been – without at the same time surrendering the creative energy which it generated.

This approach created an autobiographical vacuum which Cardus was quick to exploit. Not for nothing had he spent all those evenings in the steamy atmosphere of the Free Library, Dickenson Road, devouring the work of a man whose genius for portraying the fads and foibles of Victorian England has never been equalled. There is an unmistakeably Dickensian flavour to much of Cardus's account of his childhood. Slums, prostitution and broken families; moonlight flits to avoid the bailiff; the good times spent in the relative opulence of Manchester's spreading suburbs – Timperley and the like – while either mother or aunt plied their trade upstairs; months of ill-health and the dark days spent at the nearby Board school; carrying baggage from the now defunct Central Station to the Midland Hotel to earn the pennies needed to get into Old Trafford; frantic early-morning dashes across a scarred and blackened landscape to watch his idols perform, and endless evenings imitating their feats on the brick crofts of Rusholme; devouring great literature by candle or gaslight until either frost or failing eyesight intervened; pushing a handcart laiden with planks, serving an apprenticeship as a pavement artist, and boiling type in a printer's works; braving the elements to hear the Hallé from the nether regions of the Free Trade Hall and then the long walk home.

None of these episodes would have been out of place in *Hard Times* or *Nicholas Nickleby*: but herein lies a problem. The difference between Dickens and Cardus, as far as their purpose in writing was concerned, should be found in the distinction between fiction and autobiography. But even after due allowance is made for artistic licence, there are great swathes of Cardus's autobiographies where the vision of what he would like to have been intrudes so forcefully as to all but obliterate what he had been and was. If his childhood adventures at first sight seem a trifle unlikely, when seen against the background of the conditions a slum child would have confronted they take on a conformation little short of miraculous. To make any sense of Neville's early years, the reader has to reconcile his own account with, firstly, the relatively few factual details included in the autobiographies and, secondly, all that is known of the prevailing social conditions in late nineteenth-century Manchester.

'Born in a slum' and raised 'in one of the worst areas of Manchester in one of Manchester's worst times', wrote Bill Grundy in terms which could leave no one in any doubt about the signal impact which the experience of poverty was supposed to have had on Neville's mind, character and development. Almost without exception, Grundy's obituary-writing colleagues followed suit, each perpetuating the legend of the sickly, short-sighted child from Rusholme who overcame abject poverty to find international renown, and each seemingly unaware of the role Neville himself had played as both the subject and architect of that legend. No one, it seems, was prepared to consider the possibility that the story of an inveterate raconteur, as told by himself, may have gained something in the telling. 'Why should they have done?' you might ask, and with good reason. The account of his childhood in *Autobiography*, *Second Innings* and the rest makes compelling and convincing reading. Yet for all its excellence it still suffers from one simple, but fundamental weakness. Like a new jig-saw puzzle, some of the pieces don't fit together. The closer one looks at the circumstances of Neville's birth and childhood, the more mysterious they become.

Poverty and pauperism, or rather the difference between them, provide the key to some of these puzzles. 'Manchester was my place of birth, in a slum,' Cardus told us in *Autobiography*, and on several occasions thereafter. To appreciate the full implications of this bland statement, it has to be remembered that for much of the nineteenth century Manchester was a phenomenon quite unlike anything the world had previously encountered – a city which had grown in the space of less than fifty years from provincial insignificance to be the centre of the world's largest urban agglomeration, and which had acquired in the process a physical identity which was to stamp it as the 'shock city' of the nineteenth century. This identity owed much to an 'unconscious tacit agreement' as a result of which, in Frederick Engels' words, 'the working-class districts are most sharply separated from those parts in the city reserved for the middle-class. Or, if this does not succeed, they are concealed with the cloak of charity.'[6]

Visitors to the city were often struck by the enormous material gap which separated rich from poor, and by the contrast between the great wealth which the working-classes were helping to create and the misery in which they lived. As one contemporary put it, the merchants of Chorlton-on-Medlock, Ardwick, Cheetham Hill and Pendleton lived

> in free, wholesome, country air, in fine, comfortable houses . . .
> and the finest part of the arrangement is this; that members of
> this monied aristocracy can take the shortest road through the
> middle of all the labouring districts to their places of business
> without ever seeing that they are in the midst of grimy misery
> that lurks to the right and to the left.[7]

The first fifty years of the nineteenth century were undoubtedly Manchester's worst. The English language struggles to do justice to the slums of this period. Set alongside enormous concentrations of wealth and imperturbable gentility, these god-forsaken holes contained levels of destitution and squalor rarely, if ever, equalled in civilised society. Samuel Smiles may well have believed that 'the Gods had placed labour and toil on the way leading to the Elysian fields', but for the inhabitants of the 'classic slum' it must have seemed an unconvincing argument. While Frederick Engels' political allegiances may have led some to doubt the absolute objectivity of his judgements, Doctor John Kay had no axe to grind when he wrote of the Manchester slums:

> The habitations . . . can scarcely be said to be furnished. They
> contain one or two chairs, a mean table, the most scanty
> culinary apparatus and one or two beds loathsome with filth. A
> whole family is often accommodated on a single bed: and
> sometimes a heap of filthy straw and a cover of sacking hide in
> one indistinguishable heap, debased alike by penury, want of
> economy and dissolute habits. . . . To this fertile source of
> disease were sometimes added the keeping of pigs and other
> animals in the house with other nuisances of a most revolting
> character.[8]

Outside, conditions were little better. An innocent mill-owner, caught short whilst on a visit to the city, once found himself in the greatest difficulty, as the following embarrassed outburst confirms: 'I have had to go to half a dozen privies before I could get one without pollution. . . . Finally, I proceeded up Union Street and have been compelled to skulk behind a wall.'[9] The 'privies' to which he referred usually faced the street and lacked doors, drains and seats. It was customary for 'two females to go together and for one to stand outside and spead her garments to screen the other'. While that most urbane of historians, Professor G. M. Young, may have used more refined language to record his 'inevitable conclusion that [by 1860] an increasing portion of the population of England was living under conditions which were not only a negation of civilised existence, but a menace to civilised society', the plain truth was that most of the people spent most of their time literally in the shit. Not surprisingly, this did little for their general physical well-being and absolutely nothing for their chances of survival. 'Half the children,' wrote Edwin Chadwick in his seminal *Report on the Sanitary Conditions of the Labouring Population*, 'died under the age of five, and Manchester was notorious for its high general death rate.'

Cardus, of course, never witnessed the industrial slum at its worst. No one would dispute that by 1889, the year of his birth, the conditions described so graphically by Engels, Kay and Chadwick lived on only in the memory of those lucky enough to survive them. In Manchester, for example, the passing of new public health legislation had prompted the establishment in 1846 of the first municipal cleansing department which employed six men and two horses and carts 'to remove night soil and domestic rubbish'. It was only several months later, after both the horses had died and the carts repeatedly collapsed, that the authorities decided on a more forthright approach. On 5 May 1846, the Council voted £3,000 to be spent on cleaning the city. 112 men with 50 horses and carts were employed: each week they emptied about a thousand privies and ashpits, removing more than 2,000 cartloads of rubbish. By the end of the operation, the cost had risen to £8,000 of which, to the consternation of the Borough Treasurer, only £2,500 was recovered through the sale of manure.

Financially unprofitable though they may have been, the efforts of these early sanitation authorities did succeed in removing the worst excesses of urban-industrial progress. Slums still existed, as the residents of Salford would confirm, but they were no longer of the character which prompted even the most hardened of contemporaries to wonder whether a city as dirty and unattractive as Manchester could ever be fit for human habitation. By the time young Neville (or Fred, as he was then known) started to wander the streets, many of those accretions of dirt and filth which dated from the Industrial Revolution had been consigned to the rubbish heap and history. That the conditions he experienced were, by modern standards, totally disgusting is probably true, but at the same time entirely irrelevant. Cardus's descriptions of his upbringing make sense only if judged by contemporary standards. When Joseph Brotherton, M.P. for Salford, asked in the course of a Commons debate on the Factories Bill in 1847, 'Shall it be allowed that to eat, to drink, to work and to die be the lot of a large portion of our fellow countrymen?' the reply he received from Sir James Graham, callous and insensitive though it may sound today, amounted to a succinct expression of contemporary values: 'I grieve to say that not only in this country but throughout the whole of this world of sorrow and care, the lot of eating, drinking, working and dying must ever be the sum of human life amongst a large portion of the human family.'

Victorians accepted poverty as a fact of life: the poor, they reflected, are always with us, always have been and always will be. And for long periods, the poor themselves seemed happy enough with this state of affairs. Looking down rather than up the social ladder, the first priority as they saw it was not to penetrate the fleshpots of the middle classes but to avoid the fate of the pauper. Pauperism was an all-embracing condition which afflicted every aspect of a man's life. Once deemed a pauper, he lost personal status, individual freedom and political rights. Thus, when Neville wrote of 'poverty', as likely as not he was referring to a blessed state in distinct contrast to 'pauperism' – a condition to be proud of, not ashamed; for at the end of the day it was one step up from the ignominy of the work-house.

The final reason for treating Cardus's autobiographical accounts of his childhood with some caution is that, contrary to popular belief, he was not born in one of Manchester's worst areas. In fact, had he been born four years earlier Neville would not have been a Mancunian at all, since Rusholme did not become a part of the city until the Extension Act of 1885. Before then, it had existed as a separate township, jealously guarding its independence in the face of repeated approaches from the ever-expanding metropolitan borough to the north. In the end, it was the unlikely issue of sewage that made annexation unavoidable. After the Sanitation Act of 1866, the Public Health Act of 1875 and the River Pollution Act of 1878, small riparian authorities like Rusholme could not hope to avoid being saddled with the costs of litigation if they failed to install

sewerage and draining facilities to prevent untreated sewage empty-
ing into the rivers which flowed through Manchester's boundaries.

Before the Industrial Revolution, Rusholme had existed as a
sleepy, rural parish. Even as late as 1801, its population numbered
only 726. There followed a century of rapid growth in the course of
which the peripheral areas of Manchester, Rusholme included,
grew faster than the centre, only to find themselves absorbed into a
vast, amorphous metropolis by a municipal marriage of convenience. By 1901, the once proud township had given way to an
urban borough, even though by this time its population had risen to
over 19,000. Unfortunate though it may appear today, Rusholme
enjoyed a better fate than many of its neighbouring boroughs. One
by one, they were forced to sacrifice not just territorial integrity but
also their souls. By the end of the nineteenth century, many had
succumbed to a dulling uniformity of condition and appearance
which left great swathes of Manchester distinguishable only by the
arbitrary convention of a municipal boundary. This was the
Manchester that Neville saw on that balmy afternoon in May 1912,
as he gazed down from the windows of the train taking him to new
work in Shrewsbury and new worlds beyond. These were the 'rows
and rows of dismal houses with backyards full of old cans and
bedsteads and torn oilcloth; the long vistas of streets with lamp-
posts and corner shops' which, he tells us, 'had nurtured me since I
was born'.

At this point, many of Cardus's devotees must have sat back and
reflected on the curious turn of events which had led them to read
sixty pages of autobiography and still know little more about its
subject than when they had started. The closer one looks at
Autobiography, the clearer it becomes that much of its appeal stems
from the questions which are raised but never answered. How could
an imagination so vivid and fertile have emerged from a setting so
grey and uninspiring? How could a talent which was to produce
some of this century's best journalism have survived the grinding
poverty of back-street Manchester? It is a measure of Cardus's skill
as an autobiographer that two volumes later the majority of his
readers, though generally still none the wiser, had neither lost
interest nor were willing to admit defeat. Unfortunately for them,
there was no relief at hand. The autobiographies were as much an
instrument of confusion as a source of truth. If there are answers,
they aren't to be found in his own narrative nor in that last, departing

view from the railway compartment all those years ago. For the train to Shrewsbury did not pass within eyeshot of Rusholme.

[IV]

In 1889 the neighbourhood in which the Carduses lived had not yet come to resemble the 'festering and wretched suburb' which Ruskin described in *Sesame and Lilies*. Unlike much of Manchester, Rusholme was still a place of enormous contrasts. To the south-west lay the arboreal splendour of the Platt Estate and the village of Fallowfield, whilst in the opposite direction, only a mile from Neville's birthplace, Victoria Park remained a haven for those most estimable members of Manchester's banking and commercial fraternity whose carriages, every Thursday night following the weekly Hallé concert, 'swung by iron gates and curved along drives to massive turreted stone houses, at the base of them broad stone steps leading up to the portals, flanked by lions *couchant*'.[10]

But it was not in 'sequestered purlieus' such as these that Neville was destined to spend his early years. He was born and raised in a more densely populated network of streets referred to in the 1871 Census as Enumeration District 61 – 'part of the township of Rusholme, bounded on the north by Regent House, South by Fallowfield, East by Victoria Park and Didsbury Road and West by Moss Side'. Many years before, harvesters from Ireland who had come to work for the farmers around Rusholme lodged in the vicinity of Moor Street, just around the corner from Summer Place, and the fact that the word 'cardus' appears in some Irish dialects has led to speculation that Neville's dynasty may have originated on the other side of the Irish Sea. Whatever the case, by the time the youngest member of the Carduses of Summer Place was scampering the streets, the Irishmen, and the handloom weavers who also used to inhabit the area, had long since departed, both victims of the inexorable logic of industrial change. In the 1880s, Summer Place was at the centre of a bustling, colourful cosmopolitan community. Artisans, teachers, clerks and constables lived side by side with families displaced by one or other of those tides of human migration which spread European stock to all parts of the globe. Theirs was not a world of slums and and paupers, poor though many undoubtedly were.

It is hard to conceive of a setting more likely to fire the imagination and ambition of an impressionable, intelligent young lad. Slaughter-houses, the Rusholme brewery, a menacingly-named 'people's institution' and the first 'real' ice-skating rink in England (a facility which at first 'had great trouble in getting a good quality of ice') all lay between Summer Place and the pleasance of Platt Estate and Victoria Park. Walking to the Board school in Grove Street, young Neville would have come upon colonies of Germans, Jews, Armenians, Swedes and, most noticeable of all, Turks. The presence of these exotic communities was enough to attract even the most genteel of Victorian families to Rusholme. The following entry in the diary of a contemporary confirms the popularity of the district: 'We always enjoyed a walk in Rusholme because we might be rewarded by the sight of a Turk, or even two Turks, gravely pacing in carpet slippers with red fez and black beard.'[11]

As well as creating a largely inaccurate impression of Rusholme, Neville's portrayal of himself as a product of the slums does little justice to Manchester itself. While no one would deny that there had been times when parts of Manchester, for example Salford, represented as barren a landscape as mankind has ever created – a cultural desert whose only salvation was to be discovered post-humously in the genius of Lowry – the city itself could offer as rich and diverse a programme of literary, theatrical and musical talent as anywhere in Europe. Tomes have been written about Manchester's debt to its immigrant population and in particular the German community who, it has been said, 'mingled Beethoven and Brahms with business in Portland Street'. Important though this infusion of new blood may have been, the seeds of the cultural tradition of which Cardus became part had been sown amongst the indigenous population many years before. Public concerts were being held in Manchester as early as 1744, and from 1770 the city could boast an annual season of concerts organised by the Gentlemen's Concert Society.[12] In a different sphere, Faucher was only one of many to draw attention to the existence amongst all sections of the com-munity of an extraordinary appetite for culture and learning. Writing in 1844, he noted:

> The almost exclusive occupation of the inhabitants of Manchester, in manufacturing and commercial pursuits, is unfavourable to the cultivation of literature and of the arts which require leisure and studious habits. . . . But, although

Manchester may not be fitted to produce or cherish this class of talent, it is not slow to appreciate it and patronise it.[13]

Even the working classes, whose life style and conditions of existence were scarcely conducive to an appreciation of greater literature, music and art, displayed the same yearning for culture. By the second half of the century, a survey of working-class behaviour in Lancashire would have identified two typical responses to poverty: on the one hand, there was the world of the toper and, on the other, that of the 'enlightened' working man. Those who fell (literally and metaphorically) into the first category were easy to spot and even easier to forget, but the second group was made up of an altogether different type of person. Consider by way of example the case of Joseph Livesey who, after beginning life as a lowly apprentice, rose by dint of his own efforts and talent to become a much favoured figure amongst the Lancashire *literati* towards the end of the century.

Anxious for information and having no companions from whom I could learn anything, I longed for books but had not the means to procure [them]. . . . I seldom got a meal without a book open before me at the same time, and I managed to do what I have never seen any other weaver attempt – to read and weave at the same time. . . . For hours I have read by the glare of a few embers left in the fire grate with my head close to the bars.[14]

As a result of his concern with self-improvement Livesey, like Neville, became very short-sighted. Other, less dedicated, souls took an easier route to erudition via 'periodical publications' and the free library. Again it was Faucher who drew attention to the extraordinary profusion and popularity of libraries in nineteenth-century Manchester. 'There are few communities in the world,' he observed, 'which are more emphatically reading communities than Manchester and the manufacturing districts of Lancashire. . . . Its literary institutions are numerous, and possessed of extensive libraries.'[15]

In their own way, the Carduses were part of this enlightened tradition. Though it may well have been the case that by the time Neville was born his grandfather's taste in reading did not extend much beyond the three 'bibles' – the 1607 version, the *Manchester*

Guardian and the *Sporting Chronicle Handicap Book* – the important point was that he was literate. In 1889, this alone put him in a class apart from the great mass of manual labourers. Elsewhere in his autobiographies, Neville recalls how his grandfather had once attended a Mechanics Institute, a foundation originally established to advance the cause of working-class education. It is an interesting insight into the values and ambitions of the Cardus family that Robert's attendance at an Institute came at a time when that foundation was coming under increasing criticism for 'attracting persons of a higher rank than those for which it was designed' and for having 'abandoned practical science in favour of literature, recreation and entertainment'.

With the far-reaching changes in society during the Industrial Revolution, the pursuit of culture gradually came to be seen as a 'different and superior social idea', at first providing relief from the all-pervading influence of the cash nexus but by the end of the century encompassing 'a whole way of life, material, intellectual and spiritual'. As befitted the city which, more than any other, epitomised the new industrial order, Manchester rose to the challenge of this shifting pattern of social taste. With the Hallé (under firstly the eponymous Sir Charles and then Dr Hans Richter) established as its crowning glory, the city played host to an impressive array of musical, intellectual and theatrical talent. Cardus himself recalled a week which

> began with a new Galsworthy play at the Gaiety occupied by Miss Horniman's repertory company, a Brodsky Quartet concert on the Tuesday, a matinée by Réjane on Wednesday, a Hallé concert with Richter and Busoni on Thursday, and on Friday a production of Ibsen's *Ghosts*, in camera.[16]

Add to this the presence of C. E. Montague, James Agate, Allan Monkhouse and Ernest Newman at the *Manchester Guardian*, Samuel Alexander and Stanley Jevons at the University, and MacLaren, Spooner and Tyldesley at Old Trafford, and it is easy to see why many consider this to have been Manchester's golden age.

Thus, contrary to the impression he worked so hard to create, Cardus was the product neither of a slum, nor a cultural desert. Born of a generation which lost two out of every ten children born before they reached the age of ten, he not only survived but also enjoyed a relatively healthy, untroubled childhood. Of course life at Summer Place had its ups-and-downs: with no regular income to rely on, the family was particularly vulnerable to the vagaries of economic fortune. 'One day,' he tells us, 'Summer Place made shift with bread and dripping and 'potato-ash', and the next day would be heard by the neighbours feasting deep into the night.' But somehow they managed to make ends meet, a feat which did not go unnoticed. No doubt to Neville's subsequent chagrin, his family came to be looked upon by their neighbours as rather superior folk.

Others in Rusholme were not so fortunate. The early years of the present century were difficult times for Manchester. As the once-mighty cotton industry entered yet another slump, so cases of individual hardship multiplied. Newspapers carried banner head-lines announcing the 'terrible distress' which had befallen the city and its inhabitants. Rusholme may not have fared as badly as some of the traditional working-class boroughs, but it could not entirely escape what are now quaintly termed 'the knock-on' effects of recession. There was, for example, the small matter of the 700 unemployed labourers who descended on Rusholme from all parts of Manchester as soon as word got out that the Local Government Board, in an initiative which anticipated 'job creation schemes' by over seventy years, were intending to fund the construction of a large lake in Platt Fields.

Against this background even the mundane, humdrum world of Summer Place had its advantages. By contemporary working-class standards, the house was extremely well-appointed. Not only did it boast a bay-window but also, more significantly, a toilet – albeit in the backyard. In *Full Score* Neville recalls 'the morning's bowel evacuation, which took place, by the way, in an outdoor shed, done upon a wooden stool, whence the wind blew upward'. Appallingly primitive though this must sound today, in 1889 it ranked as a refreshingly sophisticated arrangement. As we have seen, Manchester's reputation for radical thinking did not extend to the delicate subject of sanitation and domestic hygiene. It was not until 1872 that the city adopted a policy of replacing the notorious 'privy middens' with pail-closets, a decision which marked the beginning of the equally notorious 'Dolly Varden' era. The Dolly Varden in question was not a person but a popular brand of scent, and the ironical reference was to the arrangement whereby 'low carts with a dozen compartments [which] collected the pails from the houses . . . and as they were drawn through the streets, sometimes three together, the stench was nauseating'.[17]

Before anyone runs away with the idea that the ownership of a pail-closet stamped the Carduses as the lowest of the low, it is worth noting that in 1897 Dr Niven, the local Medical Officer of Health, reported that Manchester was one of only four out of seventy-eight 'principal towns' in the United Kingdom still advocating the use of pail-closets. As late as 1902, only 45,686 (37%) of the 151,471 sanitary conveniences in Manchester were of the water-closet type. Privy middens and pail-closets weren't totally replaced until 1917.

Elsewhere in his autobiographies, there are other indications that the picture of the 'uneducated boy from an illiterate home' was not entirely accurate. Not only were his grandparents clearly not illiterate, but it was Beatrice who, by his own admission, was first responsible for encouraging her nephew to read 'reasonably good books'. Nor was the family so poor that they couldn't afford more than the occasional trip to the music hall, and a reasonable supply of clothing for Neville, including a 'sailors suit' to be worn only on Sundays, and a special belt and coloured tie to adorn his cricket kit. And material possessions weren't the only benefit bestowed on young Neville which suggest that his was not an orthodox slum upbringing. How many other children in Rusholme, or the whole of Manchester for that matter, were lulled to sleep by arias from *Norma* sung by their aunt?

The abiding impression of the Carduses is of a modest but unlucky family who, through no fault of their own, were deprived of a regular breadwinner at a time when English society offered little protection to the weak and the vulnerable. Haunted by the spectre of penury, they struggled to maintain the trappings of material respectability by any means available to them: hence Neville's early involvement in the delivery of the domestic laundry which his grandmother took in. The predicament in which they found themselves generated an inescapable feeling of apprehension and anxiety, echoes of which are to be found in George Orwell's description of his own family background in *The Road to Wigan Pier*.

I was born into what you might describe as the lower middle-classes . . . a sort of mound of wreckage left behind when the tide of Victorian prosperity receded. . . . In the kind of family I am talking about there is far more consciousness of poverty than in any working-class family above the level of the dole. . . . Practically the whole family income goes in keeping up appearances.

From his frequent references to slums and poverty it is clear that from a fairly early age Neville was affected by a similar consciousness, though in his case it prompted a response very different from the conspicuous consumption that Orwell observed. Sharpened by the early loss of a father, by the unconventional antics of his mother and aunt and by his own powers of imagination, it was to be the catalyst which fused ability and ambition into an unshakeable determination to escape the empty drudgery of working-class life.

2
Discovery

'A wanderer is man from his birth.'[1]

[I]

Following Neville through his recollections of adolescence is like pursuing a familiar figure through a swirling, patchy fog. Occasionally a well-known shape looms out of the mist to reassure the reader that he or she is still on the right track, but the overall effect is one of gradual disorientation. We continue to read partly because the journey itself is a pleasant experience and partly because we are fascinated by the prospect to be revealed once the fog lifts. Cardus once claimed that he was probably 'the last of the romantics', and nowhere is this disposition more clearly in evidence than in the chapters of *Autobiography* which describe his teens and twenties. The narrative itself contains few surprises as both the setting and the central theme had been foreshadowed earlier. Having deliberately cast himself adrift from the bosom of his family, in *Autobiography* if not in fact, Cardus had no option but to portray himself as a 'little waif' wandering the streets of Manchester in search of the 'happy isles' which, once discovered, would provide spiritual and material sustenance for the rest of his life.

The challenge would have been too much for most writers. Presented with a once-in-a-lifetime chance to create their own graven image, but totally lacking the necessary wit and skill, the average hack would have floundered between fact, fantasy and pure fiction. That Neville avoided this fate was due both to the skill with which he prepared his readers for what they were about to receive and to the quality of his writing. Nevertheless, an over-dependence on the purple passage can create its own problems. 'Ce que j'adore dans la musique,' wrote Goncourt, 'ce sont les femmes qui écoutent.' The danger in high-quality writing is that the reader may come to prefer the thing written to the thing written about. The key to Cardus's skill as an autobiographer lies in the way he turned this possibility to his own advantage.

Readers of *Autobiography* and *Second Innings* were party to a delightful deception. Where they might have expected a detailed chronicle, instead they found a series of highly personalised images etched in some of the richest, most alluring of textures. This literary collage had a mesmeric quality. It created a sense of empathy, not false but partial. Under its spell, few readers realised that throughout the early chapters of his autobiographies Cardus was indulging in a spot of harmless *legerdemain*. These pages present not one life history but two. The first (and largely hidden) describes a young man's advance to maturity; the second contains the substance of a literary legend which had been forged in the course of a long and fertile career and finally cast in a flat in Sydney. Dovetailing the two stories demanded the utmost dexterity, particularly as Cardus looked upon autobiography as a source of salvation, a means of making his own past 'come out right'. In places the marriage is less than perfect: sometimes details cannot be reconciled; elsewhere we find different versions of the same episode. Neither weakness seriously impaired Neville's self-image, but both demonstrate how much can be learned about a person from the facts he chooses to invent about himself.

The early years of this century were the best and worst of times for young Neville. On the one hand, there was the excitement of adolescence and the first visit to Old Trafford in 1900; two years later, the end of formal education. After five years of compounded misery, he finally turned his back on the despised Board school, on Miss Barthwick 'of yellow visage, and hair pointed straight down the middle', on 'the three R's, a list of dates . . . some geography about peninsulas being nearly surrounded by water . . . and Scripture every morning at nine o'clock'. Free at last, he looked about for work, though with no great sense of urgency. The Protestant Ethic never weighed heavily on his mind, much less his spirit. Many years later he was to write, 'I didn't want to work for my living. I define work as an occupation you would give up tomorrow if you inherited £50,000,' and added as an afterthought, 'I sometimes wonder what would happen to this country if everybody suddenly inherited £50,000. Not five per cent – not even one per cent – would stay in their jobs.'[2]

1901 was the *annus mirabilis* of young Neville's hero, J. T. Tyldesley – 'Mercutio and D'Artagnan rolled into one', as Neville was later to portray him. 3,041 runs, including 9 centuries and a top score of 221, flowed off his bat during a season when the Old Trafford wicket 'imperilled knee-cap, breast-bone and Adam's apple alike'. 1902 saw the arrival of Joe Darling's Australians, including the incomparable Victor Trumper. For Neville the summer was one long holiday. Supported by Beatrice's boundless beneficence (until Karsa's money ran out), he acquired a new cane-handled bat and an indelible memory of Trumper's century before lunch in the Old Trafford test match. So great an impression did this immortal innings leave on Neville that years later he would write of Trumper:

> His cricket burns in my memory with the glow and fiery hazard of the actual occurrence, the wonderful and consuming ignition. He was the most gallant and handsome batsman of them all. . . . In my memory's anthology of all the delights I have known, in many years devoted to the difficult but entrancing art of changing raw experiences into the connoisseur's enjoyment of life, I gratefully place the cricket of Victor Trumper.[3]

Here a word of caution is in order. It is very tempting, but exceedingly dangerous, to use Cardus's accounts of cricket and cricketers as biographical fodder, or to derive seminal insights into the development of his personality from prose prepared with only half an eye to history. Whether or not the young Cardus actually attended the matches he recalled is a question of fact; whether it matters or not, one of taste. After all, Shakespeare missed Agincourt. It would have been a matter of supreme indifference to Neville himself to learn that that in *Autobiography* he dated his first appearance at Old Trafford as the summer of 1902, whereas elsewhere this event is recorded as having taken place two years earlier. His recollections of the Homeric feats of MacLaren, Tyldesley and Trumper owed as much to 'emotions recollected in tranquillity' as to the first-hand observations of 'thoughtless youth'. With this in mind, it is as well to bring to the reading of Cardus on cricket just a pinch of salt whereby the extravagance which was a hallmark of his art may be balanced.

Forty years on, Neville was to recall the summer of 1902 as the high-spot of his childhood. Thereafter, things took a turn for the worse. Poverty became a real threat. The conditions he witnessed when, as an agent for a burial society, he ventured into the 'underworlds of Gorton and Salford and Hulme' in pursuit of weekly premiums on insurance policies, left him prey to a lifelong dread of penury. Even at the height of his fame the vision of destitution still returned to haunt him. In Sydney, for example, his reaction to his agent's advice that *Autobiography* 'was going to be a winner' was 'And thank the Lord it was. Otherwise I would have been in today's equivalent of the work-house.'[4]

As far as Neville was concerned, his problems really started at home – wherever that was. The family had already left Summer Place by the time Grandfather Robert died in October 1900. The next port of call was Claremont Street, but from then until 1916, when Neville turned up at 154, Fallowfield Road, the precise whereabouts of the Carduses is a complete mystery. 'The family broke up' was as much as Neville was prepared to disclose. The deaths of his grandparents were merely noted. Beatrice's demise occupied little more than a paragraph at the end of which her nephew, with just a touch of disapproval, recalled that:

> She became inexplicably compassionate about an elderly man who for years had been the gardener at a house where she picked up a temporary job as laundress, deep down in the cellar, two days a week. She married him, kept him and bore him a daughter and died at the age of twenty-eight.[5]

Then, without so much as a farewell glance at his mother, Cardus politely but firmly closed the door on that chapter of his life and, unimpeded by memories too painful or too uncomfortable to contemplate, set out on the first stage of his journey to Mount Helicon. Within a sentence, youth had become but a memory: 'After the breaking-up of Summer Place and the passing of Beatrice I lived precariously for a while. . . .'

[II]

The next ten years saw Neville acquire the values, attitudes and habits of a lifetime, and the raw material of an identity which was to find its definitive expression in *Autobiography* nearly half a century later. It was a time of improvement; improvement in life chances, in material conditions and in cultural standards. Though the world's first industrial economy may have been displaying disturbing signs of structural weakness, Manchester was still moving forward; more slowly, it is true, than in her heyday, more slowly too than many of the European nations which had industrialised in Britain's wake, but nevertheless still moving forward. 'Relative decline' was a term Mancunians were not familiar with. Optimists to a man, they displayed an unshakeable faith in those self-sustaining properties of progress that had underpinned economic activity for the best part of a century. From the smoke and din of Trafford Park to the civic splendour of Albert Square, there was a lasting buoyancy about public and private discourse which reflected a deeply held belief in the ability of British economic and political institutions to weather the storms ahead, from whatever quarter they might come, of whatever force they might be.

Neville's advance to manhood epitomised this optimism. Imbued with all the enthusiasm of youth, he embarked on a personal voyage of discovery. Though no records of his exact course have survived, some idea of its range and direction can be gained from the early entries under 'Cardus' in the index of *Second Innings*.

> ... *joined public library*, 42–4; on novels and novelists, 44; *discovery of Dickens*, 44–54, 69–70; *discovery of metaphysics*, 71f; cricketing memories and *experiences*, 82, 84f; at Board school; *professional cricketer; awakening interest in music*; desire to become *lieder* singer ...

It was a very earnest young man who surveyed the future from an uninspiring room somewhere in south Manchester. Where he spent the next decade is less important than the manner in which he occupied himself. The picture he bequeathed to us shows a young man rendered homeless by an unhappy and unavoidable series of events, making his way in the face of great adversity, sustained by an unquenchable zest for life. Home, he tells us, was not his mother's residence, but 'a single back room in a Manchester lodging [where I was], so cold in the winter for want of a blanket that I collected newspapers and periodicals to pile on my bed over my feet.'[6]

The choice of imagery in this passage is interesting. By subtly insinuating an association with the world of the tramp on his cold, bleak park-bench, Neville succeeded in enriching his narrative and exciting his readers' sympathies to the point at which they were unlikely to think too closely about the impression being created. This latter reaction was crucial. Throughout the early chapters of *Autobiography*, the reader was encouraged to feel that though the experiences being described may have been beyond his or her ken, nevertheless their romantic appeal warranted, even demanded, instant and uncritical acceptance. Had this tactic misfired, his public might well have concluded that the story was no more than an elaborate variation on a familiar theme, and not the substance of a miraculous metamorphosis which led Neville from Rusholme to the foothills of Parnassus.

The effect of this subterfuge was to camouflage elements of normality in Neville's upbringing. Look again at the 'discoveries' and 'experiences' listed in the index to *Second Innings*. Stripped of mystique, they appear the predictable manifestations of a process of physical and mental maturation known simply as 'growing-up'. Each entry is evidence of a widening of interest and association; each denotes a staging-post on the way to a mature identity. Cricket and culture were the central pillars of the identity he coveted. As was only fitting, the former had first run on his imagination. Like generations of boys before and since, Neville lived for the game. During the day his thoughts seldom strayed far from the sward; in the evening he and his pals hurried to the rough strip of 'brick-croft' behind Summer Place which served as their pitch, there to ape the exploits of their heroes as long as daylight permitted. 'One evening,' he recalled, 'I would announce that I was Lockwood and about to bowl fast; the next evening I might change myself to Rhodes and bowl so slowly that the ball scarcely reached the block-hole. It all depended upon what the day's county cricket scores chanced to reveal and extol.'[7]

These great battles were no place for the squeamish or faint-hearted. With a fervour born of innocence, the players scorned conventional notions of politeness and decency as they strove to inject an element of brutal realism into their performances. My favourite picture of young Neville recalls just such an occasion one evening in 1899. Earlier that day, the tragic Johnny Briggs had been carried off the field at Headingley after suffering the first of a series of epilectic fits which were to lead to his death only three years later. The news reached Neville as his own test match was about to begin, but somehow the element of personal tragedy had been lost *en route*:

> An excited urchin, Sammy Ogden, a little late into the action that evening, came tearing over the earth even as I was setting my field in the character and gestures of A. C. MacLaren; and my long-stop was the youngest of the Moffits next door, who wasn't really qualified for big cricket because he hardly reached as high as the wickets. With the awful tidings from Leeds hot in his mouth, Sammy Ogden appeared upon us like a messenger in a Greek play. 'What's the matter?' we asked. And again like a messenger in a Greek play, he broke into blank verse:
>
> > Briggs 'e's gone and 'ad a fit at Leeds,
> > Taken off the field 'e wos today;
> > And England can now only bat ten men.
>
> Messenger Ogden's news heightened the drama of our own test match in the dusty sunshine of that hot summer. The youngest Moffit immediately acted Johnny Briggs having a fit; and as MacLaren (myself) and the eldest Moffit (Joe Darling, the Australian captain) led him off the field he made spit in his mouth to represent foam.[8]

The hours spent locked in mortal combat on that dusty plain did not go unrewarded. Two members of the group were destined to join the ranks of county cricketers and Cardus himself became a more than useful performer. Many a batsman was lulled into a false sense of security by the sight of the bespectacled young man at the bowler's end, only to fall victim to the cricketer's equivalent of the 'old one-two'. One legacy of his years in the Rusholme 'nursery' was an uncanny ability to spin an off-break 'so that it would whip upwards viciously straight at the most important and tender part of a man's anatomy'. In those days, the 'box' was not the indispensable appendage it is today. With a ruthlessness which totally belied his amiable exterior, Neville 'seldom hesitated, as soon as a batsman came to the crease, to let him have a quick one bang in the penis; after which a quick, simple straight one would invariably remove him from the scene'.

Years later, during a lecture at the Purcell Rooms of all places, Sir Neville was to return to the theme of the cricket box. His story centred on the formidable personage of Dr W. G. Grace who, as befitted a medical man, was a strong advocate of the box. 'Every young man should have one,' he used to say. During one match, 'W.G.' was approached somewhat sheepishly by a young man who, it transpired, lacked this vital piece of equipment. 'Make one out of chicken wire,' the great man thundered. This advice was duly followed and the young man proceeded to enjoy an injury-free afternoon. The only problem was that every time the ball hit this newly-fashioned guard, it went 'ping'. After a while, during which he had been hit all over the place by his protégé, Grace could contain his anger no longer. At the end of another disastrous over, he went up to the young man and observed tartly, 'My dear chap, I said a cock-box, not a music-box!'

At this point in his recollections Neville indulges in a character-istic *volte-face*. After setting himself up as a young man who by dint of hours of lonely practice had perfected a knack for bowling off-breaks which placed him in great demand in the local leagues, he then abruptly drops the subject. Save for a few anecdotes about an early match in Whalley Range where he returned the stunning figures of nine for fourteen, an incident in the wilds of Worcester-shire when he smashed a county fast-bowler for successive boundaries to win the game, and a much later occasion when he came within an ace of bowling his former hero, A. C. MacLaren (none of which shed any light on his professional career), the details of his exploits on the field were driven quietly but firmly into a dense, censorial, autobiographical mist from which they were never to emerge.

But even this strategy did not satisfy Cardus's deeply felt need to rid himself of the taint of active participation in cricket – as a professional. The game which in childhood had inspired absolute and total devotion was in later years destined to be downgraded to the status of a passing fad, a childish diversion bereft of intrinsic appeal. Time and time again in the successive volumes of autobi-ography, Neville went out of his way to erase from the reader's mind any suspicion of a lasting emotional affinity for cricket, or any other sport for that matter. The familiar association between Cardus and cricket originated as an historical accident and survived long after it had ceased to have any basis in fact largely because of the quality of his writings on the game. In reality, Cardus declared,

> I am not a man who is interested in sport. I have attended only one race-meeting in my life. I have never seen an English Cup Final. I have seldom known that it was Derby Day until the next morning's newspapers. I cannot play any card games.[9]

If the sporting dimension of cricket did not stimulate Cardus, what was the source of its attraction? Surely no one would spend the best part of twenty consecutive summers, day-in, day-out, at cricket grounds as far removed as Maidstone and Manchester just for the money? The answer lay in the extra-sporting dimension of the game, the characters he met and the range of human responses they illustrated. Whether the players in question would always have recognised themselves as the subjects of the delightful cameos which captivated the *Manchester Guardian*'s cricketing audience for a generation or more is open to doubt, but for Cardus they provided irrefutable evidence in support of his contention that, 'There are many things about cricket, apart from the skill and the score. . . . To go to a cricket match for nothing but cricket is as though a man were to go into an inn for nothing but drink.'[10] Not only did he never consider cricket as an appropriate subject for his pen 'in the years when I was trying to equip myself as a writer', but looking back, 'It is pretty certain that if I were young today I wouldn't become devoted to first-class cricket and wish to write about it.'[11]

And so on. So emphatic are these rejections of cricket, so frequent their appearance, that the sceptic might be forgiven for suspecting that by the time Neville came to recall his youth he had become slightly embarrassed at having treated such a simple pleasure so seriously. For, despite his protestations, the fact remains that throughout his late teens and early twenties cricket was a central theme in his life. A bowler of quality, much in demand in the local leagues, he organised his annual calendar with one aim in mind: to leave the summers free to make a living as a professional. During these months, he played three or four times a week for different teams on different grounds around Manchester; achieving various degrees of success, but always earning enough money to support himself in tolerable accommodation and, most important of all, acquiring that 'professional' insight into the game which some critics hold to be the essential difference between his music and cricket commentaries. When Neville wrote of the problems he had experienced in finding regular work, of 'the cul-de-sac of casual labour' which at one stage seemed to threaten his future, the fault did not lie entirely with the local labour market, difficult though this undoubtedly was. The truth of the matter was that between the ages of eighteen and twenty-two he was happy enough doing 'all kinds of menial work', as long as this arrangement left him free to enjoy the bliss of an uninterrupted summer's cricket.

Where and how Neville's winters were spent is predictably unclear. Depending on which volume of autobiography you turn to, he might have been absentmindedly doodling on a high-legged stool in Hugh Fleming's office in Bridge Street or pushing a hand-cart up Brook Street for a joiner and builder named Ed Moses or boiling lead in a print room. Whatever the truth, our impression of the adolescent Cardus remains the same. Intelligent, articulate and carefree, he was blessed with an unquenchable capacity for joy, and an equally irresistible determination to indulge this gift whenever and wherever possible. The results were often unpredictable. 'One summer evening,' he recalled, 'I suddenly ran like mad down the street, impelled by a strange ecstacy of happiness; there was no special cause for this outburst, and I had not known the like of it; it was pure joy at the thought that I was alive and young.'[12]

By the time Neville started to write autobiographies, this simple spontaneity had long since given way to a more sober, measured approach to life. The change is most evident in his references to cricket. Where once he had thrilled at the sight of a cunningly flighted off-break or the sound of a perfectly struck cover-drive (though he always claimed that shortsightedness prevented him from hitting many of these), now the game took on a different significance. 'Cricket helped me to a balance at the bank,' he reveals in *Autobiography*, while in *Second Innings*,

> the point to be emphasised is that it was through cricket that I escaped from the seemingly blind alley of my lot in an existence as a clerk, handyman or any pitiful job; for I had no visible means of support, no technical training whatsoever, and no capacity to 'rough it'. Cricket opened my door of escape;

cricket brought to me enough economic independence whereby to educate myself.[13]

But the lasting association between Cardus and cricket, both in his eyes and in those of his public, was not based on financial considerations. At an early stage in his career, Neville identified in the traditional pastime of flannelled fools a rich, but largely ignored, aesthetic seam, and it was the skill with which he exploited this reserve which was to set him apart from all other cricket writers and, with the exception of Bernard Darwin, all other sports writers too. His emphasis on the aesthetic, as opposed to the physical, technical or competitive elements in cricket may at times have been exaggerated, but it was, and remains, his hallmark. Bearing this in mind, it is perhaps strange that Cardus devoted so little time to explaining why he placed such stress on the aesthetic, or even what he meant by the term.

In the absence of any word from the master, many observers have been tempted to speculate. For example, it is very easy to equate the development of a new style of reporting with a young journalist's natural concern with creating his own niche in a highly competitive profession. Seen in this light, Cardus's emphasis on the aesthetic element in cricket was no more than a strategic affectation. Alternatively, it has been suggested that the style of writing which Neville developed was his way of bridging an uncomfortable social and cultural chasm which divided the two worlds he was to frequent, and of resolving some of his own identity doubts in the process. Thus one critic has recently argued that Cardus 'may even have felt he was slumming, culturally speaking, when he was at Old Trafford rather than at Hallé concerts or at the theatre. So he needed to elevate cricket by high-brow comparisons with the world of art.'[14]

Both interpretations contain a measure of truth, but neither gets to the heart of the matter. That in presenting cricket as a performing art Cardus created a new journalistic genre is undeniable. No one before or since wrote about the game quite like 'Cricketer'. Nor is there any doubt that at the beginning of his career in journalism Cardus set out to infuse his columns with culture. His was to be a different order of reader. 'When I began to go to cricket matches for the *Manchester Guardian*,' he recalled, 'I wrote above the heads of the average reader who turns in his newspaper for cricket reports: Hobbs was not enough for me as Hobbs. I had to see something aesthetic in him, or a symbol of something, or as a sculpture, with clouds of glory about him. . . .'[15]

Poor old Jack! 61,237 runs, 197 centuries, and still 'Cricketer' wasn't satisfied. Who was the precocious pup who dared to suggest that England's greatest batsman was somehow inadequate? Contrary to speculation, he was neither an ambitious *arriviste*, nor a graceless philistine who saw style as a short-cut to fame. It was Hobbs's misfortune, so some would have it, to catch 'Cricketer' at a moment when he was particularly conscious of the need to establish himself. Cardus's style was more than just an expression of his personality: it was one means by which he formed that personality, and in the end it became part of the personality itself. His determination to transform the reporting of cricket into a medium suited to his personal tastes was thus not a meretricious ploy, but a carefully fashioned response to a growing awareness of the breadth of his cultural appetite. If cricket was to occupy a central place in his life, the conventional presentation of the game had to be recast in a form congruent with his cultural predilections and responsive to his literary talents.

[III]

Culture was for Cardus the critical motive force behind his pursuit of identity. It was also the mould within which the public persona that came to embrace both 'N.C.' and 'Cricketer' was cast. The beginning of this process dates from the moment the young boy first followed his inquisitive mind through the doors of the Dickenson Road Library into what were for him the uncharted regions of great literature. From this time until the day ten years or so later when he finally became the Neville Cardus we now recognise, this young man travelled extensively across the face of Western European culture, stopping here and there to steep himself in a particular tradition, without once straying more than sixty miles from Manchester.

His route was not the product of cold, logical planning. Dipping and winding along the undulating contours of literature, theatre, philosophy and music, it more closely resembled the wanderings of a happy-go-lucky rambler than the itinerary of a seasoned traveller. Sometimes the need to affirm the privileges of youth caused him to fly in the face of every established canon of taste. Elsewhere the pilgrimage ground to a halt while homage was paid at the shrine of some long-forgotten sage. Sudden changes in pace and direction were the order of the day; above all, progress had to be visible.

The starting-point for this cultural grand tour was the music halls of Manchester: Pitt Hardacre's Comedy (housed in the then very splendid Midland Hotel where Rolls wooed Royce) and Miss Horniman's occasionally notorious Gaiety Theatre. As he watched the shows and pantomimes from the distant, precarious gallery rail, the great comic actors of the day – Harry Randall, Little Tich, Dan Leno, Harry Weldon, Wilkie Bard and the incomparable George Robey – animated a great tradition of pantomime dame. Mother Goose, Widow Twankey and the Ugly Sisters may seem a far cry from Brünnhilde, Norma and Donna Anna, but for Cardus they were the stuff of which dreams were made.

Robey held a special place in his affections, partly because of his unrivalled capacity to communicate with ordinary people and partly because he too was an avid cricketer. Neville liked to tell of the day he saw Robey batting in the nets at Lord's against none other than Jack Gregory, one half of the great Australian fast-bowling partnership of the 1920s. Always the actor, even off stage, Robey was heard to mutter as Gregory's first ball whistled by, 'I mean to say . . . well, I mean to say.' As Cardus grew older, he could not resist the temptation to over-intellectualise when discussing Robey and the tradition he represented. In a radio interview towards the end of his life, he was to claim that 'music hall was the epitome of the working classes: it put the pavement on the stage and made art of it'. Later in the same programme, the interviewer (Peter Cotes) asked Cardus what he had meant by describing Robey as 'Rabelaisian and Gothic'. The old 'pro' was not caught out so easily. Spotting the googly a mile off, he was content to pad up. 'Robey,' he said, 'was definitely Rabelaisian, but I've no idea what I might have meant by Gothic.'

From the grease-paint and slapstick of the music hall, Neville 'graduated' to higher things. Though cricket continued to dominate his summers, the next ten years were to see him broaden and develop his tastes and knowledge. The pursuit of identity commenced with a vengeance. Reading constituted the first challenge. As a boy, he had thrilled at the daring deeds of Maxwell Scot, Sidney Drew and Henry St John in Alfred Harmsworth's weekly, *The Boy's Friend*. Many a summer evening was spent waiting for the London train to bring the latest edition . But the discovery of a new world neatly stacked behind library doors strained his loyalty to Maxwell

Scot and his friends to the limit and it was not long before he forsook these ripping yarns for the world of Jerome K. Jerome and true literature. Ironically, much of the impetus behind Neville's earliest forays down the shelves was apparently provided by his 'semi-literate' grandfather. Concerned at his grandson's choice of reading matter, the old man took him aside and offered the following guidance: 'Read proper books, young man, proper books. Don't waste your money on novelettes.' (The fact that the work in question was *Anna Karenina*, and that according to the Register of Deaths the old man had died at least two years before he came to make this remark should worry the reader no more than it worried Cardus.)

Neville was evidently much moved by his grandfather's strictures (if such they were) for within a few months he had embarked on a formative voyage through the works of Charles Dickens. 'Discovering Dickens is one of the few important events that occur in mortal life,' he observed later with uncompromising candour. He himself discovered Dickens 'after much tramping the streets from lending library to library', the breakthrough coming not a moment too soon as only a sentence later Cardus felt impelled to write off a substantial section of humanity. 'I am still of the opinion that human beings can confidently be divided into broad classes; those who have it in them from birth onwards to appreciate Dickens and those who haven't. The second group should be avoided as soon as detected.'[16]

Fortunately, Neville felt able to place himself in the first category, and from this honoured station proceeded to generate prose which, at its best, revealed an imaginative power and a richness of expression even Dickens would not have been ashamed of. In such passages, he succeeded in infusing the average and the mundane with unsuspected originality. But when the vital spark was missing, the fall from grace was drastic. The burnished narrative slipped all too easily into a miasma of exaggeration, irrelevance and self-indulgence. Moreover, there were moments when Cardus was so overwhelmed by his admiration for the likes of Nickelby, Weller, Pecksniff and Mrs Gamp that he succumbed to the temptation to paint himself in unmistakeably Dickensian colours. Consider, for example, the following passage from *Second Innings*:

> On a winter night, in my cold attic, with newspaper piled high for warmth on my bed, in a garret-room uncarpeted, even without oilcloth, bare boards and sometimes the sound of a

mouse gnawing away at one of them, a candle burning a small circle of gloom, I read for the first time the scene in *Pickwick* where Sam Weller composes a Valentine. . . .[17]

After devouring Dickens for the best part of a year, Neville turned his attention to the works of Thackeray ('strictly works written by an accomplished author'), Meredith, Hardy ('who meant as little as the long arm of his coincidences'), Conrad and, with 'labour and conceit', Henry James. All this by the time he was twenty. Not content with consuming others' prose, he turned his hand to preparing his own and, after the shortest of apprenticeships, came up with a novel about a millionaire in a sumptuous mansion who 'held the listeners spell-bound, by the profundity of his ideas and the lambent flame of his irony'. The manuscript was never submitted for publication.

Even at this early stage, it is a little difficult to accept at face value Cardus's thumbnail sketch of his teenage self as 'one of the shyest, most self-conscious of youths'. The more one delves beneath the surface, the clearer it becomes that this portrayal owed as much to wishful thinking as to objective self-appraisal, an impression reinforced by the other details of his life which Neville subsequently released. Once securely ensconced in the musty ambience of the lending library, it was literally and metaphorically only a short step from literature to philosophy. 'One darkened afternoon' he chanced upon G. H. Lewes's *A Biographical History of Philosophy*, and in that moment 'made one of the most far-reaching discoveries of my life'. It was not his first brush with philosophical thinking (a year earlier he had wrestled with G. W. Foote's atheistic heresy, *The Freethinker*), but it proved to be by far the most significant.

'How many books do we read in a lifetime,' he asked later, 'of which we can say that they open doors in our consciousness, that after reading them we are different, and that even as we turn the pages we feel sight coming where there was no sight?' Through the clearing mist, young Cardus saw stretched out before him the engaging prospect of the philosophic mind – Locke, Berkeley, Hume, Kant and Schopenhauer, all stacked neatly on open shelves awaiting his selection. None were to be disappointed. By the time his second autobiographical volume went to print, Neville felt sufficiently *au fait* with the Western tradition of philosophy to offer his own assessment of its competing giants: 'I can always return to

Schopenhauer,' he wrote, 'the only writer in metaphysics with grandeur of imagination.' The lad from Rusholme had travelled far.

But it was music more than any other cultural activity that captured Neville's imagination during these formative years. He was a late starter. Born into a household lacking any musical instruments and raised on a diet of music hall melodies, he was sixteen before first getting to grips with the classical repertoire. Once ignited, however, his passion for music soon became all-consuming. For a while cricket became little more than an 'also-ran'. Neville had entered a state of grace, and (for several years) scores, results and averages, details which have fascinated generations of children, barely registered. 'To this day I can remember most important details in the history of cricket except any concerning the four summers from 1908 to 1912; I have to consult *Wisden* when these seasons are under discussion. . . . No, I was lost in music.'[18]

This total immersion took several forms. Always possessed of a reasonable voice, he now took lessons from a professional tutor (named in *Who's Who*, but nowhere else, as Charles Egan), initially with less than happy results. But in time determination and dedication achieved their just rewards in the form of 'an engagement or two'. As many of these bookings – a Saturday night 'smoker' for local freemasons – did not offer a captive audience for performances of *Die Winterreise*, we can only presume that on occasions Neville must have been within a whisker of sacrificing his art at the altar of Mammon.

Fortunately, not all his apprenticeship proved as compromising. Every fortnight he attended concerts at the Royal Manchester College of Music at which the Principal, Dr Adolf Brodsky, the tutors and Samuel Langford, the music critic of the *Manchester Guardian*, assessed performances from the awful proximity of the front row, occasionally inclining a head or pursing lips in a way which to the *cognoscenti* implied either salvation or eternal damnation. Once in a while, Dr Brodsky led his own quartet in performances which went 'beyond the printed symbols and quavers and semi-quavers to the source of musical life itself', and afterwards to the comforts of the Brodskys' home in Bowden where all was *schön* and *gemütlich*.

To round off the week, every Sunday afternoon during the winter Neville walked four miles from his home to meetings of the

'Brotherhood' at the Islington Hall, Ancoats, where in the space of a few hours he experienced the intellectual and verbal wizardry of George Bernard Shaw venting his Socialist spleen on such opiates as the Ten Commandments, and a young, unknown tutor from the Royal College playing Beethoven's Opus 111 in a manner which prepared the audience for 'baptism into music as a spiritual fact'. In Neville's own words, 'I did not understand the language, but I heard the voice.'

With a mystical communion with the Almighty under way, it is perhaps an appropriate moment to stress that there was, and is, more to good music or any other art form than the aesthetic impulse. When Neville came to recall his initial sorties into culture from a vantage point forty years on and 12,000 miles distant, he may well have seen them as an *entrée* to a higher spiritual plane, but at the time they possessed a very different significance. Just as Shaw had laboured painstakingly to build the character of 'G.B.S.', so Neville spent much of his late teens and early twenties busily shaping his own identity. The end-product of his endeavours, the Neville Cardus known to music- and cricket-lovers the world over, was unique: the production process itself, a phenomenon known to psychoanalysts as 'identity work', was not. From time immemorial, young people have experienced a similar wish to discover and express their individuality, and Neville was no exception to the rule. If anything, the motley examples of men and women handed down by his kin provided an even greater incentive to find a richer, more fulfilling world.

The last years of Edwardian England were a vital period in Neville's emergence. While the rest of the country was basking in those last, palmy days before the outbreak of war, he was engaged in an intensely personal debate, a process of self-enquiry fired and fuelled by culture. The existence he worked so assiduously to create was unmistakably highbrow. Culture, he felt, bestowed on its worshippers both substance and style. He needed to be different and was only too happy to be labelled 'an intellectual snob'. He hungered after great literature, fine minds and beauty; hence the endless journeys to libraries, the long walks to and from concerts at the Free Trade Hall, the hours spent at the University listening to Samuel Alexander expound upon the mysteries of metaphysics and Bernard Bosanquet pursue the elusive Hegelian distinction between Mind and Object. His 'education' was planned with all the precision of a military campaign. Nothing was left to chance: 'I compiled a cultural schema when I was veering towards the twenties, a plan of campaign: so many hours a week to that subject, so many hours to this.'[19]

Armed with this 'Schema of Culture', and a 'Review of Literature' for good measure, Neville set off in search of a new world. On the way, he observed several time-honoured conventions. 'Identity work' often requires a distaste (if only temporary) for institutions like the family and schools, and a preference for complex, novel or arcane pursuits which would be frowned upon in conventional circles. In recent years, the novels of Kafka, the music of Stockhausen and the plays of Pinter have enjoyed a special following amongst the young partly because they satisfied these criteria. Other important conditions are the availability of an accessible peer group to identify with and the potential for sexual arousal, albeit on a lofty intellectual plane! It must also allow plenty of scope for factional rivalry between supporters of the leading artists of the day – Callas versus Tebaldi, Domingo versus Pavarotti, to quote but two recent examples; and finally, for those so inclined, it should also open up opportunities for further learning and the acquisition of obscure expertise. Ideally, the activity should easily be associated with a highly visible group of followers and have provision built into it for a degree of permissive behaviour which would otherwise be deemed undesirable. University students' rag stunts and the antics of the 'promenaders' are cases in point.

It takes no more than a quick glance to see how much of Neville's early life fits this pattern. Parents were dropped; relatives (with the exception of Beatrice) ignored; school and teachers denounced; new discoveries in literature, music, drama and philosophy noisily devoured – and it was a rich feast!

Elgar, Shaw, Wells, Ibsen, Nietzsche, Strauss, Debussy, the French Impressionists; our first taste of Stendhal, the de Goncourts, J.-K. Huysmans – these last were rather late reaching England, or at any rate Manchester: then before our eyes had been accustomed to the fresh vista, the Russians swept down on us – Dostoievsky, Turgenev, Tchekov, Moussorgsky, Rimsky-Korsakov and the ballet. It was a renaissance; the twentieth century opened on a full and flowing sea; thus we emerged from the Victorian Age.[20]

For all his supposed shyness, Neville seems to have experienced little difficulty in finding or creating suitable peer groups. As a young boy, along with Johnny Howard, Billy Clegg and Harry Pinkerton, he was a founder member of 'the Gang', a group of 'back-street' reprobates who revelled in a form of delinquency which Cardus, consistent to the last, described as a 'kind of art for art's sake'. As the hours of thoughtless youth passed, the Gang was superseded by a more sedentary and cerebral band whose staple diet was culture and who met in summer outside the gates of Alexandra Park, and in winter at a Lyon's Café on the corner of Albert Square. At each venue, Neville and his fellow 'young Turks' ('W' and his enterprisingly named brother, 'EW'; the gammy-legged Scottish Marxist, Bobby Burns; and Herbert Ramsbottom) met 'not to air (our) economic grievances, not to 'spout' politics and discontent, but to relieve the ferment of our minds. . . .'[21]

These Socratic encounters were usually triggered off by a particular event or performance, but soon raged like an uncontrolled forest fire across a tinder-dry cultural landscape. One day the subject might be the respective merits of Bancroft and Wolf; the next day, Richard Strauss and 'modern' music; the next, Busoni, and so on. The importance of not being found intellectually wanting on these occasions required detailed preparation. Arguments had to be clarified, references checked and quotations memorised. Here was an ever-present incentive to extend the bounds of knowledge.

Yet as important as the substance of these meetings was the sense of group identity they fostered. For Neville and his friends, the acquisition of culture was very much a collective experience. Wherever possible, first performances were attended *en masse*. Elgar's 1st Symphony was deeply etched on Cardus's memory, not necessarily because it represented a landmark in the development of English music (many would argue that the 2nd was a superior piece), but because his presence at its first performance by the Hallé under Hans Richter on a cold, foggy December night in 1908 was a cultural *rite de passage*. Attendance on such an auspicious occasion served to place him in an elect as heir to a great tradition of European culture.

Of all the characteristics of identity work only the sexual dimension does not figure in Neville's accounts of his coming-of-age, though there are good reasons for believing that he deliberately chose to underscore his achievements in this sphere.

The emerging picture of Neville at this stage of his life is not, as legend would have it, one of a solitary young man forced by circumstances to plough a difficult furrow through hostile terrain, who found solace in cricket and salvation in a mystical union with music. Far from being extraordinary, his childhood seems to have conformed to a familiar pattern, so much so that when the moment came to recreate these years a degree of recasting was needed before they would come into line with the image he had subsequently acquired. The key to the changes which occurred during this period lies in Neville's determination to distance himself from his past, and to create a fresh identity more in keeping with the world he hoped to frequent. The clearest indication of what was afoot is to be found in nothing more striking than a change of name. Today the world knows and speaks only of Neville Cardus, but in his early days back in Manchester Neville went by the name of Fred. In practice, the phasing-out of Fred was only a gesture, but it symbolised a sea-change. 'Fred' conjured up uncomfortably vivid memories of a forgettable childhood. It wasn't so much that things had been bad as boring and mediocre. A real, impoverished working-class background can offer hidden benefits. Tarted up here and there, it can be made to seem a romantic, even stimulating, experience, but a childhood spent in the slightly more prosperous Summer Place conferred no such blessings. 'Neville', on the other hand, smacked of a different world where urbane circles engaged in animated, but always civilised, discussion, and cultural and intellectual excellence was the ultimate goal.

By 1912, this 'most self-conscious of youths' had acquired his majority and a self-confidence which allowed him to write to Jerome K. Jerome 'telling him that I thought his novel was "literature"', to take Forbes Robinson to task for providing an inadequate portrayal of Hamlet, and to present the dominant figure in English music, Dr Hans Richter, with a petition for performances of modern French music – a request which, it has to be said, cut little ice with 'the All-Father'. 'Mod'n French musik,' he retorted. 'Zer is no mod'n French musik.' The name of Neville Cardus had also made its first appearance in print as the author of a learned piece in *Musical Opinion* entitled 'Bantock and Style in Music'. Still only twenty-one, his ambitions had yet to crystallise, but already the two influences which were to determine the course of his life over the next fifty years had begun to make their presence felt. The first was a passion for writing; the other an affection for the *Manchester Guardian* and all it represented.

[IV]

Shrewsbury appears in Neville's memoirs as a magical interlude. He was appointed to the post of assistant professional at the school in the spring of 1912 on the strength of some impressively consistent bowling performances in the local leagues around Manchester. Having applied for the job purely 'on spec', he had long since forgotten about it when, several weeks later, a letter arrived from the Head of School announcing his success. From the moment the Shrewsbury train steamed out of London Road Station bearing the new assistant coach, two pairs of spectacles and a tin box containing his worldly chattels, the scene shifts to an Arcadian paradise, 'a green and wooded futurity . . . richness in the open air of England; trees and the murmur of summer in the distance'. Through the lush green foliage, we catch a glimpse of 'the most beautiful playing-fields in the world, spreading and imperceptibly mingling with the pasture land of Shropshire'.

Characters move dreamily across our view as if on an impressionist canvas. Cardus himself enters, a little apprehensively at first, but with growing assurance as his qualities are recognised. Other eminences come and go; the Headmaster, Dr Cyril Alington, shortly destined to move to even greater glory on Agar's Plough; Attewell, once of England and now the school professional, exponent of the front-foot technique, a Midlander through and through; Wainwright, his successor, a thin, dour Yorkshireman fond of his ale and of playing back; and in the background, the distant rumble of a world disappearing in the mud of Flanders.

Shrewsbury made an immediate impression on Neville: in his own words, it was as though he had shed a skin. In a letter to an imminent visitor written during the summer of 1916, his last at the school, he confessed, 'I really envy you – because I remember so well the pleasure – keen pleasure – of my first visit here.'

Forget about the nervous, frail young man of *Autobiography* whose first appearance at the nets reduced his pupils to hysterics and his employer to despair. Those opening deliveries may have been a little erratic, but then the greatest of us need a few looseners before striking line and length. The young man who arrived at Shrewsbury

School early in May 1912 did not need to be persuaded of his talents. Lean and fit after years of league cricket, mentally prepared by those evenings at the Lyons Café, Neville felt confident of holding his own even in the exalted surroundings he now occupied. There was no question of being overawed. After he had been at the school only a matter of weeks, the new assistant coach took issue with no less a figure than the Headmaster on the merits of a particular translation of Euripedes' *Medea*, a bold move considering that Neville knew nothing of Greek. For good measure, he also read the Koran. Energetic and confident, there must have been times when Neville's company became almost oppressive.

When he first read the advertisement in the *Athletic News*, it must have seemed like a heaven-sent opportunity. Unlike his existing job as a clerk in the marine insurance company of Hugh and Christopher Fleming, the position of assistant professional offered the best of all worlds. Summers spent in a beautiful setting full of cricket; time to devote to reading and writing; a salary which, if carefully husbanded, would be sufficient to finance a winter's uninterrupted study of literature and music; the inspirational presence of Alington and his colleagues; a new world less than fifty miles from Manchester. Nor was he to be in any way disappointed.

In their different ways, both Attewell and Wainwright proved to be congenial colleagues. The former snored and the latter drank, but neither succeeded in upsetting the mood of high seriousness which descended on Neville during a large part of those summers. He quickly settled to the routine of school life, establishing a happy rapport both with boys, who called him 'Sir', and masters alike. Alington, in particular, soon warmed to the earnest endeavour of his new coach and when, at the outbreak of war in 1914, the Headmaster's personal secretary rallied to the flag, no one was surprised when Neville assumed his responsibilities. For the next three summers, he occupied a small room next to Alington's library in School House. The partnership was broken only by Alington's departure for Eton in the autumn of 1916.

During his first months at Shrewsbury, Neville was content to confine his role in school life to coaching. All his spare time was devoted to reading and writing, either in the school library where he studied as diligently as any of the pupils, or back at his lodgings. But it was not long before his reputation spread. His knowledge of music made him a natural target for the Musical Society, a challenge which Neville neither could, nor wished to, resist. Before long 'Fred Cardus', assistant cricket coach, had reappeared as 'J. F. N. Cardus', organiser and presenter of lectures in aid of the 'British Prisoners of War in Germany' fund. On one of these occasions, Neville took as his subject 'The Art of Song: An examination of the principles of the art-lied, with illustrations from Loewe, Schubert, Schumann, Franz, Brahms and Hugo Wolf', and featured such local celebrities as Miss Grace Pound and Miss Dora Pickering. Unfortunately, no records (written or otherwise) of the evening have survived.

One of the great advantages of working at Shrewsbury was that it allowed Neville to remain in close touch with friends and events in Manchester. It was nothing for him to slip away from the nets at the end of an afternoon's practice, rush down to his lodgings, change and then, almost in one movement, leap aboard the train to Manchester. The two-hour journey gave him ample time to recover his breath before setting out on another headlong dash through the streets of Manchester, finally to arrive at the Quay Theatre only minutes before Thomas Beecham entered the pit and the curtain rose on, say *Falstaff* or *Madam Butterfly*.

Towards the end of his stay at Shrewsbury, Neville struck up a close friendship with a gentleman by the name of George Popper. Throughout the summer of 1916, the two kept up a regular correspondence, Popper providing all the latest news and gossip from Manchester and Cardus replying with a mixture of learned discourse and intimate personal detail which forms an instructive contrast with the portrait he was to create thirty years later. The exchange of letters began shortly after Neville's return to Shrewsbury in late April 1916, for what was to be his last summer at the school. By this time he had moved from his original lodgings at 14, Cross Hill to a 'high social plane in Shrewsbury apartments (not lodgings)' at 21, Colon Crescent. From the tone of his first letter, the return to the school had not been the uplifting experience of previous years. Later we discover why. He was missing Manchester's cultural programme, and finding the eccentricities of the Headmaster's typewriter almost more than mortal flesh could bear:

21, Colon Crescent
Shrewsbury

Dear Popper,

Thrice lucky you – these next few weeks! Remember to murmur a consoling prayer for me 'tween acts – you can include it among the usual supplications for Singer's Souls. My own soul is probably past caring for since I found this damned typewriter.

Keep your eyes on Douglas. What a frantic existence his must be just now. No doubt he will die a spectacular death during 'Boris'.

I must confess that I'm not happy here this year, and I have cursed most eloquently my folly for coming away.

Let me hear from you at once, and give me all the news and your impressions of the opera.

Yours,
Fred

Take note – I also live in a Crescent!
You are not the only meritocrat.

Popper, who lived at 33, Victoria Crescent, Eccles, evidently complied with 'Fred's' request for only a couple of weeks later another letter (this time on headed School House notepaper) was on its way to Manchester. The tone is still resentful, but life evidently had its moments:

Shrewsbury
12 May 1916

My dear Popper,

I will risk swelling your head by telling you that I have formed a better idea of the opera in Manchester from your notes than from all the critics! Sammy's notices so far have quite lacked that definite-ness that good criticism demands. A first-grade critic, I take it, must be able to find phrases that apply to a given work, apply to it *inevitably, and to that work only*. If the critic can succeed at this, and in addition, possesses a style that is unconsciously self-revelatory – then we get a Pater, a Newman.

Manchester has not had a musical critic of this nature since – er – say last winter but one! . . .

I mourn for having missed 'Boris'.

You will forgive all this rather prosy stuff in a letter, but in this wilderness, I have no opportunity to talk much – so I must let off waste-matter in my letters. . . .

Edith comes today – so I shall be happier. Probably you think I am a sorry philosopher – but that is because I am a very good lover!

> Best wishes,
> Fred

Thanks for your offer to keep me supplied with Langford's notices etc – but Edith sends me everything! I hear that Sheldon has been engaged for the opera season by the *Daily News*.

So far Newman has not been to the opera. He was in Birmingham on Monday and Tuesday. I am in close touch with him here.

So the truth is out. The young man who was later to write of himself, 'the history of my sex life could be interestingly and comprehensively told on a post-card' and 'girls don't exist for me – I did not sleep with a woman until near middle-age' was in reality supremely confident of his amatory prowess. The lady in question, Edith Honorine Watten King, later to become his wife, was an extraordinary person in her own right. Though she remains a shadowy figure throughout the autobiographies, Edith was in fact very close to Neville and destined to play a crucial, if unconventional, role in his career. In 1916 she was a schoolmistress, but devoted much of her spare time to amateur dramatics. As likely as not the two first met at a theatrical evening. and from then on Edith became a regular member of the Lyons Café set.

Another interesting feature of this letter is its unmistakable self-assurance. Irrespective of whether he is praising Popper, laying into 'Sammy' (none other than Samuel Langford, *Manchester Guardian* music critic in succession to Newman, and elsewhere in the autobiographies described as the 'greatest of all writers on music'), or explaining Wagner, Neville positively oozes confidence. He is quite prepared to take issue with anyone, even Ernest Newman, the music critic of the *Birmingham Post* and probably the most influential voice of the day. It seems from this letter that Neville and Newman already shared a 'close' relationship. But it is neither to Newman nor Langford that he is referring in the mysterious second paragraph. The identity of the 'musical critic' does not become clear until *Who's Who* is consulted. There, in an entry nestling between 'Cardinall, Sir Allan Wolsey' and 'Cardwell, George', we discover that the music critic of the *Daily Citizen* (Manchester edition) in 1913 was none other than one Neville Cardus.

Edith, it transpires, was also friendly with Popper. In a letter dated 20 May 1916, Neville expressed his 'immense gratitude [to Popper] for so splendidly entertaining Edith'. Later on in this letter, we also discover Popper's guilty secret. He was a German immigrant and hence subject both to close police supervision of his movements and public vilification. By early 1915, a combination of rapidly rising casualty figures and stories of enemy atrocities resulted in attacks on premises bearing foreign-sounding names becoming common-place. In Salford, for example,

crowds of young people and women congregated in the vicinity of shops owned by persons with German names and attacked them with some degree of violence. The crowd in the early morning numbered several thousands and began by jeering outside the shop and house of Mr Herman Pratt, pork butcher, of New Road. Then the more daring spirits threw stones. By the time every window had been smashed the police had lost control of the crowd. Receiving no reply to their jeers, the rioters, surging forward, broke down the shop door or scrambled through the window and tossed pork cuttings and everything they could find into the street. . . .

The premises were completely wrecked. 'I have never seen anything like it before,' said a constable who took part in an attempt to check the rioting. 'There would be many a breakfast table set better this morning than it has ever been. Folk went off with sides of bacon, brass curbs and fire irons. One woman complained to the police that she had only been able to procure a pot of dripping.'[22]

Whether Neville appreciated the risks he was running in befriending a Hun we will never know, but it was a mark of his loyalty that he stood by Popper at a time when many would not have thought twice about removing his name from their visiting lists. Not for the first or last time in his life, Neville showed a complete disregard for such niceties. Besides, in a city whose commercial and cultural life owed so much to its middle-European immigrants, it was in many ways no bad thing to have friends with guttural accents.

And so the relationship prospered. Popper kept Neville abreast of all the comings and goings in Manchester where the Beecham opera season was in full swing, and Neville replied with his own brand of comment and criticism. However self-opinionated some of his observations may seem today, there is no denying the breadth of knowledge they reveal. By this time, Neville was totally absorbed in art, the kind of 'art' which, according to his intellectual mentor, Walter Pater, 'comes to you proposing frankly to give nothing but the highest quality to your moments as they pass, and simply for those moments' sake'.

Burning with Pater's 'hard, gem-like flame' was all the rage amongst those who, like Neville, equated aesthetic ecstasy with 'success in life'. Hence the last lines of his letter of 20 May:

> The Compulsion Bill troubles me not, although, as Hugo has it *'les hommes sont tous condamnés avec des sursis indéfinis'*. But *I*, at least, have three certain months to burn 'the hard, gem-like flame'.
>   And I *will*.
>
>   Best wishes,
>   J.F.N.

The correspondence continued throughout the summer term. On 22 May, Neville returned some opera notes Popper had sent him, and ventured a few thoughts on 'old Gounod's Romeo':

> No doubt you suspended for the time being all recollection of Shakespeare. Personally I can usually get amusement out of Gounod if I can drive all notions of his ostensible sources out of my mind. Just ignore Goethe; instead of *Faust*, call the opera *Edwin and Angelica, or Hush, Hush, Hush, here comes the bogie-man*, and it is a certain evening's relaxation.

By 6 June Neville had completed a brief synopsis of a long article he hoped to write about 'Moussorgsky and Opera' and sent it to Popper for his comments, adding that 'Newman has seen it, and is encouraging.' His letter ended with a plea:

> Keep me well supplied with correspondence – Edith can't be eternally writing.
>
> > Eternally,
> > Fred

Edith evidently wasted few opportunities to visit 'Fred', for on 17 June Neville confided to Popper, 'Edith's here this week and we *are* burning the gem-like flame.' The beginning of July saw two important developments in the relationship between Neville and Popper. Firstly, after a correspondence lasting over three months, they decided that the use of first-names was in order:

> > Shrewsbury
> > 4 July 1916
>
> Dear George,
> (I have been wondering how long it would take you to call me by my Christian name, and no doubt you have been indulging in similar speculation!) . . .

To celebrate this breakthrough in human relationships, Neville invited Popper to spend a few days in Shrewsbury, a suggestion which was quickly and gratefully accepted. The only apparent obstacle was George's unfortunate birthright, but Neville was optimistic that a solution could be found. As he put it: 'If only you can get that P'liceman fellow in a genial mood, then I can guarantee you some very delicious days.' In the event, the greatest threat to Neville's plans came not from the vigilance of the Eccles constabulary but the strength of anti-German feeling amongst the landladies of Shrewsbury. This misjudgement proved costly, both in terms of physical effort and shoe leather. A week later, Popper received the following rather breathless epistle, this time hurriedly pencilled on a letter card and not on headed notepaper.

                                                    Shrewsbury
                                                    11 July

Dear George,

I have worn myself to a shadder in my quest for a decent home for you. But the landladies here are afflicted with very virulent patriotitis, and I had almost given up hope when I found a very nice place, near the School, in the most select quarter of town. But they want twenty-five shillings weekly *for the rooms only*. This would mean your paying something like thirty-five shillings each week. It's exorbitant, I know, but *I* pay nearly as much. No doubt you find it nearly as costly at home and one expects an increase on holiday. It is a very nice place – and there would be absolutely no trouble about your origin. Write me at once.

                                                    Fred

One of the interesting features of this letter is the insight it gives into Neville's own style of life. For a man who was supposedly saving every penny, he seems curiously unconcerned about paying nearly 'exorbitant' rates for his accommodation. There is little suggestion here of the young man who 'could live at Shrewsbury on a pound a week and put the rest into a Post Office Savings Bank'. Be that as it may, George's visit went ahead as planned and, as far as we can tell, was a great success. Neville met him off the seven o'clock train from London Road and escorted him to his holiday home where supper was waiting. The timing of the visit had been carefully planned to coincide with a particularly busy period in the school calendar.

A couple of days before he was due to depart, George received a letter from Neville setting out some of the pleasures that awaited him:

Next week is *the* week of the term (as far as the attractions of the School are concerned – and the School is everything, I think). We start our Bumping Races on Tuesday, and nothing so vividly expresses the public school spirit as these. You really ought to have a rattling good holiday – and a *unique* one.

As well as demonstrating the strength of Neville's attachment to

George, these lines highlight an even more basic facet of his character. No matter how ostentatiously he may at times have affected a radical chic, by temperament and outlook Neville remained firmly anchored within the Establishment. The playing fields of an English public school were for him a more natural setting than the iconoclastic frenzy of the Lyons Café where socialism vied with Richard Strauss for pride of place in the race to modernity. If he had eccentricities they were to be found not in any deviant or revolutionary attitudes but in the fervour of his loyalties. During the five years he spent at Shrewsbury, he came to love the school and all it stood for.

The strength of this attachment made the final break all the more painful, though at first it seemed likely that Neville would accompany Alington to his new appointment at Eton. Certainly there were no obvious signs of anxiety or distress in the manner in which he and Edith approached the summer of 1916. Whilst he prepared for a holiday in North Wales, she continued to pursue her theatrical interests in Manchester. That particular stage was still dominated by Miss Horniman and her company at the Gaiety Theatre, a state of affairs which Edith, for one, found less than ideal. On one memorable occasion, her wrath erupted and, with Neville's evident blessing, the following ferocious missive was despatched towards the unsuspecting Popper:

> Shrewsbury
> Monday

Dear Mr Popper,

Fred has shown me your copy of the Horniman's letter. It stamps her unmistakably for what I've always been inclined to consider her – a frig and a wooden-headed one at that, with an utter lack of ability to resist expressing the *very first* thing that comes into her silly old head – her criticism of *Exiles* is just what one would expect from that highly coloured rather sexless-looking lady who stares at one from outside of waiting-rooms at railway stations . . . in the words of Shaw, 'she's an ugly old devil' – to use a war-word she's a b******* blighter.

> Best wishes,
> Edith

Shortly after this episode, Neville and Edith set off for a fortnight's holiday at Llanfairfechan where all would have been idyllic had the local newsagent been better stocked. Again, it was to the ever-willing Popper that Neville turned.

> Penrhos
> Llanfairfechan

Dear George,

This place is adorable, but the newsagents are illiberal. Send me last Friday's *New Witness*, this month's *Musical Opinion*, the *Birmingham Post* on Newman days, and any decent *Guardian*.

I cannot write to any length today: I believe it is the Sabbath.

> Thine,
> Fred

On 17 August 1916, Neville bought a post-card of the Sychnant Pass as seen from Dwygyfylchi. On it, he wrote the following message:

Dear George,

I expect to be in the Café Lyons at six tomorrow (Friday) evening. I would like to spend the evening with you.

> Fred

It was to be his last word from Wales, and his last as an employee of Shrewsbury School.

3
High Summer

'Denn eben, wo Begriffe fehlen,
Da stellt ein Wort zur rechten Zeit sich ein.'[1]

[I]

Alington's departure for Eton in the late summer of 1916 signalled
the end of Neville's stay at Shrewsbury School. He might have
returned for another summer in the nets, but without the Headmaster's inspirational presence (to say nothing of his impossible
typewriter) it was an empty prospect. For a while there was talk of a
similar post at Eton, but uncertainty surrounding his call-up (he was
eventually rejected on the grounds of poor eyesight) put paid to that
idea. At the end of his holiday in North Wales, Neville returned to
Shrewsbury to pack his bags and bid farewell to the few friends who
had stayed in school over the vacation. By early September he was
back at 154, Moseley Road, Manchester, enthusiastically contem-
plating the start of a new concert season. Alas, the next few months
failed to live up to expectations; he had little money, and work
proved disturbingly difficult to come by. After a quiet Christmas,
Neville wrote to C. P. Scott, the editor of the *Manchester Guardian*,
on 13 January enquiring whether there were any openings 'amongst
the proof-readers or in the general offices'. Two months later, his
career as a *Guardian* journalist began.

The first year was spent working alongside the likes of Howard
Spring, William Longden, A. V. Cookham, George Leach, J. V.
Radcliffe and 'Shovelton' in a reporters' room which, under the
direction of Haslam Mills, was 'the most gifted and resourceful in
the world'. But his stay in this exalted company proved to be a short
one. Barely a year after submitting his first copy – a report of a

lecture on 'Population and Militarism' by Mrs H. M. Swanwick –
Neville was called into Scott's office and asked to 'take charge of the
Miscellany column and the back-page article and write a fourth
leader now and then'. At the same time, he also performed the duties
of a part-time secretary for Scott. But again, it was to prove a short-
lived appointment. Less than a year later, Neville found himself
'entrusted with the dramatic criticism of the *M.G.*', under the
tutelage of C. E. Montague. It still comes as something of a surprise
to many to discover that 'Cricketer' didn't make his début until
1919, while 'N.C.' had to wait a further seven years for his first
appearance as principal music critic. By 1927, little more than ten
years after he had joined the *Guardian*, Neville occupied not one but
two of the most influential desks in British journalism.

At the same time as he was making rapid strides in the newspaper
world, Neville was also making significant advances on other fronts.
On 17 July 1921 Neville Cardus, aged thirty-one and a journalist by
profession, the son of a civil servant, Frederick Cardus (deceased),
married Edith Honorine Watten King, aged thirty-three and a
schoolmistress, at the Chorley Registry Office. The bride was the
daughter of John Thomas Sissons King of 'Sindow', Albany Road,
Victoria Park. The marriage was solemnised by the Registrar, Mr C.
H. Ramsbottom, and witnessed by Thomas J. Wrigley and F. J.
King. After spending the first few years of their marriage in rented
accommodation, in 1929 the couple moved to 2, Barnsfold Avenue,
Withington, a property which Edith bought from Mrs Lilian Mutter.
Unlike her husband, Edith seldom strayed far from Manchester. It
was her home and over the years she had become heavily involved in
any number of local activities. Neville, on the other hand, quickly
found that London was to play as important a part in his working life
as Manchester, and thus it was no surprise when he became a
member of the National Liberal Club in June 1931. This venerable
institution served as his London base until his departure for
Australia in 1939. During these years he stayed at the Club on
average between ten and twelve days a month, every month.

On succeeding Sam Langford as *Guardian* music critic in May
1927, Neville was able to add a European dimension to his already
extensive travels around England. Even before stumps were drawn
on the final afternoon of the County Championship, he was often to
be seen boarding the boat train at Victoria *en route* for a small town in

Austria which every autumn played host to an international élite –
and there were many who would have given a great deal to be
numbered amongst its members. Neville often took a friend along
with him on this pilgrimage. 'James Ramsbottom' – 'a lean and
cadaverous gentleman, unwieldy of limb and gait, with a kind of
Jackdaw of Rheims bedragglement of hair for covering' – went in
1931; thereafter, it was the turn of Barbe Ede, the lady he met and
fell madly in love with on Charing Cross Station, to accompany him.
Salzburg was to provide Neville with some of his happiest memories.

The years which saw the emergence of 'Cricketer' and 'N.C.' also
witnessed the establishment of a substantial literary reputation. By
1940, as well as his *Guardian* contributions, Neville's bibliography
included some 370 entries ranging in weight and substance from
books to articles in which he reflected upon a particular event – as in
'The Salzburg Festival' (*Monthly Music Review*, February 1932), or
mused upon a major issue of the moment – for example, 'Is
Bruckner Boring?' (*The Listener*, 1937), or used the pretext of a wet
afternoon at Old Trafford to indulge in a spot of idle reminiscing,
hence 'No Play Today' which appeared in *The Field* in July 1936.
1922 saw the publication of *A Cricketer's Book*, the first of six
collections of articles drawn mainly from his *Guardian* columns
which were to appear over the next fifteen years, the others being
Days in the Sun (1924), *The Summer Game: A Cricketer's Journal*
(1929), *Cricket* (1930), *Good Days: A Book of Cricket* (1934) and
Australian Summer (1937). At the same time he also contributed to
an eminently catholic range of periodicals including such bastions of
the establishment as *The Times Literary Supplement* and *The Listener*,
the slightly sectional *Empire Review* and *Nation and the Athenaeum*,
the entirely cerebral *Monthly Music Review* and *Gramophone*, the
more visual *Illustrated Sporting and Dramatic News*, and the downright salacious *Women's Cricket*.

The end of these golden years was foreshadowed in a trivial, but
nonetheless ominous, event at Lord's which Neville recalled in
Autobiography:

On the Friday morning when Hitler invaded Poland, I chanced
to be in this same Long Room at Lord's watching through the
windows for the last time in years. Though no spectators were
present, a match was being continued; there was no legal way of
stopping it. Balloon barrages hung over Lord's. As I watched

the ghostly movements of the players outside, a beautifully preserved member of Lord's, with spats and rolled umbrella, stood near me inspecting the game. We did not speak of course; we had not been introduced. Suddenly two workmen entered the Long Room in green aprons and carrying a bag. They took down the bust of W. G. Grace, put it into the bag, and departed with it. The noble lord at my side watched their every movement; then he turned to me. 'Did you see, sir?' he asked. I told him I had seen. 'That means war,' he said.[2]

[II]

These were the bare details of Neville's life from the time he left Shrewsbury to the moment he set sail for Australia at the end of 1939. In fact the circumstances leading up to his first appearance on the *Manchester Guardian*'s payroll may not have been exactly as he described them. By 1917 the young man who had once gazed hopefully up at the lighted windows of the Cross Street offices from the far distance of the pavement opposite no longer cut as sorry a figure as his autobiographies lead us to believe. Unemployed he may have been but he was certainly not downhearted nor disconsolate. Times were difficult and he had no private means, but he had friends – some of whom, notably Edith, were happy to help him make ends meet; he had contacts as influential as Newman and he had the beginnings of a reputation as a music critic; and, most important of all, he had a protective and sustaining belief in his destiny. For Neville, the last months of 1916 and early 1917 were a blessing in disguise. They gave him the chance to recharge and refine his intellectual energies before mounting the next onslaught on those citadels of knowledge and beauty which he saw as the ultimate objective. Thus the problems he faced were largely of his own making. As he explained in his letter to C. P. Scott,

I am a young student intent upon devoting his life to politics and art. In these times, however, I am finding it hard to keep alive. My particular fear is that necessity will drive me to at least suspending my studies, which happen to be at a critical and fascinating stage. I have had to educate myself, and my culture, such as it is, has been got by scorning delights and living laborious days for some eight years. Immediate employment would enable me to find the means whereby to continue my education, and I would gladly accept any position, however modest, that you might possibly be able to offer me.

These are hardly the words of a young man 'reduced to appalling shifts', nor do they convey that sense of desolation and distress typically associated with imminent destitution. 'Finding it hard to keep alive' has an overly melodramatic ring to it, and elsewhere it is clear that the author has no intention of seeking permanent, full-time employment, that his main concern is to overcome a temporary 'cash-flow' problem, and that, even at this early stage in his literary career, he was not averse to dressing up the past to suit present purposes. Witness, for example, the reference to living 'laborious days for some eight years': the truth was that he had spent much of that period scudding round the playing fields of Shrewsbury.

From the biographer's standpoint, the significance of the letter lies in the way it reveals what *Autobiography* conceals. In that volume a mature, internationally renowned figure recalled selected episodes of his life, but the inadequacies of this account cannot be attributed solely to the odd oversight and error. One of the fascinations of the Cardus legend is how its hero managed to escape a lifetime's drudgery midst the smoke and grime of industrial Lancashire. In the absence of any other explanation, the temptation (encouraged by Neville of course) has been to accept that a mystical combination of luck and fate was responsible for his success. It was an account to which Neville became so attached that by the end of his life he had come to believe most of it. Thus, in *Conversations*, he observed,

When you look back on your life, you wonder how those things happened. People with a religious turn of mind would call it the 'work of God'. I have another description for it – destiny. The longer I live, the more I come to believe in destiny. As I look back on my life, I ask: 'Why did that happen? What made me go this way instead of that way?' The answers remain a complete mystery to me.[3]

However romantic this may sound today, the fact remains that it is difficult, if not impossible, to reconcile the image of a young man content to leave his destiny in the lap of the gods with the Neville we left at the gates of Shrewsbury School – confident, forthright, sometimes self-opinionated and determined. The difference can only be explained by looking beyond the autobiographies. In 1917, Neville had a clear idea of the person he wanted to be and the life he wished to live. As the letter to Scott showed, far from sitting back and waiting for fate to take a hand, he had planned and worked to realise his cherished ambitions. There was as yet no evidence of the mystical infatuation with destiny which was to permeate the autobiographies. At this point in his life, Neville's preoccupations and outlook were strongly secular. He knew what he wanted and what he liked – his 'passions', as he used to call them – and he 'was determined to do the things [he] loved doing'.

Scott's response to Neville's entreaties, though doubtless well-intentioned, turned out to be less helpful than either would have wished. After a disconcertingly rambling interview with the great man at his home in Fallowfield, Neville was offered a position as a part-time amanuensis; he was to provide his master with verbal summaries of all the important material he did not have time to digest. Congenial and stimulating though this arrangement might have seemed, it was not long before Neville spotted its disadvantages: namely, that Scott took little notice of his efforts and, worse still, 'I did not receive a cheque or a penny's pay for my month's devoted performance.' Early in March, Neville wrote a second letter to Scott, again stressing his reduced circumstances and again asking whether there were any openings at Cross Street. This time his perseverance was rewarded. After a slight delay, the 'most famous editor of his day' responded by suggesting that Neville should come to the *Guardian* offices and speak to the head reporter – not Haslam Mills, as we were told in *Autobiography*.

                                                3, Cross Street
                                                Manchester
                                                20 March 1917

Dear Mr Cardus,

        I was away last week or would have sooner replied to your letter. If you can make yourself useful in the reporters' room I expect that would be the best opening. I think you said you had some shorthand, and I daresay you could soon improve it. I have mentioned the matter to our head reporter, Mr W. H.

Mills, who will be glad to see you at the office any morning between twelve and one, and will then consider the matter.

Yours very truly
C. P. Scott

At this point in Neville's narrative, the gap between truth and half-truth perceptibly narrows. Realising that he was well on the way to becoming the man he wanted to be, the likelihood is that he felt less inclined to embellish. Now a member of a paper which could boast as talented a collection of writers and reporters as English journalism had ever assembled, Neville's career was no longer a case of wishful thinking. Any doubts he may initially have entertained about the job evaporated as he grasped the full meaning of working for the *Manchester Guardian*. Apart from occasional health problems, the transition from nonentity to nationally, then internationally, famous journalist was accomplished with a smoothness which might turn any present-day careerist green with envy. With a certainty born only partly of *ex post facto* reasoning, the brash confidence of the former assistant professional-cum-part-time-lecturer was blended with a natural talent and determination to create a career which over the next fifty years would establish new standards of cricket writing and an unmistakable brand of music criticism.

Though Neville chose to describe the first stage of his career with the *Manchester Guardian* as his 'prentice years', it was in a sense a misleading choice of words, as a complete novice would never have been offered the job in the first place. 'Rookies' won their spurs in less exalted surroundings – in Neville's case this had been the left-wing *Daily Citizen*. Working for Scott required a combination of proven ability and high promise. Independence of outlook, moral strength, intellectual rigour, wit and clarity of expression were the order of the day; there was no place for over-embellishment or trimming. In *Autobiography*, Neville recalled how he had concluded one of his first leaders with what he thought to be a particularly apposite quotation from Lewis Carroll. The next morning, however, he was quizzed by Scott on the precise meaning of these lines. Having failed to satisfy the great man, he received the following admonition: 'Never employ any quotation of which you do not understand the meaning.'

With Scott at the head of a brilliant editorial team, it was only to be expected that initiation into the ways of 'the Corridor' would prove a demanding experience. At times, the atmosphere at Cross Street was almost seminarian in its intensity and rigour. New reporters found themselves subjected to what was as much an education of the spirit as of the pen. Preconceived notions received short shrift, though not necessarily out of consideration for the readers. 'Let them educate themselves up to us,' Scott once advised Neville. Above all else the *Guardian* required of its writers a conscientious and conspicuous regard for the English language – even if compositors later decided to add their own flavour. The manifestations of this creed were diverse. Some, like Haslam Mills, were obsessive about the tidiness of their copy: 'Take good care,' he told his cub reporters, 'over the material appearance of your writings.' A single alteration constituted a fatal blemish which damned the offending page to the wastepaper basket.

Within the confines thus imposed, Mills set great store by the quality of his opening sentence. 'Your first sentence settles all,' he would say. 'Your first sentence determines the subsequent quality and direction of the rest.' This was all very well when the muse was upon him, but on other occasions it could result in great frustration and enormous wastage of paper. One night, Neville recalled,

> . . . after he had taken an unusually long time over a notice, and after he had gone home, I entered the room with a letter to be laid on his desk. . . . On the floor at the base of Mills' desk I saw many crumpled balls of copy paper. Ah, I thought, here are his frustrated attempts. If I study them I may learn much. . . . I picked up all the crumpled papers, unrolled them, straightened them out, and studied them. There were at least a dozen, and each contained no other words, with not a single erasure, than (neatly written as ever) PALACE OF VARIETIES.[4]

Others, like Montague, were concerned more with the quality of prose than the accuracy of copy. Contrary to legend, he rarely altered a word of the drafts which came before him. Finally, there remained those like William Longden, 'nearly the oldest of reporters on the *M.G.* or anywhere else', who clung to the belief that 'the art of writing consisted in as few words as possible, arranged in the simplest and most traditional order'. No one, not even Scott, could convince him of the virtues of a more variegated prose style. Together with George Shovelton and Walter Biggs, he remained a monument to a classic tradition of reporting now threatened with extinction by a new generation of 'young lions', a category in which Neville placed himself. Whether, on the demise of these monoliths, English journalism followed precedent by descending into a veritable dark age is something that Neville declined to comment on.

Although Neville may have chosen to inject a goodly dose of naivety and youthful idealism into his letters to Scott and his subsequent self-portrayals, in the main these were not the qualities friends remembered him by. While there would be moments in his career when an unheralded shyness and diffidence betrayed the insecurities of childhood, the new *Guardian* reporter seemed to lack little by way of confidence and composure. From the start, his copy bore the unmistakable stamp of self-assurance. His were not the self-conscious, groping phrases of a man in search of a style; the challenge of the *Manchester Guardian* lay in discovering whether an existing identity could survive the stresses and strains of full-time employment, fellow journalists and the great British public.

[III]

Once he had settled into his new surroundings, the major problem facing Neville was a matter of style. Such is the telescoping power of history that it often comes as a surprise to discover that the qualities for which the famous are remembered were not theirs by gift of birth, even less by accident. Strange though it may seem today, the man whose writing is now considered to be among the finest examples of journalistic prose came to this pitch of poise, elegance and colour only after years of practice and experimentation. There is no doubting Neville's natural talents; he was intelligent, inquisitive and possessed of an acute feel for the aural and visual impact of the written word. But the ability to write was a different matter.

In the autobiographies, the great breakthroughs in Neville's career were revelational – a mystical combination of fate, fortune and divine intervention. There was, for example, the performance of Edward German's *Tom Jones* on 7 April 1907, at which a 'miracle' 'swept me into the seven seas of music, not once to be in danger of drowning, though overwhelmed here and there by enormous waves. I was a swimmer by grace.' Earlier still, he had received 'the Grace of Art' through the vision of a single MacLaren off-drive, thus ensuring that 'from MacLaren to Wagner and the romantic gesture would henceforward be a sure and natural transition, as sure and natural as the transition from the enjoyment of Tom Hayward's serene and classic batsmanship to the music of Bach.'[5]

Wondrous though this may sound today, there are still moments when Neville's emphasis on the part played by other-wordly factors in his career come perilously close to undermining the credibility of his narrative. Even the most adoring of readers must have sometimes wondered whether anyone could really have been so lucky. At these times, the sense of *deus ex machina* becomes almost transparent. By contrast, those passages which describe his early days as a writer avoid any semblance of mystical *legerdemain*. Here the learning process is described in all its mundane, arduous detail. There are no divine visitations, no Pauline revelations to relieve those terrible moments when inspiration is conspicuous only by its absence, and the writer is left to contemplate a distended wastepaper basket smirking in silent appreciation of wasted hours.

Towards the end of his life, Neville was asked to offer some advice to would-be writers. His 'eighth commandment' ran as follows: 'You must love writing as passionately as a man loves his mistress.' It would be idle to speculate on the source of this allusion, though one can almost see the flicker of a smile cross Neville's face as he weighed his words. In his own case, the first signs of burgeoning talent appeared in early childhood when he wrote and produced his own comic. From then on, fired by an insatiable appetite for great literature and the ever-widening vocabulary which was its natural consequence, his fascination with language had become a 'raging cataract', a passion which drove him to devote hour upon hour to the simple physical act of writing. The result was a primal feel for the structure, shape and sound of language which he never lost, and which left him with a lifelong distrust of all mechanical substitutes for the pen, most notably the typewriter.

Like many budding belletrists, Neville's response to the challenge of writing was a mixture of practice and imitation. Often the two overlapped. In *Conversations with Cardus*, for example, having delivered his *credo* – 'You must practice writing just as a pianist practises the piano' – he goes on to recall how

when I was seventeen or eighteen I used to sit down and write. I probably wrote a lot of rubbish, and I'd usually tear up what I'd done, but I was acquiring the habit of writing. If you can't write something original, then copy something. Get words into your system. Find a page of Bernard Shaw or Max Beerbohm and copy it with the same dedication as a young pianist who has to practise five-finger exercises.[6]

If the explicit purpose of laboriously copying pages of literature was to 'get acquainted with vocabulary' (Neville always agreed that 'you won't learn how to write by reading a dictionary; you must meet words in context put into a sentence by a fine writer in such a way that every word becomes like a note in music') then it should also be noted that the works recommended for copying all had a particular significance for him. His love of Dickens has already been mentioned. The sharpness of observation and richness of portrayal; the ability to see beneath the façades of ego and manners; the insight and irony – these were qualities Neville revered and sought to emulate. Shaw and Beerbohm were similarly much admired for their pungent irreverence, while Oscar Wilde's command of language, syntactical elegance and brilliant wit left an indelible impression upon his imagination. Other influences, however, were to prove less helpful. Early intimations of the philosopher *manqué* in Neville were to be found in an undiscerning admiration for Walter Pater and his fellow aesthetes. Their influence during his formative years was reflected in a tendency to over-embellish which, at its worst, could leave the original subject submerged beneath a welter of sensuous imagery.

Notwithstanding these weaknesses, the fact remains that by the time he started work for the *Manchester Guardian* Neville had a basic grounding in the techniques of writing and a prose style which was rich in promise, if still sometimes mannered. Combined with his imagination and determination, these qualities explain his rapid progress from the Reporters' Room to editorship of the Miscellany column and thence to the drama desk as 'C.E.M.'s' assistant, all in the space of three short years. But preferment did not mean that Neville was spared the rigorous training which Scott demanded of all his recruits. During his time in the Reporters' Room Neville covered his share of town hall meetings, public lectures and all the other humdrum events which were the staple diet of the inside pages.

Flexibility and versatility were the qualities Scott looked for in his 'young lions', and such was his distrust of 'overdone specialism' that even the most distinguished members of his team often turned their pens to improbable topics. For example, Allan Monkhouse, his literary editor, later described by Neville as 'an artist in shades so fine that compared to him Henry James was substantial, not to say carnal', was also in charge of the 'Manchester Cotton' columns, a duty which necessitated a daily visit to the Exchange. When the time came for Neville to compose his first leader, the subject Scott selected for him was concerned not with drama or music or cricket, as one might have expected, but the legal and moral issues raised by the torpedoeing of an Allied Ship in neutral waters. Finally, those who dreamed that they might some day occupy a room on the 'Corridor' had to master that assortment of local traditions and taboos which constituted the distinctive *M.G.* house-style. There was, for instance, a long list of words to be avoided at all costs. Even Ernest Newman, whose copy was normally sacrosanct, found himself taken to task by the ever-vigilant editor for using the word 'commence'. 'Under the auspices of' was another forbidden phrase. An indication of Scott's dislike of change was his opposition to any suggestion that the cinema was an art form worthy of serious coverage. In the end he was persuaded to accept a short column, but only on condition that 'cinema' was spelt with a 'k'!

Having already acquired a thorough grounding in the basic mechanics of writing, Neville found little difficulty in mastering the tricks of the journalists' trade. Only those who subscribe to the legend of innocence he himself created should be surprised at the speed of his progress under Scott. From his first day at Cross Street, effort and advancement went hand-in-hand. He thrived on a nutritious diet of hard work, opportunism and his own 'immortal longings'. The combination rapidly became the basis of a lasting relationship which consumed the rest of his working life, sometimes to the extent of blinding him to whole areas of human activity. Living, as he did, in a world continuously racked by manifestations of human fallability, it is one of the unusual featues of Neville's character that he rarely showed any interest in the 'problems' of modern society. He never voted. War, political conflict, economic depression, unemployment (subjects uppermost in the minds of many of his contemporaries), left him unmoved, even bored, except when they threatened an aspect of civilised society that he valued. His own elemental struggles were to be found on the landscape of

Wagnerian mythology or in the mental turmoil of a Mahler symphony rather than on the Somme or at Dunkirk or in Hiroshima.

Idiosyncratic though this outlook may seem to a generation
constantly assailed by reports of crisis and disaster, it goes to the
heart of Neville's personality. In the opera house, the theatre or the
concert hall, distanced from the reality of personal anguish by
scores, scripts and the ritual of curtains, raised platforms and
applause, a finely honed sensitivity allowed him to distil aesthetic
beauty from the deepest distress. In real life, that same sensitivitity
was the source of his greatest vulnerability. He found the pain and
suffering of others profoundly disturbing and often unendurable. As
he grew older, he found the thought of visiting sick or immobilised
friends like Jonty Solomon, for example, too distressing to contemplate. Even when Edith was gravely ill, he found hospital visiting
almost unbearable. When it became necessary for him to go into the
Nuffield Clinic after his last illness, his fears were captured in a
single sentence: 'Edith never came out.'

[IV]

Such was the strength of Neville's reputation as a music critic that
many of his readers failed to realise that his career as a drama critic
came first, and only then did he move on to cricket and music.
Though this order might not have been to Neville's liking, at the
time there was no alternative. Sam Langford occupied the
Guardian's music desk in a manner exactly befitting the shambling,
shaggy colossus portrayed in *Autobiography*, and the County Championship had been suspended for the duration of the war. Fans of his
cricket writings found it equally difficult to believe that Neville never
actively sought the post of cricket correspondent. However much he
had enjoyed playing and watching the game, he would never have
voluntarily given up a whole evening to writing about a subject he felt
to be fundamentally lacking in intellectual challenge. Compared
with music or drama, cricket had little to offer the budding aesthete.
Hence his assertion in *Autobiography* that 'if anybody had told me
that I was destined to make a reputation as a writer on cricket I
should have felt very hurt'. Ironically, many years later when he
came to reread some of his early match reports, he found that they
contained some of the finest prose he ever wrote on the game.

For once, Neville was being entirely truthful when he wrote that

'Cricketer's' birth was 'sheer chance'. The decision to move the young man who had so recently taken over the Miscellany column to be second drama critic was as much a reflection of the predicament in which Scott suddenly found himself in 1918 as a recognition of any special talents which Neville may have laid claim to. Montague, one of the most influential drama critics in the country, had spent much of the war away from the *Manchester Guardian* and when he returned it was to concentrate on leader-writing and private authorship. Allan Monkhouse was seriously ill at the time, while Arthur Wallace spent long periods out of the country. The way was thus open for Neville to explore new worlds. For the next few months, he led a hectic existence.

As editor of the *Manchester Guardian*, C. P. Scott led by example. His own schedule typified the rigour of the organisation he owned and ran. 'Every night, or early morning,' Neville recalled, 'after the first edition was off the machines, he [Scott] put a muffler round his neck – no overcoat despite the terrible Manchester winter – and he rode home for miles on his bicycle.' On one such journey, the inevitable occurred – he fell off.

A policeman came to his rescue, picked him up and after seeing that no bones were broken said: 'You ought not to be out as late as this, sir – in this weather.'

Scott told him that he had been working late. 'Gawd!' said the policeman, 'at your time of life? And may I ask, sir, who do you work for?'

'The *Manchester Guardian*,' replied Scott.

'Well, all I can say is this, sir,' said the policeman, 'the *Manchester Guardian* ought to be bloody well ashamed of itself keeping an old man like you out this time of night.'[7]

It goes without saying that if the editor could do it, so could his staff. If the effectiveness of this style of leadership is to be judged by the status of the *Guardian*, there is little doubt that Scott must be numbered amongst the greatest of editors. As a forcing-house for young talent, his paper ranked second to none, but at considerable cost. Scott's regime placed enormous strain on his key employees, none more so than Neville who, in addition to holding the drama portfolio, also continued to serve as the 'All-Father's' unpaid personal assistant. In his own words, 'he was a drama critic until after midnight, and a humble factotum at ten o'clock next morning'. Yet, as he was at pains to stress, 'no one dared complain of weariness to Scott'.

Thus it was not altogether surprising that the spring of 1919 found Neville confined to bed for eight weeks with a serious pulmonary condition. What could not have been predicted, however, was the train of events which flowed from this unpropitious scene. Anxious that his protégé should return to the fray as soon as possible, yet equally determined to ensure that recovery should be complete and lasting, the then news editor, W. P. Crozier, an optimist by nature, prescribed by way of convalescence a few days in the sun at Old Trafford. As an afterthought he added that, should Neville feel so inclined, he might like to try his hand at reporting one or two games. It may have been a case of divine inspiration or a purely fortuitous suggestion in the best traditions of British decision-making: whatever the explanation, the events that followed are now firmly established in the folk-lore of English journalism.

For want of anything better to do, Neville followed Crozier's advice and went to watch Lancashire playing Derbyshire in the recently resumed County Championship. Finding that the day passed pleasantly and with little strain, he ventured to prepare some copy. At first, this was rejected by the sub-editors on the grounds of excessive length, but later it was reinstated in full on the explicit instructions of Scott. A precedent had been created, and almost before Neville realised what was happening a household institution had been born. A christening was hurriedly arranged to pre-empt criticism from those long-standing *Guardian* readers who might not have understood how 'N.C.' could appear simultaneously on both the sports and the arts pages. The only difficulty was that no one could think of an appropriate name for the infant prodigy until, in a flash of inspiration, Madeline Linford, then Crozier's personal secretary, came up with 'Cricketer', a by-line so stunningly unexceptional that it was instantly accepted.

Despite the encouraging public response to his first efforts, it was some time before Neville was prepared to treat this new-found outlet for his energies as anything other than a 'spare-time affair' for which, as he observed on several occasions, he received no additional remuneration. In *Autobiography*, this initial reluctance was put down to the fact that he 'simply had no intention of writing on cricket for any length of time'. And there was certainly nothing in 'Crick-eter's' first reports to prepare his readers for what was to come. Drawing his audience's attention to the striking orthodoxy of these pieces, he went on:

> You will observe how conscientiously I observed the unities . . . how I entered into the freemasonry of the cricket reporter of the period. . . . I fitted myself into the idioms and procedure of sports writers of 1919. I should have been the most flabber-gasted individual in the world if anybody gifted in prophecy had told me as I sat at Old Trafford on that Monday in June 1919 that in another year or two I would be more or less famous up and down the land as a writer on cricket.[8]

For all its appealing modesty, there is something disconcerting about this statement. It is too straightforward to be entirely convinc-ing and smacks of retrospective simplification. It is hard to imagine Neville ever being quite so ingenuous. While his dismissive reaction to the idea of writing about cricket could be attributed in part to a natural distrust of anything new, a more potent explanation lay in the feeling that no matter how popular his reports might prove to be, the subject itself could never be compatible with the lofty intellectual aspirations set out in his 'programme of self-development'. In other words, becoming a cricket writer meant coming to terms with a subject he felt to be intrinsically unworthy of his talents.

Mercifully, the dilemma was resolved for him when early in 1920 the *Manchester Guardian* asked him to become their cricket corre-spondent on terms which he couldn't refuse. 'Cricketer's' existence was secured, and a legend launched. Given security of employment, and finding himself in the enviable position of being able to enjoy all that was best in cricket without sacrificing his beloved music, Neville proceeded to blaze a trail which in less than five years took him to a position of pre-eminence amongst contemporary sports writers, and to great personal happiness. Between 1920 and 1939 he pursued first-class cricket around England and across continents, stopping off at grounds as far apart as Sheffield and Sydney, and writing on average 8,000 words a week – nearly two million in all.

It was the best of times to follow Lancashire cricket. Between the wars the Club won the Championship outright on five occasions, a record bettered only by their mortal rivals from over the Pennines.

During those same years, only three other counties enjoyed any success at all. On the resumption of first-class cricket in 1919, Lancashire found themselves in a better position than most of the other counties. Though Harold Garnett, T. A. Nelson, Egerton L. Wright and W. K. Tyldesley of the pre-war side had been killed, the nucleus of a comparatively strong team remained. The batting was particularly formidable. Ernest Tyldesley headed the averages and his brother, Johnny, though now forty-six, was still capable of great innings. Against Gloucestershire, the brothers shared a partnership of 218 in under two hours, of which Johnny made 170, including 7 sixes and 17 fours. Just below Ernest in the final lists came Harry Makepeace ('Old Shake', as he was known) and Charlie Hallows.

At this time the bowling was the weak link, with much depending on Harry Dean, Lol Cook and two more Tyldesleys, Dick and James, but from 1922 the line-up was immeasurably strengthened by the arrival of Cecil Parkin. The difference he made can be gauged from his record in Championship matches that year: 172 wickets at 17 runs apiece. Parkin was not everyone's favourite; that redoubtable patrician, Sir Pelham Warner, once observed that he was 'something of a genius as a bowler, but he had too many tricks and too many balls of different type, so that it was not easy to place the fields accurately for him'. Parkin's views on Warner were unfortunately never recorded. As a player, 'Cec' was noted for an abundance of stamina, which was convenient for Lancashire as James Tyldesley died early in 1923 and Cook was to suffer a complete loss of form. But he was much more than an honest workhorse – only one other player in the history of the game has opened both the bowling and the batting for England against Australia.

During the first six years of the post-war Championship, Lancashire were rarely out of the top five counties at the end of the season. In 1920 it looked as though the coveted title would be theirs, until at twenty-two minutes past six on the last afternoon of their last match Middlesex beat Surrey to steal the honours. Well though Lancashire undoubtedly played during these early seasons, the unfortunate fact was that Yorkshire were playing even better. From 1922, the White Rose reigned supreme for four consecutive seasons, an achievement which lent an added tension to the 'Roses' matches. Today's games are only a pale shadow of those dour, unyielding encounters when Yorkshire (with Robinson, Rhodes, Waddington, Kilner, Macaulay and E. R. Wilson) and Lancashire (with Parkin, Makepeace, Hallows and the Tyldesleys) often waged wars of attrition to decide no more than first innings points. In 1922, for example, with five overs to go Yorkshire's last pair needed five runs to win. In the end the game was drawn, but not before the tension had proved too much for many spectators. In the heat of the moment, one poor fellow whose only crime was impartiality suddenly found himself confronted by a formidable figure from Huddersfield:

'Arn't you Lancasheer?'
'No, I am not,' came the spirited reply.
'Then where's t'a from?'
'From London,' now with a trace of apprehension.
'Well, keep thi clipper shut. This game's got nowt to do with thee.'

This was the spectacle and the atmosphere which awaited Neville as he settled to his new task. He loved every aspect of the game, and his own experiences as a player enabled him to bring an element of technical insight to his reports which others' lacked. Nevertheless, the basic ego problem remained. How was he to reconcile a style of writing created in anticipation of a career devoted to European culture from Shakespeare to Schoenberg with the dissonant reality of 'a snick through the slips', 'a long hop', 'a sticky dog' and 'rain stopped play'?

As so often proved to be the case, Neville's gift for *a posteriori* reasoning would later come up with a solution not available at the time. As the importance of cricket in his life was retrospectively diminished to the point at which he could declare 'never have I regarded my cricket as more than a means to an end: that end being music and the savouring of life by a free and civilised mind', so cricket's contribution to his bank balance and his reputation was commensurately reduced until the once famous association of Cardus and cricket appeared as little more than a pleasant, but irrelevant, interlude in a lifelong odyssey. In 1920, however, Neville took cricket rather more seriously. His new responsibilities necessitated a fundamental change of habits and of outlook. The long afternoons of earnest conversation with other would-be intellectuals in the secluded corners of the 'Café Lyons' were a thing of the past. From now on his life would involve regular and extensive travel, and it would be inextricably linked to the fortunes of a simple game and the delights of mass entertainment.

That the transition to this new milieu was effected so smoothly was partly due to Neville's boundless enthusiasm and partly to the prosperous condition of Lancashire cricket. With no disrespect intended, had he been asked to cover Northamptonshire or Somerset 'Cricketer' would never have been born. But Lancashire was a different proposition. One of the most successful teams in the Championship, based at one of the most famous grounds in the world, Lancashire County Cricket Club had an aura of greatness about it which few rivals could match. Steeped in tradition and folklore, it provided a perfect setting for Neville's love of spectacle and atmosphere. The coincidence was crucial. There is little doubt that had he been offered a free choice of 'desks' Neville would not have opted for cricket, and 'Cricketer' would have remained forever a twinkle in Crozier's eye. But when Crozier outlined his proposal, Neville was enough of a realist to see that however much he might have coveted Sam Langford's job, 'Cricketer' offered immediate advantages and benefits which he could not afford to turn down. The music desk would have to wait – for seven years, as it turned out.

Many literary figures have come across cricket in their travels, as often as not their attention having been attracted to something peculiarly English about the game, its setting, its players or the values it (usually) exemplifies. Not until the arrival of 'Cricketer', however, had a writer devoted a major part of his literary talents and energies to the game. As his friend and one-time publisher, Sir Rupert Hart-Davis, once noted: 'Neville's writings on cricket were not the work of a cricket reporter turned literary, but the first flights of a prose-writer whose subject happened to be cricket.' His response to the prospect awaiting him in the late spring of 1920 reflected the two concerns uppermost in his mind: the advancement of a professional career, and the continuing pursuit of culture. At first sight, cricket might have seemed an unlikely conveyance to either destination, but Neville saw the future differently. If the subject was too modest to capture and hold the reader's attention, then he would enhance its status; if it was too bland to sustain the discerning literary palate, then he would enrich it with lavish metaphor and rich imagery. From the start Neville's prose style was consistent with both his intellectual preoccupations and a dawning realisation of the aesthetic power of language. From the beginning, too, it was a style that bore the seeds of its greatest weakness – the likelihood that, sooner or later, the reader would find the medium a more engaging achievement than the feats which it sought to recreate.

Lancashire's recent past gave Neville every reason to hope that he would find a fair leavening of skill, style and character at Old Trafford during the summer months. After all, the deeds of Hornby and Barlow, Spooner, Tyldesley and Archibald Cambell MacLaren spoke for themselves and, as a former professional himself, Neville was well placed to judge the potential of the current team. The beauty of his new position was the access it gave to both past and present. Looking back through his early columns, nothing leaves a greater impression than 'Cricketer's' ability from a very early stage in his career to recreate the past and blend it with the present. Though those who value historical accuracy above all else will always question Neville's fondness for the historic present, others continue to find a paragraph of Cardus as satisfying as a whole volume of *Wisden*.

The argument will no doubt rumble on; to expect a final resolution one way or the other is, I suspect, to mistake the issues at stake. It is not a simple question of fact versus fiction, as some would have it, but of a preference for different orders of reality; whether, by nature or training, we look for an objective record of events – as on a score-card, or whether we prefer to let verbal and literary richness immerse us in a reality equally vivid, but largely subjective. There is no question that cricketers are but men, yet on occasions Neville would have them be gods; but consider how much would have been lost had this tendency to excess been cauterised early in his career. Neville tended to use history not as a substitute, but as an alternative. When rain intervened, or his cricketers' abilities temporarily deserted them, or he simply lost interest, 'Cricketer' turned to the deeds of bygone heroes to illustrate those qualities in man that he valued most highly.

So it was that many of his purple passages revolved around invocations of character rather than reconstructions of perform-ance. It was part and parcel of his art: where there was a dearth of character, he would unashamedly create, reasoning that the loss of such a vital ingredient could only impair the reader's vision of 'reality'. One of the finest pieces of cricket prose I know is

'Cricketer's' description of Tom Richardson's bowling against the Australians in the last innings of the Manchester test match in 1896. Neville, as far as we know, was only seven at the time and was not even at the match. Those who were present, however, have confirmed that the event was almost as glorious as the chronicler's reconstruction. Australia needed to make only 125 to win; Richardson's face had lost its customary smile:

In Australia's first innings he had bowled 68 overs for seven wickets and 168 runs. Yet he was here again, bowling like a man just born to immortal energy. And four Australian wickets were down for 45 in an hour. If only England had given the Australians a few more runs, the crowd wished out of its heart – if only Richardson could keep up his pace for another hour. But, of course, no man could expect him to bowl in this superhuman vein for long. . . . Thus did the crowd sigh and regret. But Richardson's spirit *did* go on burning a dazzling flame. The afternoon moved slowly to the sunset – every hour an eternity. And Richardson *did* bowl and bowl, and his fury diminished not a jot. Other English bowlers faltered, but not Richardson. The fifth Australian wicket fell at 79, the sixth at 95, the seventh at 100. The Australians now wanted 25, with only three wickets in keeping, McKibbin and Jones – two rabbits – amongst them. 'Is it possible?' whispered the crowd. 'Can it be? Can we win . . . after all? . . . Why, look at Richardson and see: England must win. 'This man is going to suffer no frustration. He has bowled for two hours and a half without a pause. He has bowled till Nature has pricked him with protesting pains in every nerve, in every muscle of his great frame. He has bowled till Nature can no longer make him aware that she is abused outrageously, for now he is a man in a trance, the body of him numbed and moving automatically to the only suggestion his consciousness can respond to – 'England must win'. . . . With nine runs still to be got by Australia, Kelly gave a chance to Lilley at the wicket and Lilley let the ball drop to earth. The heart of Richardson might have burst at this, but it did not. To the end he strove and suffered.[9]

Looking back at early examples of the style which was to double summer sales of the *Manchester Guardian*, one is immediately struck by their enthusiasm and freshness. They were unmistakably the work of a man on the threshold of a new world; a man who, in seeking to put his stamp on a subject previously dismissed as trifling, turned to prose to justify his presence in this unlikely backwater; and a man who was looking to cricket to confirm a growing conviction that, in matters of human exchange, 'the style is the man'. With all these considerations in his mind, Neville entered what he later called his 'yellow' period as a cricket writer. Predictably, it was to be distinguished by 'a very conscious art'. Images and metaphors were prepared well in advance; often all that remained was somehow to fit the day's play around them. The end-product often bore the tell-tale signs of this strategy. In places, layers of prosaic artifice lay so thickly as to all but submerge the spontaneity and authenticity which his critics were happy to dub the *sine qua non* of good reporting. The blame can sometimes be laid elsewhere. Neville probably never saw W. G. Grace in the flesh and thus his evocation of him in 'The Champion' was of necessity an exercise in imaginative reconstruc-tion, with all the difficulties and dangers which this entailed. Elsewhere, however, as in the description of his childhood hero, J. T. Tyldesley, whom he certainly watched on more than one occasion, Neville's exuberant inexperience betrays him. The 'slash stroke, that upper-cut over the slips' heads' was the invention not of 'Johnny' Tyldesley but of 'Johnny' Briggs. (It may be doubted whether Briggs ever got out in any other way.)

Some *M.G.* readers may have looked to Neville's columns for the soundness of their technical commentary – their criticism, for example, of the two-eyed stance, which had abolished the cut and the off-drive and made that side of the wicket 'as dull as a winter's day' – but most, I suspect, will have read and re-read them for the pictures they conjured up of great batsmen and great bowlers in action. Pursuing his own career led Neville not only to seek satisfaction in style but also to explore the relationship between style and personality. MacLaren, Ranjitsinhji, Spooner, Trumper, Duff, Shrewsbury and Lucas – these, he told his readers, were stylists. Not one of them performed in the manner of the others. They expressed in cricket their own private and immortal souls, using bats as other men used violins and brushes. They were, in short, artists. And Neville went on to declare that every one of Hirst's innings was an autobiography – it almost told you what his politics were. 'So with MacLaren. Once you had seen him at play, masterfully putting balls to the boundary – nay, he dismissed them from his presence with a wave of an imperial bat – you knew the man.' Brearley, a fast bowler by trade, was 'like the wind in Dickens that roared "Ho! Ho!" all over the countryside till, tiring of inland fun, it scampered out to sea and with the other zephyrs made a night of it,'[10] while C. B. Fry 'deliberately turned his mind and spirit inside out for all the world to look at'.

That others may have seen those heroes differently, or that they may at times have had difficulty in recognising themselves amid 'Cricketer's' vivid metaphors, does not necessarily detract from the merits of his columns. Neville would have liked to be considered as much of an artist as the 'flannelled fools' he portrayed. If the reader is willing to grant him this wish, then it doesn't matter if 'Cricketer's' images' were drawn just a shade larger than life. The very extension of this latitude places all his excess and exaggeration in the realm of artistic licence where different rules apply. Whatever conclusions the reader comes to, it cannot be gainsaid that the first five years of 'Cricketer's' reign saw the creation of a new genre of cricket-writing which, at its best, was worthy of comparison with the finest examples of English journalism. One example will suffice:

> A bat, indeed, can look an entirely different instrument in different hands. With Grace it was a rod of correction, for to him bad bowling was a deviation from moral order; Ranjitsinhji turned a bat into a wand, passing it before the eyes of the foe till they followed him in a trance along his processional way; George Hirst's bat looked like a stout cudgel belabouring all men not born in Yorkshire; Macartney used his bat for our bedazzlement as Sergeant Troy used his blade for the bedazzlement of Bathsheba – it was a bat that seemed everywhere at once, yet nowhere specially.

During the early '20s Neville established a routine which was to last until the outbreak of war in 1939: 'Summer after summer up and down England,' he tells us in *Autobiography*, 'with my eyes on green grass for hours and my face receiving the brown of sun and air.' For a while Manchester remained his only home, but as rail travel occupied ever more of his time, a base in London became a necessity. For anyone possessed of even the slightest liking for cricket, it must have seemed a good life: for Neville, it was unalloyed bliss.

I saw the blossom come upon the orchards in Gloucestershire, as we journeyed from Manchester to Bristol, and I saw midsummer in full blaze at Canterbury; and I saw midsummer dropping torrents of rain on the same lovely place, the white tents dropsical: 'Play abandoned for the day.' I saw the autumn leaves falling at Eastbourne. I have shivered to the bone in the spring-time blasts at the Parks at Oxford. In a *Manchester Guardian* article I congratulated the keenness and devotion of two spectators who at Leicester sat all day near the sight-screen, from eleven until half-past six, in spite of an east wind like a knife. Then, as I was finishing my notice, a thought struck me. 'But,' I added in a final sentence, 'perhaps they were only dead.'

. . . From Old Trafford to Dover, from Hull to Bristol, the fields were active as fast bowlers heaved and thudded and sweated over the earth, and batsmen drove and cut or got their legs in front; and men in the slips bent down, all four of them together, as though moved by one string. On every afternoon at half-past six I saw them, in my mind's eye, all walking home to the pavilion, with a deepened tan on their faces. And the newspapers came out with the cricket scores and a visitor from Budapest in London for the first time expressed a certain bewilderment when he saw an *Evening News* poster: 'Collapse of Surrey'.[11]

The speed with which Neville moved to the top of his profession seems even by present-day standards to be little short of indecent; to many of his older colleagues the margin must have seemed even narrower. In April 1920 'Cricketer' anticipated the start of the new season with an article in celebration of cricket, and so began a tradition which again was to last until 1939. In the first such piece, entitled 'The sweet o' the year – especially for cricketers', all the ingredients which would soon distinguish Neville from his predecessors, contemporaries and successors – wit, elegance, insight and a goodly measure of self-indulgence – had been assembled. The mould was ready for casting.

Happy is it that one is in no danger of missing a jot of the sense of the event when one begins a new season. Let it be a balmy April day, and how can we fail to catch the joy which comes as we feel the air filling out our flannels, making us luxuriously loose at the neck, and passing over the body with a gentle caress? Good Lord, we must ask ourselves, what lives do we lead in the winter? How absurd now seems to be the best Melton overcoat in the world, and the softest of silk scarves! This is the sweet o' the year.

The occasion has its pains and penalties, none the less. A batsman sends his willow like a flail, and hits a half-volley! Heaven help me, he might ask himself, why do they make bats so impossibly heavy? How, in the name of justice, do they expect a mere mortal to hit a ball so outrageously small? Yet once upon a time, the distraught man tells himself, he was known to hit it – aye, even to the boundary! Will he ever accomplish the feat again?

So, too, does the bowler have his moments of misgiving, as he strains his creaking joints into activity after the winter's period of coma. The problem with him is to get the ball even half-way down the pitch, and he is thinking of writing an indignant letter to the papers asking the M.C.C. to go in for a projectile whose specific gravity might conceivably be within human power to control with dignity.[12]

According to legend, although 'Cricketer' was nurtured on a Lancastrian diet, the event which finally secured his reputation took place in 1921 on a field far removed from Old Trafford. The most famous match ever staged at the Saffrons, Eastbourne, arose out of a challenge issued by A. C. MacLaren, nearing fifty and absent from first-class cricket since 1914, to Warwick Armstrong, captain of the all-conquering Australians of 1921. The story of how this greying patrician's motley assortment of unsung, unfancied amateurs defeated the mighty tourists (McDonald, Gregory and all), has been recounted too often – particularly by Neville himself – to bear re-telling in full. It is enough to recall how, having been forewarned of the impending clash, Neville found himself the only reporter on the ground when the teams took the field. For a while it seemed as though the majority had been correct in their decision to sit this one out. MacLaren's team were skittled before lunch on the first day for a disastrous 43 and by the end of play the Australians had made 174. It looked for all the world like another facile triumph for Armstrong's men. What happened on the following morning has passed into cricket history and the Cardus legend.

The young reporter, by now resigned to the prospect of humili-
ation, took the precaution of sending his luggage to the station
before leaving for the ground. When MacLaren was bowled first-
ball by McDonald, his precautions seemed well founded. Neville
was already on his way to the exit, *en route* to the Oval to try to recover
his reputation, when Aubrey Faulkner and Hubert Ashton began to
put together the stand which was to last till nearly the end of play that
day, leaving the Australians needing 196 to win. How on the final
day, with the *Guardian* still the only major paper represented, C. H.
Gibson's inspired bowling left Armstrong's team 28 runs short of
their target, and Neville with the only scoop of his career is one of
cricket's most treasured memories. Doubtless the event contributed
mightily to Neville's fast-growing reputation but, as tends to be the
case with Neville's most famous fables, some of the details turn out
on closer examination to be a trifle inaccurate. Surrey were not
simultaneously engaged in battle against Yorkshire at the Oval; as
Wisden confirms, they were involved in an 'epic' encounter with
Middlesex at Lords which was to decide the fate of the County
Championship. This slip was typical of Neville. Like all inveterate
story-tellers, he was sometimes prone to embroidery. In the case of
'MacLaren's match', having told the story on endless occasions
before he came to write *Autobiography*, it is not difficult to imagine
how, by then, fact and fiction had become more or less
indistinguishable.

Similarly intriguing is the mystery surrounding the circumstances
of Neville's entry into the Holy Estate of matrimony. Edith and he
had enjoyed a relationship which today might be described as a
common-law marriage ever since the Shrewsbury days. What finally
decided them to formalise their relationship is anyone's guess. As
Neville was in many respects a very conventional person, he may
well have felt that, with a regular income and a good job, now was the
time to keep Edith 'unto the manner born'. Alternatively, it may have
been that Edith, tiring of the informality of their partnership,
decided that the time was right to satisfy at least some of the typical
expectations of persons of her pedigree and position. Whatever the
case, the two were married in a civil ceremony on 17 June 1921.

In *Autobiography*, Neville recounted how on the morning of the
ceremony he went first to Old Trafford, where Lancashire won
the toss and Makepeace and Hallows opened the batting. After
watching for a few minutes, he repaired by taxi to the Chorlton

Registry Office where he 'committed the most responsible and irrevocable act in a mortal man's life'. After the Register had been signed, he returned to Old Trafford to discover that Lancashire had prospered to the tune of 17 runs: Makepeace 5, Hallows 11, and one leg-bye.

Unfortunately for Neville (though I'm sure he was fully aware of the danger), cricket numbers amongst its followers a peculiar species of zealot that thrives on a daily infusion of facts and figures culled from *Wisden*. After the publication of *Autobiography*, it was only a matter of time before one representative of this strange breed decided to delve more deeply into Neville's narrative. Geoffrey Copinger, who laid bare Neville's deception, discovered that Makepeace and Hallows opened the batting for Lancashire only once in June 1921 (in a completely different match) when Harry made 4 and 24 'retired hurt' and Charlie 109 'not out' and 0. Thereafter Makepeace was out of the side for a month and the two didn't bat together again until August. *Sic transit gloria mundi.*

[V]

By 1926, Neville's world had altered beyond recognition. Gone were the years of vaulting ambition and echoing uncertainty. Now he was a man of substance, with a wife and prospects. The real and the autobiographical lives were not set on convergent courses. His reputation was beginning to extend beyond the relatively narrow world of *Guardian* readers. Two collections of his cricket essays, *A Cricketer's Book* and *Days in the Sun*, had already appeared. His publisher in each case had been Grant Richards, a gentleman who described himself as an 'old literary sportsman'. As, by all accounts, Richards's attitude towards publishing combined elements of spontaneity, intuition, dash and risk more usually associated with amateur batsmen in the golden days of Ranji, Fry and Spooner, it was no surprise that he built up a list of authors which included Shaw and Masefield, and still managed to get into desperate financial straits on more than one occasion. A man of great verve and charm, he evidently found little difficulty in consuming the profits of his publishing activities.

It was to this 'bloom of clothes' and 'brilliance of monocle' that Neville chose to send 'in a dishevelled state . . . a packet made up of newspaper cuttings' which became *A Cricketer's Book*. At first sight,

Richards wasn't especially taken with Neville's offering, but in the end, persuaded more by the *Guardian* connection than anything else, he agreed to publish. After a brief disagreement over the selling price – Neville favoured a shilling or half-a-crown, but Richards would 'have nothing to do with a cheap publication' and fixed the price at six shillings – the book duly appeared. Although neither Richards nor Neville 'made a fortune', both were happy enough to produce two further collections of Cardus essays. Thereafter they parted, and Neville's next book, *Good Days*, went to Jonathan Cape.

Through his business dealings with Neville, Richards was drawn to several conclusions about the character of his author which make interesting reading, particularly in the light of the image which Neville subsequently acquired. Recognising quality when he saw it, Richards readily acknowledged that he was proud to have been associated with Neville, but, he added in an autobiography entitled *Author Hunting,*

> ... my friend is a most difficult author to handle. In spite of the fact that the first proposal came from him – the result, I suspect, of some friends urging – he will not believe that his stuff is worth reprinting, and the getting of a second and third book out of him was as difficult as anything I have ever experienced. . . . An austere and sensitive soul.[13]

It was an observation that most friends, colleagues and associates would confirm.

Happy, secure and (by and large) satisfied: this was Neville Cardus at the end of 1925. His first years with the *Manchester Guardian* had seen great success; 'Cricketer' was now a household figure; his hallmark a style both distinctive and unique which, as it matured, was to become the envy not only of the freemasonry of sportswriters but also of the wider community of journalists and writers. Yet even this record of achievement could not have prepared Neville for the success to come. First, there was Lancashire C.C.C.; in April, 1926, the county stood on the threshold of its greatest days. Secondly, there was music; Sam Langford died in May 1927, and with his passing the way was clear for Neville to extend his responsibilities to include that form of creativity which he had always regarded as the *ne plus ultra* of all art forms.

To say that Lancashire had not given ample warning of their

potential would be unfair. From the re-start of county cricket in 1919 they had been a force to be reckoned with, but in those days they had suffered from a lack of decisiveness and consistency at the critical moments. If ever there was a case of 'men making history', it was E. A. McDonald's transformation of Lancashire's fortunes between 1925 and 1930. Ted McDonald, born in Tasmania, on 6 January 1892, first came to the eyes of the British public in 1921 when, together with Jack Gregory, he was largely responsible for the drubbing that Warwick Armstrong's party inflicted on English cricket that summer. He only played in eleven test matches, but in those games he managed to establish himself as one of the great fast-bowlers of all time. Imagine then the excitement amongst Lancashire supporters, to say nothing of the team itself, when the news broke that McDonald had decided to settle in Lancashire and, once fully qualified, would be available for the county. After three years in league cricket, he began his new career with Lancashire in 1924, by a happy coincidence the same year as the county recruited a new wicket-keeper – George Duckworth from Warrington.

The addition of McDonald and Duckworth transformed Lancashire from a powerful team into one which at times bordered on the invincible. At first, it seemed that circumstances might conspire to prevent the county capitalising on its newly acquired assets. In 1924 rain ruled out a finish in all but two of the twelve matches played at Old Trafford. In 1925, however, Lancashire had no one to blame but themselves. After running neck-and-neck with Yorkshire for most of the season, with McDonald taking 205 wickets, they faltered in the final weeks and finished third. But in 1926 Leonard Green took over the captaincy from Jack Sharp and led Lancashire to three successive Championship titles. His was probably the strongest team ever to represent the Red Rose. To complement the bowling of McDonald, Parkin, Sibbles and Richard Tyldesley, Green could mount a formidable array of batting talent. In 1926, for example, Ernest Tyldesley scored 2,365 runs at an average of 69.55, and between 26 June and 6 August he hit a half century or more in ten successive innings, a feat only Bradman has equalled. In 1928, Charlie Hallows scored 1,000 runs in May and, together with Watson, put on more than a hundred runs for the first wicket on twelve occasions during a season in which Lancashire remained undefeated.

These great feats stirred Neville's imagination to a degree which sometimes severely stretched even his literary abilities. In the early days, pre-selected images and metaphors littered his copy. The effect was 'consciously picturesque' – where once the reader had imagined the wicket as a dusty, scarred strip of mottled turf, now in 'Cricketer's' column he was presented with an Elysian paradise where all was 'blue sky and green grass'. Though Neville openly acknowledged the extent to which he overwrote during this, his 'yellow' period, at least partial justification was at hand. 'In the beginning of anything,' he wrote in *Autobiography*, 'you must take risks and explore your palette entirely.' But by the mid-1920s, the days of 'lyric gush' had begun to give way to a mood 'tinctured with satire if not with open irony'. In his own estimation, 'Cricketer' became less concerned with the score-board (a curious judgement as even the most fanatical of his readers would have been hard put to produce many examples of reports overburdened with statistics), less intoxicated with his own literary powers, and instead concentrated more on the field of play and the figures who occupied it. 'It was then that I began to see cricket as something more than a game. To me, Woolley and Hammond and Jack Hobbs were like actors in a play, and I wrote about them not only in terms of runs and strokes but also in terms of individual character. I found myself as deeply engrossed in cricket as in a symphony orchestra.'[14] And for all his later statements to the contrary, cricket never totally lost its hold on his imagination. As Rupert Hart-Davis pointed out in his introduction to *The Essential Neville Cardus*,

. . . almost any fine summer's day will find him at Lord's, high in the Press Box, wandering from the Tavern to the Long Room and back, or sitting alone in one of the stands. Even those minor games for which the match-card used to promise 'Band if possible' draw him in. He smokes a pipe and carries a book under his arm. Often he seems not to be watching the players at all, but experience has shown that little escapes him. If one eye is on the Eternal Verities, the other is firmly fixed on Denis Compton.[15]

Eight of the Lancashire side of the late '20s were good enough to play for their countries; Ernest and Richard Tyldesley, Makepeace, Watson, Hallows, Iddon and Duckworth for England, and of course McDonald for Australia. With so much talent on display, the danger was that 'Cricketer' would soon show those tell-tale traces of flabbiness and a tendency to repeat which are the all-too-familiar consequences of over-indulgence. That this threat rarely material-ised was largely due to the skill with which Neville focused his eye as much on character as on technical ability. The beauty of 'Cricketer's' life was that in travelling from match to match he had a chance to observe players, on the field and off, at first hand. He could watch their eccentricities, their foibles, their pet hates and superstitions, and most of all their humour. At the end of the day, the combination of these details and his vivid imagination gave to 'Cricketer's' match reports an insight, an originality and a colour which no other journalist has matched. They were the raw material from which he created the characters of English county cricket; men like Cecil Parkin, 'tall, erect, his black hair shining', who sang the pop songs of the day as he walked to his mark and who once confided to Neville that 'when the time comes that I can't play any more, I'll do as the Romans did. Aye, I'll get in a hot bath and – cut mi ruddy throat.'

In the evenings, too, Neville lived close to his players. The Lancashire team, he observed,

> . . . sat in their pub, gently drinking and talking over the day's play. At half-past ten, the Captain would say, 'Now boys – bed. One more for the road.' The waiter would come, and 'Dick' Tyldesley would say: 'Noa, skipper, noa. Enough's as good as a feast.' Pause as the waiter still waited. 'Well, mek it half-a-pint.' Another pause, shorter, then 'Ah well, Ah might as well mek it a pint.' Every night the same formula, the same effort to resist, the same compromise.'[16]

Critics have argued that Neville too often let his imagination run wild; that in striving to enliven and enrich his subject matter he portrayed its principal characters in a manner which bore little or no resemblance to their mortal form. 'So what,' his apologists would reply; and indeed, were it not for the fact that side by side with his propensity to exaggerate 'Cricketer' also tended to neglect technical detail, the criticism would carry little force. As it was, lacking a firm, factual definition, and imbued with his own romantic energy, some of 'Cricketer's' heroes acquired an ethereal character which rested uneasily besides their dour, northern birthright. In these cases, Neville wrote as a painter, not as a photographer. His descriptions often owed as much to his inner feelings as to empirical observation. He wrote what he imagined, but sometimes, falling prey to his own reputation, he wrote not as he felt but as he imagined his audience would have expected him to feel. Not that the end product was unacceptable; Cardus's work never was – even when, expecting an account of a match between Gloucestershire and Lancashire, the reader instead found himself experiencing the purest evocation of midsummer beauty in the Cotswolds, all under the masterly heading of 'Lancashire's Steady Batting'. Nor should it be forgotten that there were many occasions on which 'Cricketer's' powers of imagination took him directly and effortlessly to the truth. When he wrote of Frank Woolley's batsmanship, 'The lease of it is in the hands of the special providence which looks after things that will not look after himself', it mattered not one whit that the great Kent player understood the passage to be a reference to the doubtful reliability of his back-play. Such are the perils of advanced literacy.

By focusing the attention of the cricketing public on events at Old Trafford, Lancashire's triumphs had the effect of further extending the potential size of 'Cricketer's' captive audience, and Neville was by now far too wily to pass up such a golden opportunity. During the summers of the late 1920s, he followed Colonel Green's team from ground to ground, devoting the greater part of his energies to their glory. Other sides attracted his attention only when Makepeace, McDonald and Co were not performing. Tests were given priority only after much heart-searching; and even then he sometimes left too early and had to imagine the critical phase of play. Even Lord's, the headquarters of the game, saw him only once or twice a season.

Of all the matches in the Championship calendar, two stood out as being of a different substance. The rivalry between Lancashire and Yorkshire had of course exercised a major influence on the course of English history long before county cricket was dreamed of. With the advent of less violent methods of resolving conflict, their traditional enmity had been channelled into the relatively peaceful context of bi-annual cricket matches. By the time 'Cricketer' came to take his place in the Press Box, these encounters were at the height of their popularity. Twice a summer, over the Whitsun and August Bank Holiday weekends, the tribal clans gathered; 30,000 partisans baying in ferocious unison at the merest prospect of advantage. 'It's a rum 'un, is t'Yorksheer and Lankysheer match,' one of the players recalled, 'T'two teams meets in t'dressing room

on t'Bank Holiday; and then we never speaks agean for three days –
except to appeal.' No quarter was asked or given; concentration was
intense and risk-taking a mortal sin; maidens occurred in profusion;
and umpires were 'luxurious superfluities'.

With his love of spectacle and character, 'Cricketer' revelled in
these occasions, their unique atmosphere bringing both the best and
the worst out of him. Between the two wars, he saw every match.
Whenever the game was lacking in interest, he would unashamedly
embellish to restore the richness of the occasion. The players he
treated as actors; the greatest – Rhodes, Sutcliffe, Tyldesley,
McDonald and Paynter – had no need 'of a remoter charm, by
thought supplied'. Endowed with an abundance of talent and a
presence to match, they were the equal of any occasion. Others,
however, owed their reputation and a place in history as much to
'Cricketer's' prose as to their own abilities. When the muse was
upon him, Neville's imagination could create the most endearing of
cameos from the most unlikely of subjects. Characters arose from
his pen in a form that no score-board could convey.

Emmott Robinson was perhaps his most memorable creation.
During a career with Yorkshire which began only after his thirty-
sixth birthday, he scored 9,446 runs, including 7 centuries, aver-
aging 24.53, and took 892 wickets for just under 22 runs apiece,
figures which, in *Wisden*'s view, represented the achievements of a
'noted all-round professional'. To 'Cricketer', he was a

> grizzled, squat, bandy-legged Yorkshireman, all sagging and
> loose at the braces in private life, but on duty for Yorkshire he
> was liable at any minute to gather and concentrate his energy
> into sudden and vehement leaps and scuffles. He had shrewd
> eyes, a hatchet face and grey hairs, most of them representing
> appeals that had gone against him for leg-before-wicket. I
> imagine that he was created one day by God scooping up the
> nearest acre of Yorkshire soil at hand, then breathing into it
> saying, 'Now, lad, tha's called Emmott Robinson and tha can go
> on with new ball at t'pavilion end.'

Together with Wilfred Rhodes, Emmott Robinson controlled the
destinies of Yorkshire cricket on the field of play. There was a
captain of course, an amateur in keeping with social convention, but

more often than not he served in a consultative capacity, usually from a far distant point in the outfield. In Neville's eyes, the little all-rounder became the apotheosis of Yorkshire cricket and Yorkshire character. Column after column carried references to his consummate canniness, strength of character and earthy humour. All of which was vastly entertaining, and may even have been true, but there was one snag: it was only a matter of time before a liverish reader stopped to ask how it was that such an extraordinary person came to be playing cricket (for Yorkshire), and why, if he was so exceptional, wasn't he playing for England. Happily, when it came to the crunch, 'Cricketer' turned out to be a lot more resilient than at first seemed likely. Faced with a reader intrepid enough to suggest that many of the characters described in his columns owed more to imagination than observation, Neville fell back on the simple act of denial: 'No, I didn't invent Emmott Robinson,' he would say, 'I enlarged him. . . . My imagination drew out of him what was natural and germane to his character.'

It says much for the quality of 'Cricketer's' columns, and for the loyalty of his readers, that very few people publicly challenged the acceptability of his reports. At their best, Neville's powers of imagination proved gloriously entertaining, but whenever he was even slightly off form the artifice showed through. It showed through to Neville himself, or perhaps he saw it through the eyes of Dick Tyldesley who, after reading one of 'Cricketer's' reports, was heard to mutter, 'Ah'd like to bowl at t'bugger some da-ay.' At the time no one knew how Emmott Robinson felt, but many years later he put the record straight in a deliciously tongue-in-cheek contribution to Neville's seventieth birthday celebrations:

Ee, by gum, just fancy that – me havin' a chance ta write summat abaht t'chap 'at ewsed ta write sa mich abaht me! Ah ewsed ta think 'at he took t'mickey aht o' me sometimes be what he said abaht when we wor laikin' Lenkysheer, but nooabdy injoyed it moore nor Ah did. They wor reyt happy days, and nooabdy did moore nor Neville Cardus ta mak 'en happy days. Ah'm reyt gled he's got ta 70 not aht, and Ah do hooap he makes it a hunderd. . . .

By the early 1930s a distinct change had come over 'Cricketer's' reports. The flowery, romantic abandon of his early years had given way to an altogether more detached, sardonic descriptive style. Less space was devoted to colour, climate and atmosphere; more attention was paid to the players as characters, and to imputing motives for their seemingly incomprehensible activities. In reporting the Roses matches of the early 1920s, 'Cricketer' had tended to linger in his scene-setting to such an extent that already slow-moving encounters became positively statuesque. Take the August Bank Holiday match of 1926, for example, a game which never advanced beyond a dour struggle for first-innings points. Perhaps, it was for want of anything better to do that 'Cricketer' chose this moment to indulge in one of his Elysian reveries:

Never has Old Trafford made a handsomer sight; 45,000 sat (or stood) there rank on rank, happy as schoolboys, happy in their grumblings. May not an Englishman have his grievance, let it be the Government, the income tax, Mr Cook or Frank Watson? It is the sign, as Meredith puts it, of our affection for a thing that we can complain at it occasionally without loving it the less. At three o'clock there was no place on earth where I would rather have been than at Old Trafford. Torrents of sunshine fell on the ancient field, the multitude was drenched in them. And the superb pavilion stood in the summer light, and during the silences that came over the game from time to time, it seemed to commune with itself – perhaps with the mighty past it has known, in those days when a Johnny Briggs would risk a match against Yorkshire by tossing up a slow ball audaciously, and when a George Ulyett was brave enough to accept the challenge and make a lion-hearted bid for victory. White clouds sailed in the blue sky; a gentle wind sent the Lancashire colours rippling in the air. Shadows fell black and tiny in front of the cricketers, like soft pools.

Six years later, while traces of this propensity remain, it was the players who now absorbed his attention and the mood, from being overtly naturalistic, is now mercurial in its mischief:

On Saturday afternoon at Bramall Lane, in wintry blasts and under a gloomy sky, a six was hit by Mitchell in the presence of several witnesses. The cold was enough to drive any man out of his senses and to be fair to Mitchell, he hit a six off a no-ball. . . .

Frankly I was sorry that Mitchell so far forgot himself. It is really not an extenuation to say that the six was struck from a no-ball. For if we look closely into the matter, the fact emerges that a no-ball enforces and compels by artful suggestion the hitting of a six. A man of Mitchell's strength of will ought surely to be equal to any such insidious ways. A six on compulsion! Zounds an' he were at the strappado or on all the racks of the world he would not hit a six on compulsion. Let him ask Emmot Robinson. . . .

In the second over of the morning, Sutcliffe was bowled by Booth, but it was a no-ball. Later in the day, Sutcliffe was caught from a 'skier' from a no-ball; it is a pity we cannot have a Lancashire and Yorkshire match played entirely with no-balls.

The same mood was upon 'Cricketer' when the match came to its close:

Yorkshire beat Lancashire here at twenty-five minutes to six by an innings and three runs. . . . The stand for the last wicket was diverting. Duckworth made some astonishingly fine hits off Bowes, but refused to run lest the fast bowler should get at Booth. Booth hit Leyland for six with a magnificent drive and generally enjoyed himself.

But Duckworth, after nursing the bowling for a quarter of an hour, skied an attempted drive and was caught behind the bowler, to the accompaniment of a howl of joy from 10,000 Yorkshiremen. . . .

[VI]

Sam Langford died in May 1927 at the house in which he had been born sixty-three years before. He had been principal music critic of the *Manchester Guardian* since Ernest Newman's short and fiery reign came to an abrupt end in April 1906. Not many remember him now, certainly not as many as recall his predecessor and successor, but in his day Langford was a respected and influential figure. Though both he and Newman were short in stature, there the resemblance ended. Indeed, the marked difference in their outward appearance had led some to wonder whether they were even of the same evolutionary stock. In Neville's words 'a mixture of Socrates,

Moussorgsky (as depicted by Repin) and Brahms ... small and podgy, with shaggy whiskers and a dome of a forehead ... loose in his old clothes as an Elephant', Sam Langford 'waddled over the earth, seldom lifting the soles of his boots from the ground', while Newman 'rather resembled a hard-boiled egg'.

Beneath the surface the differences were just as striking. Newman had been intended for a career in the Indian Civil Service until ill-health dictated something rather less onerous. Having determined where his future lay, Newman set about discovering and understanding culture with a thoroughness and dedication which may even have inspired Neville's own 'cultural schema' – though he would never have admitted it! Rejecting what he saw as the cloying subjectiveness of conventional criticism, he set out to create an 'objective science' of music criticism which focused exclusively on the object under observation, the anatomy of music. To emphasise the radical change involved, he took as his by-line the name 'Newman' (his real name being William Roberts) and eventually adopted the name as his own. By the time he came to the *Manchester Guardian* in December 1903, he had already published substantial works on Gluck and Wagner. By contrast, Sam Langford came, as Neville loved to recall, literally from the earth. Earthiness hung about him all his working life; he came to concerts with 'traces of his allotment clinging to his boots'. His father, a nursery gardener, soon realised that although his son may have loved the soil he was more at home with Bach than with business, and sent him to study piano under Carl Reinecke in Leipzig. Alas, his ambition was to be thwarted and, having discovered that short, stubby fingers were not ideally suited to the keyboard, Sam returned to Manchester and after a while began to contribute notices as Newman's deputy.

From the start it was clear that the principal and his assistant were cast in very different moulds. Compared with Newman, Langford had little experience of music criticism and none at all of writing. His first contribution bore all the signs of a difficult birth, though later in his career he was to become renowned for the speed with which he dispatched copy – 1,200 words in little more than an hour, written with a battered lead pencil to the sound of date stones being projected from between his pursed lips to the four corners of the room. He was, as Neville wrote later, 'as man and critic, at Ernest Newman's extreme'. Not for him the barbed wit and acid tongue with which Newman assaulted Mancunian complacency and the massive, monolithic presence of Dr Hans Richter. He could never have suggested after a notoriously uneven performance of Berlioz's *Romeo and Juliet* that Dr Richter's acquaintance with the score was of neither 'close nor long duration'. Nor would he have attempted to emulate Newman's acid dissection of performance:

> Men do not go through feverish scenes like that at the end of *Romeo and Juliet* with an air as if they were posing for a statue of Morpheus. . . . The orchestra was no better than the principals . . . a good deal of the orchestral music was as much like what Berlioz meant it to be as a cheap oleograph is like a Whistler.[17]

Nor, finally, would it have been for him to mount Newman's savagely witty onslaught on the 'absurd' practice of 'concert opera'.

> Mr Harrison, ignoring Venus while he was singing, divided his glances between the audience and his book. While Venus was addressing her most seductive strains to him, he was generally scanning the galleries. When he in turn poured his soul out to Venus, she had nothing else to do but look over his arm and follow the music in his copy. And this was Venus and Tannhäuser![18]

Yet Langford's output as principal music critic was such as to leave his readers in no doubt that here was a man in the true tradition of *Guardian* criticism established by George Freemantle and Arthur Johnstone. Newman, on the other hand, was always seen as a maverick. In Johnstone's eyes, music criticism 'relates music to the rest of human experience rather than treating it as a separate science' and thus, by implication, the 'objective' analysis of performance was relegated to a position of secondary or partial significance. Johnstone saw music 'as a comment, at several removes and after strange distillation, on life and experience'. In Langford's hands, the art of music criticism was returned from its temporary resting place within the analytical confines of Newman's 'objectivity' to the realms of empathy and experience. In the process, he extended Johnstone's earlier articulation of the *Guardian* creed to a point at which music became not a distanced, reflective 'comment' on reality, but an extension of human consciousness. He 'did not conduct a post-mortem on the inert score of composition', Neville once wrote of

Langford; 'he put the living, sounding musical organism under an X-ray'.

Langford rarely committed his thoughts on music criticism to paper, preferring to let his notices speak for themselves. Here again, the contrast with Newman is striking. In Langford's world, the realms of the intellect and of the heart were scarcely distinguished. He believed that 'a man can absorb only what he needs, by imaginatively experiencing and living in a subject'. It followed that this congenial man of the soil often found himself at odds with the high moral and intellectual tone of Scott's editorship. Montague's writing, he was once overheard to say, would benefit 'from a spade or two of dung out of my garden'. His own columns were a potent mixture of powerful intellect and cultured prose; they epitomised a style of writing then championed by the *Manchester Guardian*, but now largely extinct. This sea-change, and Langford's writing skills, are perfectly illustrated in the following piece taken from a notice of a Beethoven piano recital, written 'on the night':

The last sonata of Beethoven offers surely the most striking illustration there is of that unity in seeming contrasts which is the secret of the highest genius. Here is nothing, apparently, but a grim contrast between the starkest tragedy and that calm and eternal faith which is the only healer. Somewhere in the soul of this music's creator, those elements are reconciled and fused. He tells us little of the process, only of its results. The final variations approach so nearly to a mechanical perfection that the contemplation of its nearness almost brings a shudder to the mind. Yet where shall we find music more divinely separated from the mechanical than those first variations whose existence seems to be the blissful stirring of an inward life? The apotheosis of the shake with which this sonata ends and in which the whole mechanical construction and subtlety of this sonata finds its solution may be likened to those studies of light with which Turner in his last years baffled his beholders. The comparison is not far-fetched, nor a comparison with the moving glass, the smoothest of all poetic rhythms, in which Dante turned his verse . . .[19]

Langford's death left the way clear for Neville to realise his greatest ambition. However much he may have enjoyed playing and watching and writing about cricket, there can be no doubt that as his intellectual horizons had widened music had come to occupy an ever more important place in his life. The account of how he came to be principal music critic makes great play of how lucky he had been:

> It all happened, even yet again, in the chanciest way. Scott never went to concerts and was not musical. By sheer vicissitude of international politics the Russian singer Rosing entered Scott's life; they became friends and Rosing stayed at The Firs with Scott while he gave two concerts in Manchester. Langford wrote on the first of these recitals, and though he appreciated the art of Rosing up to a point, he was much too deeply enmeshed in the style and musical form of German *lieder* to see eye to eye with Rosing's and Moussorgsky's methods.
>
> Scott sent me the tickets for Rosing's second concert. I felt awkward about it. . . . I don't think Langford took it very well at the time. . . .[20]

But if we look beneath the surface of the autobiographies the reality is a little different. The post of principal music critic came his way not just because (some seven years earlier) Scott had earmarked him as a likely successor on the strength of a sympathetic review of a long-forgotten Russian, but also because he, Neville, wanted the job, and previous experience had shown him that his ambition had a handy knack of translating itself into reality.

From the moment when, as a young man, he had first perceived the beauty of music Neville had sought to broaden and deepen his appreciation of its substance. 1927 had marked the culmination of a period of preparation in which he had studied music as diligently as ever Leonardo had studied anatomy. At the centre of this process of self-instruction had been Neville's fervent desire to cultivate a mastery of the art of *listening* to music, a faculty he defined as the 'imaginative and non-egotistical reception of music', and which he later claimed to be 'an art *sui generis*' beyond the reach of 'exultant' musicians. Attending concerts, recitals and operas; talking to performers; debating and discussing with the likes of Langford and Newman – by all these means he sought to become 'an enlightened listener'. In the process, he augmented his ambitions to the point at which succeeding Langford became more an expectation than a dream.

When Scott, recognising a talent which, if carefully handled, could follow in Langford's footsteps, suggested to Neville that he should continue his studies and possibly spend some time on the continent acquiring 'experience and standards', the instruction (for that was what it amounted to) was naturally counted as an honour rather than an additional imposition. Encouraged by Scott and guided by Langford, Neville strove to acquire that ability to identify and communicate the essence of music which in time was to make him one of the most influential critics of his day.

As his studies continued, so his self-assurance grew. The same confidence that had led him to take issue with Newman over the relative merits of Bantock and Wolf also found expression in a willingness to introduce himself to J. M. Barrie, to place his literary wares before Grant Richards and to indulge his readers' fantasies with delightful reconstructions of matches such as 'Shastbury' and a 'sentimental journey' to Lord's in the company of Jolyon Forsyte. And yet beneath this buoyancy, there remained a certain angular diffidence. Until he felt he knew his heroes not as performers but as friends, a shyness that at times bordered on deference permeated his manner. That engaging mixture of professional confidence and personal reticence which lingers in the memory of many of his closest friends was already firmly etched on his character.

One of Neville's first acts on succeeding Langford was to set about editing a collection of his predecessor's *Guardian* notices.[21] Looking to the future, it was not an entirely unblemished prospect that greeted the new principal music critic. After Beecham's war-time efforts had made Manchester one of the most exciting music centres in Britain, if not Europe, the conservative elements in the city's music community had succeeded in re-imposing their stultifying orthodoxy on both programmes and, too often, performances. After Sir Thomas had almost single-handedly shaken the city out of its pre-war complacency, personal problems had obliged him to withdraw from public life. After much agonising, the Hallé Society appointed a young Irishman, Hamilton Harty, to be its new principal conductor. At a stroke, much of the vim and vigour went out of Manchester's musical life. International figures were still attracted to the city – Richard Strauss, for example, conducted the Hallé in 1922 in a programme which included *Don Juan, Till Eulenspiegel*, and nine of his songs – but increasingly the atmosphere was reminiscent of Wordsworth's lament:

Wither is fled the visionary gleam?
Where is it now, the glory and the dream?'

Money was at the root of the problem. Despite the concentration
of wealth to be found in industrial Lancashire, the Society's finances
were far from sound. The limitations thus imposed found their way
inscrutably to the conductor's podium. Some, like Langford,
believed that for all his brilliance Harty lacked the technical and
interpretative powers expected of a successor to Hans Richter. A
harsh judgement perhaps, but there was no doubting the innate
conservatism of Harty's musical perspective. 'The Hallé concerts,'
he once told a friend, 'are for established composers.'[22] No great
orchestra can remain entirely impervious to changes in the classical
repertoire, but under Harty the Hallé certainly did little to further
the cause of 'new' music. When, in 1923, Harty revealed his
intention of introducing 'novelties' into the orchestra's programme,
more than a few eyebrows were raised; but it turned out that he was
thinking of Vaughan Williams's *Sea Symphony*, Strauss's *Alpine
Symphony*, Berlioz's *Symphonie Funèbre et Triomphale* and his own
arrangement of Handel's *Music for the Royal Fireworks*. 'The new
wind sweeping through music in the South,' Michael Kennedy has
noted, '. . . was felt only as a whispering breeze in Manchester.'[23]

When, at the age of thirty-eight, Neville took over Langford's
mantle, he was thus bound both by prevailing taste and the tradition
of *Guardian* music criticism. Those who criticise 'N.C.' for con-
centrating on music's soul at the expense of its anatomy should
always remember that 'subjective' criticism was then the order of the
day – even Newman had so far failed in his attempts to overturn
orthodoxy. But then 'N.C.' would never have been swayed by
such heresy; as well as having been raised on a diet of Johnstone and
Langford, he was temperamentally and intellectually at one with the
tradition they articulated. Consciously rejecting the canons of
'scientific' criticism, he was to spend the next forty years leading his
readers through innumerable adventures of the soul amongst the
masterpieces of the classical repertoire.

From the start, the journey was not without its incidents. Like
many new appointees, 'N.C.' was eager to make an early impression
on his audience. As Harty was then the principal conductor of the
Hallé, it was perhaps not surprising that he soon found himself the
target for some of the new critic's most scathing observations. Like

Langford, Neville remained unconvinced of Harty's stature. Super-
ficial interpretation, mannered phrasing and erratic tempi were
among the weaknesses 'N.C.' chose to highlight. Relations between
the two men soon became more than a little strained. When Neville,
quoting a member of the audience, observed that Harty had
surpassed even Richter in the length of time he had taken to
complete the Adagio of Beethoven's Ninth Symphony, matters
finally came to a head. The outraged conductor protested to C. P.
Scott about his music critic's habit of bringing a stop-watch to
concerts, adding that such methods were surely better suited to the
Press Box at Old Trafford. Neville's response was to threaten to
attend Harty's next concert equipped not with a stop-watch but an
alarm clock.

Although he claimed that relations eventually returned to normal,
'N.C.'s' reviews of the Hallé concerts from 1927 until Harty's
departure in 1933 could have done little to smooth ruffled feathers.
He was particularly harsh on Harty's choice of modern music. After
a performance of a symphony by Karl Atterbury which the composer
later admitted he had written as a joke, 'N.C.' asked: 'Why do we
get, more often than not, the second-rate things in modern music at
the Hallé concerts nowadays?' A performance of Harty's first
American 'novelty', Gershwin's *An American in Paris*, prompted him
to suggest 'a 150 per cent tariff against this sort of American
dry-goods'.

It was not long before Neville's forthright notices began to upset
members of the Hallé Orchestra as well as its conductor. At a time of
rising unemployment and falling audiences, it wasn't hard to understand why players, many of whose livelihoods were at stake, should
resent 'N.C.'s' criticism of their performances. When in 1928 he
ventured to suggest that, compared with the Philadelphia Orchestra,
'the labours of the best English orchestra must seem those of a lot of
well-intentioned amateurs',[24] the fierceness of the Hallé's reaction
forced him to beat a hasty retreat, claiming that he had been
referring to orchestral standards generally and not specifically to the
Hallé.

Looking back over 'N.C.'s' coverage of the last years of Harty's
conductorship, the abiding impression is one of balance and fairness. If his views sometimes gave offence, then this is surely no less
than should be expected of any critic worth his salt. If at times it
seemed as though he was being unduly hard on those who were

doing their best, then it must also be remembered that Neville, a man who had been raised in one of the richest musical traditions England has known, was writing on the ebb-tide of Lancashire's fortunes. All over the county the range and quality of cultural life was plainly not what it had been, but in Manchester the decline was particularly acute. The city's cultural strength and vitality had been sapped by the debilitating impact of economic decline and the dispersal of its German community. The conversion of Miss Horniman's Gaiety Theatre into a cinema was a sure sign of the times. By the mid '20s, few notices bore the by-line 'C.E.M.' since, in Montague's own words, 'scarcely any serious theatre exists here now'. The malaise soon spread to the *Guardian* itself. The policy of 'Manchesterisation' might have worked in 1910, but in 1925 it could not succeed. Too often an exceptionally gifted group of journalists found themselves confronted by raw material plainly unworthy of their talents. Faced with this unhappy prospect, it was no surprise that Neville's eyes and ears turned towards London and Europe.

[VII]

Mrs Cardus, meanwhile, was enjoying life in her own inimitable way. Marriage had made as little difference to her way of life as it had to her relationship with Neville. She doted upon him, his mind, his wit and his world: he saw her in a variety of roles – mother figure, companion, counsel and audience. However eccentric their partnership may sometimes have appeared, the Carduses cared deeply for each other, and continued to do so for the forty-six years of their marriage.

Edith was a unique character. Why Neville chose to devote so little attention to her in the autobiographies is a mystery. Some have suggested that he couldn't have described their relationship without offending his own ego; others that he did not feel free to discuss intimacies which may have explained their association. Whatever the reason, this neglect of her is a strange comment on an incurably generous, loyal personality. Edith used to say that she had first met Neville when he was 'selling nails in Boswell Street'. How much truth there was to this story no one can tell, but it would have been quite in character if Edith, conscious of the young man's talents and aware of his strained financial circumstances, decided to provide a little encouragement. Marriage combined the best of all possible worlds. It cemented their mutual affection and allowed her to provide a home life which he could enjoy without having to defy the moral sensitivities of the day. 'A warm-hearted, generous nature,' one of her closest friends noted, 'prompted Edith to regard Neville much as she would have viewed an attractive stray cat of which she could be very fond without depriving it of any natural independence.'

Her world centred on her work as a teacher and on a host of extramural activities of which amateur dramatics took up the most time. During the day she was 'Mrs Cardus', art teacher and form-mistress at the Ducie Avenue Central School for Girls, around the corner from the Whitworth Art Gallery and only a mile or so from Rusholme and Fallowfield Road. In the evening she became Edith Cardus, active supporter of the Unnamed Society, an experimental theatre company favoured by the local intelligentsia and directed (rather dictatorially) by Frank Sladen-Smith, who also wrote many of the Society's plays. These were the avant-garde pieces of the day – intellectual, idiosyncratic and fantastic in conception.

The company's productions were staged at the Little Theatre in Lomax Street, on the Salford side of the Irwell. Entrance cost very little, perhaps because, as the programme suggests, Sladen-Smith had other means of raising money: 'The programme will be continuous except for an interval of ten minutes during which a silver collection will be taken. It is found that the cost of production averages half-a-crown for each person present.' What happened to non-contributors was not revealed. Edith's particular contribution to the Society centred on the wardrobe room. Here, under the rigorous direction of Gwendolen Griffiths, she helped in designing and making costumes, though strangely enough no one can recall ever seeing her with a needle in or to hand. Actors, it was said, often took the stage in a mass of safety pins.

Edith's appearance suited her character. As her photographs suggest, and friends confirm, the impression she created was more that of an interesting individual than an attractive woman. With thick-lensed glasses and a distinct penchant for extravagant colours and styles that were anything but 'stylish', she came across as slightly eccentric, well-meaning and concerned. Unlike Neville, whose interest in politics stopped at politicans, Edith believed in getting involved, as they say in Whitehall, at the grass roots. As one of her friends put it, 'she was a great one for causes'. She enjoyed a small private income, but this didn't embarrass her in the least. To Edith, political convictions and private life were, and should remain, totally separate.

Unlike Neville, however, she treated money with little respect. Blessed with a generous and spontaneous nature, she was prone to moments of extravagance. Foreign travel was one of her particular weaknesses. Knowing next to nothing about foreign currency, she tended to organise itineraries on the assumption that extra traveller's cheques could always be obtained. Once, during a holiday in Capri with Marjorie Robinson, she suddenly took it into her head to discover how much money she had, and to this end proceeded to empty the entire contents of her handbag on to the deck of the small boat they happened to be on at the time. Most of the coins immediately disappeared between the boards of the deck. There then ensued a great to-do with deck-hands and fellow passengers outdoing each other in their attempts to rescue the good lady's money. It was a while before calm was restored, and by that time Edith had seen the funny side of things. When a few members of the party turned to commiserate, they were a little taken aback to find her seated in a deckchair, convulsed in laughter, and pointing at the bowels of the boat where her money had come to rest. That Edith was easily moved to laughter should not obscure the more serious aspect of her character, however. Only a few days later, she was terribly upset by the slums of Genoa.

For Neville, succeeding Sam Langford was perhaps the greatest moment of his life, but for Edith it meant above all that her husband would now be away as often during the winter as he already was during the summer. Not that this upset her unduly; she was far too self-sufficient to worry about being left to fend for herself for extended periods. Strange though it may have seemed to others, it was an arrangement which suited the Carduses admirably. Edith could continue to enjoy 'doing her own thing' in her way with her own people, while Neville was provided with a secure physical and emotional base from which to further his career. Whatever others may have thought, the fact that they spent so much time apart did not mean that they didn't appreciate each other's company. For more than forty years their relationship remained as close and caring as any that might have been achieved through a more conventional arrangement.

When Neville was at the height of his career, he and Edith still found time to go out together to a variety of different functions in and around Manchester. Again the partnership worked perfectly; Edith could and normally did talk to everybody who struck her as interesting, leaving her husband free to chat or muse as he pleased. A friend of theirs, Jack Goldthorpe, recalled how one evening he had met the Carduses on the way to a function at the Midland; he raised his hat (gentlemen did in those days), only to find that Neville was in a world of his own and didn't appear to notice him. At this point, Edith gave her husband a nudge and directed his attention to the slightly confused Jack Goldthorpe. Eventually Neville wandered over, still in a dream, mumbled 'They'll never make 200,' and walked on.

The Carduses never needed to live together day-in, day-out to sustain their deep mutual affection. Neville couldn't have put up with conventional domestic bliss for long, while Edith would have been horrified at the thought of becoming a typical middle-class housewife. As it was, she lived in a perpetual state of disorganisation, hated cooking and loved eating out, preferences which suited Neville down to the ground. She was also a painter; art was her world as much as cricket and music were Neville's. Edith was always bemoaning the drabness of everyday life and her remedy was to paint everything in sight. She painted the stones on either side of the path leading to the front door alternately blue and green, she painted her telephone blue, and the same paint secured it to the window sill, also painted blue. When G.P.O. engineers came to recover the phone at the beginning of the war, it took them some time to locate its whereabouts and even longer to detach it from the sill. But without doubt her *pièce de résistance* involved retrieving and painting (blue of course) a Molotov cocktail which had landed in a nearby garden. When she moved to Australia she made sure this unlikely *objet d'art* went with her – as an example, she said, of 'the sort of things England had to put up with' during the war.

Some of her closest friends believed that Edith made a great tactical error in not providing Neville with a conventional wife and home. If she had done so, the argument runs, he would have had less reason and less opportunity to spend so much time away from home. It is a case that rests on a substantial misunderstanding of the characters of the persons concerned. Neville's wanderlust, his independence and his frequent craving for solitude were central to his character before he married. Edith both tolerated and indulged his whims, never seeking to restrict his freedom. Looking back, it is comforting to see the way these two delightfully impractical and often idiosyncratic characters forged a lasting alliance out of an honest, pragmatic recognition of their differences. They made the best of what they had, and left the problems to take care of themselves. However much Neville may have chosen to underscore Edith's part in the creation and maintenance of this union, hers was the presence that sustained his emotional security. In more practical terms, Edith kept a watchful eye on Neville's mother whenever her less-than-doting son was away, and often when he wasn't. And by massaging Neville's ego and providing her own down-to-earth brand of mental stimulus, she sought to further his career. Though far from ignorant about music, she usually avoided the subject when Neville was around. Yet whenever he began to talk about a concert he had recently attended, she listened in rapt admiration.

From the moment Neville decided that no self-respecting autobiography would be complete without a few daring sexual revelations, it was inevitable that the unusual features of his marriage would become a part of the Cardus legend. For once the gossip-columnists were not to blame. Everyone who came to know Neville and Edith soon concluded that a marriage between two such distinctive individuals could not but be unconventional, yet such was the genuine affection they inspired that no one wished to intrude upon the privacy of their arrangement – no one, that is, except Neville himself. In successive volumes of autobiography he dwelt upon the peculiarities of his sexual development with a candour that would have been refreshing, but for the nagging feeling that the image being created was not entirely accurate. The letters he had written to George Popper from Shrewsbury, for example, could hardly be taken as a plea for remedial sex education classes; they were the statements of a young man with a normal, healthy sexual appetitite, and the confidence of a proven performer. It is very likely that the Shrewsbury correspondence contained a goodly measure of wishful thinking, but nevertheless the overall impression seems more plausible than the image of the *ci-devant* virgin portrayed in the autobiographies. However Neville might have wished to present himself, many of his friends saw him as having an eye for the girls, and never being averse to an occasional spot of honey-sipping. None of this worried Edith. In her bluff, northern way, she was more than a match for Neville, and knew it.

The *femme fatale* of the autobiographies – 'Milady', as she was referred to in *Full Score* – entered Neville's world in the autumn of 1928. In real life she was Hilda Elizabeth Ede ('Barbe' to Neville and his friends), wife of Elton Ede who described himself as an 'accountant, merchant banker and journalist'. According to the Cardus legend, they first met on Charing Cross Station where she laddered a stocking and he experienced a sexual *frisson* the like of which he had never felt before. Unlike other celebrated platform romances, this one survived at differing degrees of intensity for nearly eight years. Compared with Edith, Barbe was altogether a more voluptuous, cosmopolitan personality. Though they both shared an interest in cricket, it was not this that occupied Neville's thoughts when they met for dinner a week or two later. That evening, he recalled, 'her eyes were more lustrous (and alluring) than any I had ever seen before. Her high cheek bones were vivid, her natural colours. Her lips were rose red, also by dowry of nature.' Though penned some thirty years after, the choice of language is a fair guide to the state of Neville's emotions that night. In little more than an evening, with a bottle of wine to hand, he had passed beyond the point at which 'no stronger notion of her remained with me than of a pleasant woman with beautiful eyes and a large generous mouth'. He was, in a word, besotted.

Others saw Barbe in a slightly different light. One of Neville's friends remembered her as being 'dark with red lips; a sort of gypsy – very free and generous. A bit of a camp follower, I suppose.' Another described her as 'not being particularly elegant, but having terrific push'. Leaving aside the subtle differences in these assessments, no one denied that Barbe was other than a striking personality. That Neville should have fallen for someone of her appeal was in no way out of character. He delighted in physical beauty; being in the company of good-looking women satisfied his aesthetic needs and fed his ego, and if, as was nearly always the case, they could provide stimulating company too, so much the better. So it was with Barbe. For her part, though she greatly admired his writing that was only one facet of his attraction. Compared with her husband Elton Ede, who was by repute rather 'a silent man', Neville, who never stopped talking, could not have provided a greater contrast.

He wined and dined her; she accompanied him to the theatre, opera and concerts; together they visited Germany and Austria. At Salzburg she admonished the local constabulary for daring to suggest that she should observe the highway code. In Vienna she penetrated the inner sanctum of Felix Weingartner's suite at the Staatsoper to obtain tickets for a concert that had been sold out for weeks; after the concert, the conductor personally greeted her during dinner at Hartman's. All the while Neville relished her presence, and when, a few weeks later, she laid into Ernest Newman for his use of the word 'commence', his happiness was boundless. In London, she was introduced to all his famous and influential acquaintances. Beecham, by all accounts, was enchanted by the way she interrupted him in full flow with a softly murmured 'Balls, Sir Thomas, balls.' It was the same story at Lord's – C. B. Fry, who usually preferred sailing ships, was so captivated by her charms that he christened her 'Milady'.

More than once, Barbe confessed to being worried about Neville's apparent lack of a good, solid home. 'Neville', she would say, 'you need a home,' the obvious implication being that Edith's idea of home life left a lot to be desired. In this respect she never understood the Carduses, but by the beginning of the 1930s the frequency of Neville's visits to London gave her the chance to persuade him of the merits of a pied-à-terre. The National Liberal Club may have been respectable and comfortable, but as a male preserve it left her at a bit of a disadvantage. Neville, who at this time was very susceptible to her blandishments, rented a small flat in Ebury Street, close to Victoria. He always preferred to stay at the Club, but Barbe was well pleased with this new facility, and there they sampled each other's virtues.

All this time Edith remained in Manchester, cocooned and content in an off-beat world of art and drama and like-minded souls. The unscrupulous libertine could not have wished for a more perfect arrangement, but however much Neville may have liked to think of himself as a budding Don Juan, when it came to the crunch he totally lacked the remorseless insensitivity the role demanded. For months he agonised over whether to tell Edith about the Ebury Street tryst; in the end he bared his soul over dinner at the French Restaurant of the Midland Hotel. Her reaction was a mixture of understanding and indulgence. Had she been a conventional wife, she would never have put up with Neville; as it was, they enjoyed forty-six years of their own brand of marital bliss. She accepted his whims as a fact of life. 'Ee,' she used to tell an old friend, 'I like him to have his little girls. It makes him so much better tempered when he comes home. He doesn't know I know, but I do.'

In the event, Edith almost certainly knew of the affair before Neville told her. A few months earlier, by a strange quirk of fate, her brother, who owned a small builder's yard in the capital, had agreed to mend some faulty plumbing at the flat. In the time-honoured tradition of craftsmen, he turned up one afternoon, unannounced and weeks later than arranged, expecting to find Neville – but he found Barbe instead. Edith's reaction was entirely in character. Fearing for her husband's career with the *Guardian* if word of his dalliance ever reached the ears of the editor, she attempted to contact Elton Ede to seek his help in limiting the potential damage.

Neville kept the flat after the episode of the plumber, but gradually passions cooled and the inhabitants became as much good friends as lovers. Some while later, he discovered, again by chance, that he was not the only journalist to visit Ebury Street. At that point, he gave up the flat. The bitter-sweet relationship ended with Barbe's sudden death in September 1937. Though the story of the affair may have gained much in the telling, Neville had been, and remained, very fond of Barbe and she was to figure, posthumously, in several of his later works. The precise cause of her death was a combination of acute asthma (she had been a life-long sufferer) and bronchitis, but for reasons known only to himself Neville chose to play this down when he wrote to an old friend a week later:

Manchester Guardian
24 September 1937

My dear Rupert,

From the bottom of my heart I thank you for your dear letter. She caught a chill and died in twenty-four hours – peacefully. I spoke to her on the telephone last Thursday and she was full of life and laughter. I had arranged for her to go through the proofs of *Australian Summer*. You call her 'gay and courageous'. And you make me happy with the best of all words for her – 'she was so affectionate and sympathetic and attractive and brave'.

Bless you,
Neville

As was Neville's wont, there was a postscript:

Lunch with me next Wednesday at the National Liberal Club.

[VIII]

The third collection of Neville's cricket writings, *A Summer Game: A Cricketer's Journal* was published in 1929. In his review in the *Observer*, J. L. Garvin wrote, 'Amongst journalists, Mr Cardus – "Cricketer" – of the *Manchester Guardian* is a genius.' The next ten years were to see the flowering of that genius. By the mid-'30s, Neville was at the summit of his career as a journalist. Nearly all his best books, including the autobiographies and *Ten Composers*, were still to come, but the columns of his later years could not match the consistent grace, colour and charm of 'Cricketer' and 'N.C.'.

As his experience had widened, so his style had matured. Gone was the flowing excess of his early days. By now, 'Cricketer's' was a more detached and sardonic presence. In some quarters, it was even suspected that he had begun to appreciate Yorkshire cricket. The transformation was aided by the gradual disappearance of many of the characters the young 'Cricketer' had doted upon. To describe Hobbs, Woolley, Makepeace, Hallows, McDonald, Parkin, Tyldesley, Rhodes, Hirst and Robinson meant resorting to the past tense, or soon would do. A new generation – Hammond, Leyland, Hardstaff, Barnett, Paynter, Larwood, Verity, Farnes and Bowes to name but a few – now chased the headlines; all great players, but somehow lacking the romantic appeal of their predecessors.

Far away in Australia, the man who was probably the greatest of them all awaited his chance to savage English bowling yet again. Like most other Englishmen, 'Cricketer' knew next to nothing about Donald Bradman before he first arrived in England in April 1930. There had been rumours of exceptional promise but other members of that party, especially Archie Jackson, seemed a greater threat. By the last afternoon of the Oval Test, however, with the fate of the Ashes already decided, even the most hard-bitten of English supporters would have been hard put to deny that the cricketing world was a different place. 'All changed, changed utterly: a terrible beauty born.' So it must have seemed to successive English captains over the next eighteen years. After an unexceptional debut in the first Test at Trent Bridge, 'Boy' Bradman proceeded to score 254 at Lord's, 334 at Headingley and 232 at the Oval. That final triumph moved 'Cricketer' to write an 'Appreciation' which for the quality of its prose was as memorable as the achievements it celebrated:

> The genius of this remarkable boy consists in the complete summary he gives us of the technique of batsmanship. In every art or vocation there appears from time to time an incredible exponent who in himself sums up all the skill and experience that have gone before him. It is not true that Bradman has inaugurated a new era in batsmanship: he is substantially orthodox in technique. . . . But Bradman shows us excellences which in the past we have had to seek in different players; nobody else has achieved Bradman's synthesis. It is, of course, a synthesis which owes much to the fact that Bradman stays at the wicket longer than most of the brilliant stroke players ever dreamed of staying. Perhaps he is marked off from the greatest of his predecessors not so much by technique as by temperament . . . a hundred runs is nothing to him; he conceives his innings in terms which go far beyond Trumper's or Macartney's most avaricious dreams. He has demonstrated that a batsman can hit forty-two boundaries in a day without once giving the outfielders hope of a catch; he has kindled grand bonfires of batsmanship for us. But never once has he burned his owned fingers while lighting them.

Bradman's career lasted until 1948, and long before its close he and Neville had become good friends. Born of an appreciation of technical excellence, it was a relationship that came to embrace a deeper understanding of character. More than once Neville described Bradman as a 'phenomenon', while he, for his part, considered 'Cricketer' in his hey-day 'to have been the best of all writers in the cricket world'. Later he was to expand upon this judgement:

> His [i.e. Neville's] articles were superbly written and he had the most wonderful ability to sift out the important from the unimportant. . . . In his later years he dwelt to a large extent on the glories of the play he saw in his youth. Many people felt he began to live in the past but as one who, too, was an observer of

most of those great players of fifty to sixty years ago, his judgement may well have been right more often than not. I refer to him as an eccentric genius, but am proud to think that I was his friend and I am a great admirer of his work.[25]

In the aftermath of the 1930 series, most cricket buffs had concluded that Bradman was nothing more than a ruthless automaton. 'Cricketer', however, sensed that there was something more to the man. At first, he could only express this feeling as a conundrum:

The really astonishing fact about Bradman is that a boy should play as he does – with the sophistication of an old hand and brain. Who has ever heard of a young man, gifted with quick feet and eyes, with mercurial spirits and all the rapid and powerful strokes of cricket – who has ever heard of a young man so gifted and yet one who has never indulged in an extravagant hit high into the air? . . . How came this Bradman to expel from him all the greenness and impetuosity of youth while retaining the strength and alacrity of youth? How did he come to acquire, without experience, all the ripeness of the orthodox – the range and adaptability of other men's accumulated years of practice in the best schools of batsmanship? . . . While we can account for Bradman's batting by reason of its science and orthodoxy, we are quite unable to accept it – it is too old for Bradman's years and slight experience.[26]

Six years later Bradman invited Neville, who was in Australia to follow the fortunes of Gubby Allen's touring party, to his home in Adelaide. The two spent several hours together, alone, talking about cricket. Towards the end of that evening, something occurred which confirmed Neville's original feeling about his host.

At eleven o'clock he told me he would have to turn me out, as he had a call to make at the hospital. But, as the hospital was on the way to my hotel, he drove me into Adelaide, on a night of great beauty. He ran up the steps of the hospital and I waited in the car. After a short while he came back, took the wheel and said: 'I'm afraid the poor little chap isn't going to get through.' The next morning the death of Bradman's baby was announced.

Bradman asked Neville not to mention this tragedy in his report the following day. 'Cricketer' respected Bradman's wishes, but other sources were less discreet. Their insensitivity didn't prevent Australia from winning that series, but it later prompted Neville to record a tribute as sincere and perceptive as any he ever penned:

> I hope I am reticent about this night's happenings; I hope no one will misunderstand me. I want to give an idea of Bradman's character. I am tired of hearing him referred to as a run-making machine on the field, and a hard Australian off it. . . . When does a batsman who commands all the strokes and plays them rapidly and scores 300 in a day in a Test match, when does he cease to be an artist and degenerate into a 'machine'? I suppose this unintelligent objection to Bradman is much the same as an objection to Bach; it is excusable in fallible humanity to regard the illusion of mastery as bloodless and remote and automatic. But Bradman, like Bach – if he will allow the comparison – is full of blood; no other batsman today is as audacious as Bradman. His hook is the most dramatic hit seen since Jessop; it is a boxer's blow. And for all the rare organisation of his technique, nature is in it always. Bradman has not allowed enormous skill to ruin the salt touch of his original self. The *gamin* comes out in a sudden cross-bat solecism.[27]

Though it was only to be expected that on the eve of a test match their conversation wouldn't stray far from cricket, on other occasions Neville and Sir Donald devoted at least as much time to music. Once, Bradman recalled,

> . . . we were having dinner at a hotel in Nottinghamshire. I referred to a certain singer and said that she came to Australia with Gerald Moore. Neville said I had the name wrong because it was another singer, whom he named. An argument ensued and Neville became so agitated in insisting that he was right that he brushed the ash of his cigar into my glass of wine.
>
> Suddenly he got up and dashed outside the room. In a few minutes he was back and gleefully told me that he was right. He had rung up Gerald Moore to find out. But in fact all he said to Gerald was, 'Did you go to Australia as accompanyist for x?' When Gerald replied 'yes', Neville did not ask anything further.

It transpired that we were both right because in fact Gerald had been the accompanyist for both, but in different years.[28]

As well as cementing his friendship with Bradman, Neville's coverage of the 1936–37 series gave him an opportunity to see the country that was later to be his home for seven years.* In those days tours lasted six months, including ten weeks at sea, all of which Neville thoroughly enjoyed. Of all the forms of transport, rail and sea were his favourites. (Cars on the other hand were impossible – he always found them very uncomfortable.) On board the *Orion*, the team were under instructions from Allen to mingle unobtrusively and to avoid talking about cricket. Speculation about the forthcoming series was felt to be best left to the other passengers jostling for places at the Captain's table. Neville watched, listened (mostly to C. B. Fry), talked (a lot) and penned cameo portraits of various members of the M.C.C. party:

> Verity read *Seven Pillars of Wisdom* from beginning to end; Hammond won at all games, from chess to deck quoits. Maurice Leyland smoked his pipe, and Duckworth danced each evening with a nice understanding of what, socially, he was doing. Wyatt took many photographs and developed them himself. Fry, armed with a most complicated camera, also took many photographs and none of them could be developed.[29]

Charles Burgess Fry, last of the modern Corinthians, always held a special place in Neville's affections. Once they bumped into each other behind the pavilion at Lord's after something had clearly upset Fry. 'Disgraceful, disgraceful, absolutely disgraceful,' he kept muttering. 'Well, it's not so bad,' Neville replied, 'at least the batting's all right.' 'Batting, batting,' Fry snorted, 'I'm talking about the ladies' hats.' Now, like Neville, he was with Allen's party as a correspondent of one of the national newspapers. *En route* to Australia, the *Orion* passed through the Red Sea, the Indian Ocean, Colombo and the Cocos Islands before finally dropping anchor in Freemantle Harbour early on 17 October 1936. For days before, one thing had been on Neville's mind – how was he to survive for six months without music? Yet, less than a day after confiding his fears to the reporters

* Financial difficulties had led the *Manchester Guardian* to dispense with 'Cricketer's' reports of the 1932–3 series.

who had come on board as soon as the *Orion* docked, he found himself at the house of a Perth doctor listening to local students performing works by Chopin and Hugo Wolf. The gesture went a long way towards stilling Neville's immediate fears, and in the longer term helped pave the way for his war-time domicile.

The test matches between England and Australia saw one of the most dramatic recoveries in the long history of the Ashes. As he looked out over Sydney harbour after England had taken a 2–0 lead in the five-match series, even Neville was tempted to believe in the impossible. But not for long.

On Christmas Eve I stood on the rocky edge called the 'Gap', looking towards the sea. I saw the *Awatea* sail through the Heads, glowing with rosy lights. The moon was a feather, and the Southern Cross a symbol of the night and the season of the year. I thought as I looked at the *Awatea*: 'According to our present plans we leave Australia next March for New Zealand, homeward bound on that same ship. Shall we really take the Ashes with us?' A few days afterwards I could give the answer; Melbourne was prophetic enough.[30]

Inspired by Bradman, the Australians fought back to win the next three matches and thus retain the Ashes. In the last analysis, the series turned on the outcome of a personal duel between Bradman and Hammond, then without doubt the two finest batsmen in the world. One incident during the test match at Adelaide seemed to Neville to sum up that rivalry, and answer the inevitable question – who was the finer player?

On the closing morning, England needed 244 to win, with 7 wickets in hand, Hammond not out. It was the fourth match of the series, England had won two, Australia one. All our eyes were riveted on Hammond as he took the bowling of Fleetwood-Smith in a gleaming sunshine. To the third ball of the day Hammond played forward and was clean bowled. Australia won, drawing equal in the rubber; they also won the fifth. As Hammond's bails fell to the ground, Fleetwood-Smith danced, walked on his knees, went nearly off his head. And I heard Duckworth's voice behind me: 'We wouldn't have got Don out first thing in the morning with the rubber at stake.'[31]

[IX]

The Lancashire that Neville had left, and now returned to, was a troubled place. After nearly a century of economic growth and prosperity, the county had fallen on hard times. The region that had led the world to industrialisation now found its pre-eminence as a manufacturing centre under severe threat. Cotton was at the heart of the problem. In March 1917 a crowded emergency meeting of members of the Manchester Exchange passed a resolution condemning the Indian Government's decision to impose import duties on Lancashire cotton goods. It was to be another nail in an already half-finished coffin. Though the immediate post-war shortage of manufactured goods generated abnormal profits for a couple of years, the reprieve was only temporary. Between 1921 and 1928 Lancashire lost 38 per cent of her pre-war export trade in cotton piece goods. By 1930 the output from Indian cotton mills was nearly equal to the total volume of Lancashire's exports in the good old days.

The *Manchester Guardian* felt the cold draught of economic decline as acutely as the region it served. A newspaper that had grown from being a provincial weekly to international repute as the industrial revolution gathered pace now found itself confronted with the spectre of a world in which King Cotton and his acolytes counted for less and less. To add to its difficulties, this economic decline came at a time when the terms of trade were turning against 'quality' papers. The late twenties and thirties were years of unremitting, cut-throat competition within the newspaper industry as the popular papers struggled to increase their circulation figures. Fifty thousand canvassers descended upon unsuspecting, bewildered readers, offering a vast array of material inducements in return for an undertaking to become registered subscribers for two or three months. Between them, the *News Chronicle*, the *Daily Mail* and the *Daily Express* disposed of 300,000 sets of Dickens's novels, losing £36,000 in the bargain. All the popular press offered free insurance policies. Neither *The Times* nor the *Guardian* could bring themselves to descend to quite such undignified levels, though they were both obliged to introduce cheap rates to maintain their existing circulation figures. By 1936 nearly two-fifths of all *Guardian* sales were at a cheap rate, a trend which, when combined with a dramatic fall in advertising revenue, went a long way towards explaining why the paper always seemed to be on the brink of financial crisis, and why according to legend it consistently paid the lowest salaries in the industry.

While all about him seemed to be in dire straits, Neville was thoroughly enjoying life. Much had changed along 'the Corridor' at Cross Street since his arrival over fifteen years before. Many of the great names he'd once idolised had departed. Sidebotham and Mills had gone, Montague too – on 'self-rustication', as a contemporary put it. After presiding over the paper's destiny for fifty-seven years, C. P. Scott finally handed over the reins to his son Ted in July 1929, and died in the early hours of New Year's Day, 1932, at the age of eighty-six. The passing of these figures marked the end of an era and left an unenviable vacuum for their successors – Wadsworth, Haley, Anderson, Boardman, Philips, Cardus and the like – to fill. That the paper not only survived but flourished under the new regime is perhaps the most eloquent tribute to Scott's judgement and skills.

Remembering his personal debt to Scott, it was inevitable that Neville would find it hard to accept that anyone could truly succeed him as editor. For all that it had been W. P. Crozier who had launched 'Cricketer's' career, and despite the fulsome tribute contained in *Autobiography*, Neville always had reservations about the man appointed to the editorship on 6 May 1932. 'What do you expect of a man who takes his holidays at "Seaview", Llanfair-fechan?' he used to moan, forgetting for the moment that he and Edith had also visited those parts.

Under Crozier, Neville became a senior member of the Corridor. As 'Cricketer', he had already acquired an international reputation, and if there had been many who had doubted the wisdom of appointing the one-time employee of the *Daily Citizen* as principle music critic in succession to Langford and Newman, 'N.C.'s' flowing columns had soon stilled these fears. In less than ten years, he had established himself as one of the two or three most influential critics in England – a position, needless to say, he much enjoyed. As well as being obliged to spend all day watching cricket and all evening listening to music, Neville soon discovered that working for the *Guardian* conferred all sorts of unexpected advantages.

His meetings with J. M. Barrie were a case in point. Neville had been a fervent admirer of Barrie's works for many years, and on more than one occasion had actually considered bearding the great man in his rooms and refusing to leave until appointed his secretary. Now, as something of a celebrity himself, Neville struck up a friendship with the playwright who, it transpired, was a great cricket-lover – in fact seldom willing to talk about anything else – and an avid reader of 'Cricketer's' columns. For his part, Neville loved *Peter Pan* and seldom stopped talking. After a few meetings and an exchange of letters, Barrie invited Neville to spend a weekend with him in London.

The result, as all readers of *Autobiography* will know, was an episode so strange that even Neville felt bound to deny any conscious attempt at embellishment. With Sir James maintaining only the most fleeting of presences, and even then succumbing to a paralysing combination of bronchitis and shyness, Neville was shown to a bedroom and left to the tender mercies of Thurston, a butler who embarrassed Neville by insisting on attending to his personal laundry before showing him to a bathroom in which damp, soiled towels vied for pride of place with a 'rusty razor blade' and 'shaving brushes congealed in ancient soap'. Barrie's sister Maggie appeared, seemingly from nowhere, clad only in a dressing-gown. Then a young man entered the apartment, entirely unannounced and utterly anonymous, while Neville was dining alone, and engaged him in conversation about cricket for a few minutes before politely taking his leave. On the final morning of his visit, Maggie told Neville over breakfast that 'during the night she had been in communication with [my] mother "on the other side" . ud that mother and she had loved each other, and that mother was proud of me and that they, the two of them, would watch over and take care of me.' Though only he could have appreciated it, there was a consummate irony to this situation: here was Neville being confronted with messages from his mother, whom many of his friends believed to be dead, and whom he knew only too well to be alive and kicking somewhere in Manchester. In the circumstances, it was not surprising that he found himself 'ready to perspire with apprehension', and greatly relieved when Thurston's timely intervention prevented further embarrassing revelations.

Strange and even disconcerting though these events must have been, they didn't prevent Neville from returning to Adelphi House Terrace on several subsequent occasions to take tea with Barrie. There was a consistency to these meetings that underlined the very precise nature of their friendship. No matter where their conversation started, it always returned to Peter Pan, or cricket or, as Barrie's last letter to Neville aptly illustrates, both:

> Adelphi Terrace House
> Strand WC2
> 27 December 1929

My dear Cardus,

Thank you heartily for your welcome Christmas greeting. I am elated to hear that you spent those early sixpences on P. Pan and that you know when bits of him fall off. I expect the explanation is that the author is a little like Macartney and tires of seeing himself always making the same strokes. A Happy New Year to you, and we simply must see a test match together.

> Yours sincerely,
> J. M. Barrie

With the annual calendar of county championship matches changing as infrequently as the railway schedules that enabled Neville to travel from ground to ground, his life had soon acquired a symmetry reminiscent of the 'king's royal progress' in medieval times. Journeys were undertaken in

... railway trains travelling across England, myself in restaurant cars, in sumptuous cushioned privacy, gliding through the sunset after a scurry and a late and strenuous finish at Lord's; we are due now for the West, to play at Bristol tomorrow morning, and before we are through with our dinner, while we are taking coffee and liqueur, we shall have left London far behind and we shall be looking through the carriage window and see country fields in the twilight and glimpses of life mysteriously not connected with us. . . .[32]

Though Lancashire's battles remained the central organising principle of his summers, as the years went by Neville found himself wandering along to Lord's more and more frequently, sometimes to catch the youthful exuberance of a schools' game, sometimes to take in the atmosphere and let life take its natural course, trusting always in Barrie's observation – 'so many things happen to you at Lord's'. And in the evenings, there was always a dinner to savour, if not necessarily to eat. By now, the addictive attraction of dining with friends was well-nigh irresistible. Homes, clubs and restaurants: the venue mattered little and the menu even less, as Neville had neither a demanding palate nor a great appetite. 'Endless talk as good as ever was talked' – Trevelyan's evocation of eighteenth-century England might well have struck a chord with Neville. Now in his forties and mature in his own terms, there was nothing he anticipated with greater relish than an evening with kindred spirits. Though the 1930s may have been a far cry from social exchange amongst the Whig aristocracy, nevertheless Neville found that the world could still offer enough by way of talking points to sustain him in full flow for an evening.

During the winter months, though music now occupied the major part of his attention, the same life-style prevailed. From 1928 until the outbreak of war 'N.C.' covered most of the major concerts and operas in England, and a good few others in Germany and Austria when time and the *Guardian*'s shaky finances permitted. His usual schedule took in two or three concerts a week (each assessed in notices that often ran to 1500 words), a couple of dinners and as much conversation as could be arranged. In these days of advanced printing technology, tight publishing schedules and short reviews, it is easy to forget that earlier generations of critics went about their business at a very different pace. It was quite usual for the *Guardian* to publish notices days after the performance they described. It was a practice Neville heartily supported. He once described the new practice of delivering a notice of around 500 words less than an hour after the end of a performance as 'atrocious and utterly imbecile', a sentiment that hardly augured well for the latter years of his career.

After a performance, he and his fellow critics would repair to their respective offices, clubs or rooms to compose or, more usually, complete (preparing notices in advance of concerts was a time-honoured practice amongst critics) a column or two. About midnight, or later if needs be, the copy found its way to the sub-editors, most of whom would never have dreamed of cutting more than a hundred words at most. A further facility available to pre-war critics was the preparatory article. During Neville's first year as principle music critic, for example, *The Mastersingers of Nuremberg* was one of the operas performed in Manchester. To prepare his readers for this enormous work, 'N.C.' submitted an equally substantial introductory essay in which he went out of his way to stress the opera's richness as entertainment. 'It provokes the sense of natural amplitude, of a laughter as broad as ten thousand beeves at pasture,' he wrote in a manner which carried more than a hint of things to come. After the first performance Neville naturally assessed the production against the criteria he had set out. On this occasion, the beeves had been decimated with the result that in his view, 'last night's performance was unable to do more than suggest the greatness of the work'.

Mention Cardus today and it is a fair bet that most people would think immediately of 'the last of the romantics', as he once described himself, fighting to preserve beauty and feeling in the face of Newman's clinical antiseptic rationalism. This 'chalk and cheese' image undoubtedly had some substance, but it also owed a lot to the well-known professional rivalry between the two critics which was summed up most succinctly in Newman's oft-quoted but sometimes misunderstood 'sensitised palate' taunt. If, as seems most likely, the remark meant that 'N.C.' paid more attention to the spirit and impact of music than to its mechanics, then it serves to emphasise the extent to which his rivalry with Newman originated in two fundamentally different approaches to art rather than in a deep-seated personal enmity. As another critic was to put it, Newman 'probed into Music's vitals, put her under deep X-ray and analysed cell-tissue. Cardus . . . laid his head against her bosom and listened to the beating of her heart.' For much of their careers the two critics, who privately shared a considerable regard for each other, took the greatest pleasure in publicly playing up their differences. After one of Furtwängler's concerts, for example, Newman, who was never one of the German conductor's greatest admirers, was heard to complain that he couldn't follow the tempi. Neville, so the story goes, sat back, drew deeply on his pipe and savoured the moment before remarking, 'It doesn't really matter if Mr Newman didn't follow the tempi as long as the orchestra did.'

On closer examination, it is clear that neither of the men remained strictly true to the critical traditions they were supposed to represent. Newman once admitted that he wrote according 'to his lights – and his liver' (a remark which prompted an anonymous donation of a box of liver pills) and particularly in his early days some of his notices revealed a capacity for prejudice which rested uncomfortably beside the image of 'calm, blindfolded Justice'. For his part, Neville would not have taken at all kindly to being described as an out-and-out romantic. Not only could he point to numerous occasions on which he had publicly stated his belief that 'the expression of romantic feeling must be controlled by the intellect', but also to various public rows with the likes of Harty, Beecham and half the Lancashire cricket team that had been sparked off by his 'obsession with detail and form'.

The 1930s were in Neville's own words a 'fruitful period'. After a sticky start, he was now acknowledged, in both England and Europe, to be a worthy successor to Langford. Tempting job offers began to come his way, including one from J. L. Garvin of the *Observer*. However much his ego may have wished it otherwise, the qualities that attracted these bids were neither exceptional intellectual profundity nor great technical insight. Unlike Newman, he was not seen as a radical influence. Introduced to music through the works of Mozart, Beethoven, Schubert, Schumann, Brahms and Wagner, his emotional affinity with the central European romantic repertoire never weakened. Mozart he considered one of the world's finest creations, the others being 'a rose (including Kathleen Ferrier) and an oyster'. 'That a Mozart was born once, and once and for all,' he once wrote, 'is a happening and consummation which beggars understanding and all known science, all psychology, biology, physics and metaphysics, and all cosmogony whatever.'

As 'N.C.' matured, his appreciation of other musical influences widened and deepened. In the 1930s in particular, it was a mark of his independence of mind that he frequently rebelled against 'the cut-and-dried metropolitan dictates of fashion' which led to concert and opera programmes being stuffed full of Mozart, Beethoven, Wagner and a little late Verdi. Following in the tradition established by Langford, he championed the cause of a then little-known Austrian composer, Gustav Mahler. Richard Strauss was another 'modern' composer whose compositions he commended, and he greatly enjoyed recounting how Newman had once adjudged the *Sinfonia Domestica* to be 'the work of a man of talent who had once been a man of genius', only to find himself a year later attending the first performance of *Der Rosenkavalier*. Of Anton Bruckner, Neville once quipped that 'like religion and matrimony, he needs faith'; but when it came to the serious business of criticism, 'N.C.' recognised more than twenty years before any other English critic (save Richard

Capell) that there was more to this strange man than second-rate
Wagnerian bumbling.

Delius was another case where Neville stood out against the
conventional scepticism of his colleagues, most of whom took the
view that a failed orange-planter from Florida couldn't possibly
warrant serious consideration. Neville thought otherwise and said
so:

> Delius has been unfortunate in his critics; they have praised
> him for his sensibility and what not; and invariably they have
> left out his music – his art – the dithyrambs of their adoration.
> He must often have prayed for deliverance from the Delians, as
> Debussy prayed for deliverance from the Debussyites. . . . In
> the nineteenth century he escaped, like Debussy, from the
> charted seas of music; he too found his island. But he was not,
> as Debussy was, enchanted out of the world by the magic of
> unexplored strands and seashores and rivers and woods, so that
> to him the sound of human sorrow came only as an echo,
> awakening no pain, no ache, no wonder and remembrance.
> Debussy was 'translated' into his own dreaming faun. Delius
> remained human and susceptible to the joys and pains he had
> known on the mainland. His music looks back on days intensely
> lived through; it knows the secret of the pathos of mortal things
> doomed to fade and vanish. At bottom Delius is pagan and
> epicurean. His music will never be familiar to a large crowd;
> and the few who come to love it will try hard to keep it to
> themselves.[33]

Elsewhere in the classical repertoire, Neville's views were much
less sympathetic. In fact, there were whole areas where he would
tread only with the greatest reluctance. Baroque music generally left
him unmoved, while much of Bach's output, his cantatas in particular, was viewed with genuine distaste. 'When I come to heaven,' he
used to say, 'I'd much rather have a Viennese waltz than a Bach
cantata.' English music (Elgar and Delius excepted) received a
similarly unenthusiastic reception in his columns. Worst of all to his
way of thinking was 'contemporary music', Schoenberg he could
take at a pinch, but certainly not Hindemith, Webern or Berg, and
only wild horses would drag him to a Stockhausen or Henze concert.
Even the comparatively orthodox Prokofiev was sometimes given

short shrift. After a Hallé concert at which his 1st Violin Concerto was performed, 'N.C.' declared: 'It has no more music in it than a crossword puzzle by Torquemada.'*

A brief glance through the hundreds of notices he prepared during the late '20s and '30s is sufficient to show where Neville was in his element. The first requirement was 'substance'; the second, substance of the right kind. In a notice of a concert given by the Hallé under Sir Thomas Beecham on 28 November 1935, 'N.C.' commented:

> One thing only was needed to give the finishing touch to last evening – before the music began, Sir Thomas Beecham should have addressed the audience and said – not one word less and not one word more – 'Gentlemen (and ladies), you may smoke.'
>
> A programme of tit-bits from Wagner does not make a Hallé concert nowadays. Hotchpotches of Wagner 'excerpts' (a terrible but proper word) play into the hands of the people who belittle the composer; they destroy his musical context and in a concert version, they present him as a noisy, rhetorical lover of the 'spotlight'.

If not 'tit-bits', then what? The answer is to be found in Neville's reaction to the announcement of the 1937-38 Hallé season: 'The foundation of any Hallé season must be, by the unwritten artistic constitution of the concerts, classic and symphonic.' Fine, the reader might have commented, but whose symphonies? Again, 'N.C.'s' views came through loud and clear:

> The programmes for the next season . . . promise many agreeable musical Thursday evenings, not exciting to the conservative instincts, maybe, but perhaps none the worse for that at this time of day, for the truth is that the time for hearing 'modern' music has gone by – in Vienna they speak of atonalism as a thing of the past. There is only one serious omission in the new Hallé schedule – the absence of William Walton's symphony. Perhaps something will be done even yet to render justice in Lancashire to a Lancashire composer who is becoming known

* The 'puzzle setter' of the *Observer*.

in most musical places in the world between Boston and Salzburg.

If these pre-conditions were satisfied, all that was needed to show Neville at his best was atmosphere and a great soloist. Then *Guardian* readers could look forward not only to a good concert but also to a memorable review the morning after.

With music, as with cricket, Neville had a gratifying habit of rising to the occasion. Two examples will suffice to illustrate this gift: the first is taken from a notice of a concert given on 11 March 1934, at which Schnabel played Mozart's Concerto for Piano and Orchestra in B flat major (K. 595), and Beethoven's Piano Concerto No. 3 in C minor (Op. 23):

The largest audience for years packed the Free Trade Hall in every part last night; the cause of this multitude was Schnabel. Strange and wonderful that the crowds should run after this high-minded artist, who pursues truth and beauty, who has no use for the usual blandishments. . . . Schnabel can move the heart with a simple chord; he can compel us to bow the head with a silent pause. The beginning of the slow movement of the C-minor concerto of Beethoven was one of the most beautiful moments the present writer has known in any concert hall; it shook the imagination like a solemn lifting of a veil. But the wonder of it happened before Schnabel struck the notes of the Largo; it was his superbly calculated pause that evoked loveliness and nobility. Only an impertinent criticism would dream of discussing Schnabel's technique, his control of form, his perfect mingling of melody, harmony and rhythm. But all this tends to overstress the spirituality of Schnabel's playing; he is a full man, who can not only watch and pray and suffer and achieve reconciliation but can also stretch his limbs vastly and laugh and – not the least this! – achieve exquisite fantasy. The third movement of the Mozart Concerto was given with the touch of true wit; the notes skipped and danced and flashed. And how sure the style! – a different laughter and energy here than the laughter and energy we heard in the rondo of the Beethoven Concerto. The humour of Beethoven was substantial; at the point of the famous and miraculous enharmonic change Schnabel's tone took on the grimness of the grotesque.

Mozart was given the laughter of the spirit; the fingering, for all its nimble dexterity, caught that grace which, because it is beyond the reach of art is, as Hazlitt says, the height of art. Here was the 'soft suffusion of the soul, the looks commencing with the skies'. This light-hearted music was infinitely touching, heard after Schnabel's reticent eloquence in the slow movement, which was pathetically withdrawn, immortal because of its great loneliness.

The second comes from the notice 'N.C.' penned after the concert on 16 January 1936, at which Bronislaw Huberman played the Concerto for Violin and Orchestra in D (Op. 77) by Brahms:

Last night's Hallé Concert was the greatest for many years; it received inspiration from Huberman, whose performance of the Brahms Violin Concerto has seldom if ever been matched in this city for intensity. To call it a performance is banal; it was a spiritual experience, a purification, vouchsafed to us by a noble artist who has come to wisdom by suffering, by finding in beauty not merely an anodyne but a new and abiding principle of life.

Huberman's playing was possessed; it transcended ordinary violin values. Somebody was heard to remark that the tone here and there became a little thin. And somebody will get to heaven one day and remark that an angel's halo is not on straight. The intensity of the adagio elevated to the profoundest poetry a movement which most players, including Kreisler, make into nothing but a lovely cradle song. . . . Huberman put his heart and soul into the slow movement; the playing told us of the thorn in the rose, the disillusionment that waits for us all somewhere – and of the consolation that time and reflection will bring. And then, in the gusto of the last movement the playing became gloriously sane as if to tell us: 'The world goes on, friends; there is work to do, and the simple things for you.' Such an artist as Huberman makes a concert a 'third of life', in Prospero's term; we must hear him again and often.

The passages illustrate the essence of Neville's greatness. It wasn't simply that his writing was elegant, witty and urbane, and his columns richly textured and well-tempered, though all these qualities were to be found in abundance. Gilbert Murray once wrote:

There is in every art an element of mere knowledge or science, and that element is progressive. But there is another element, too, which does not depend on knowledge and which does not progress, but has a kind of stationary and eternal value, like the beauty of the dawn, or the love of a mother for her child, or the joy of a young animal in being alive, or the courage of a martyr facing torment. We cannot for all our progress get beyond these things: there they stand like light upon the mountains. The only question is whether we can rise to them.

The quality that made 'N.C.' such a unique figure was exactly his way of helping others to perceive the intangible simply by rising to it himself. Returning to his pre-war notices, it makes little difference that the performances themselves took place fifty years ago, as likely as not before the reader was born. As a fellow critic notes, 'in writing about what was transitory Cardus usually managed to cast a searchlight on the eternal values'. At his best, 'N.C.' had the ability to communicate the unique and memorable aspect of a perform-ance. Whether it was Lehmann as the Marschallin, Schnabel's penetration of the Opus 111 sonata, a *lieder* recital by Gerhardt, one of Frank Mullings's histrionic renditions of *Otello* or, perhaps most poignant of all, Kathleen Ferrier's failure to utter the last few words of *Das Lied von der Erde*, was largely irrelevant, for in each case 'N.C.'s' prose helped bring his readers within sight and feel of the elemental links between art and nature; and in so doing illuminated the eternal, unchanging oneness of human experience. Simply by writing as he did, Neville probably brought more people to music than any other English writer.

[X]

As principal music critic of the *Manchester Guardian*, Neville could, and often did, meet people from all walks of musical life. Though there were times when tedium, tiredness and plain shyness made it an irksome task, for the most part he liked the business of social exchange. Conversation was one of his greatest joys, and, besides, there was no telling what useful contacts an unexpected introduc-tion might produce. As his reputation grew it would have been easy for Neville to neglect the local musical community in Manchester, but in fact he kept close links with many of the city's institutions.

Like Sam Langford, he took an active interest in the Royal Manchester College of Music, occasionally lecturing but more often enjoying dinner with members of the staff. It was a way of keeping in touch with the latest thinking (and gossip), and of course it did the College no harm to keep the ear of one of the most influential critics in the country. When time permitted, he also liked to meet and advise some of the promising young musicians in the area.

Marjorie Robinson was one who received encouragement and guidance from 'N.C.' at the start of her career. A pupil of Mullings, she came to Neville's attention after a series of promising performances in local concerts and recitals. In October 1933 'N.C.' heard her sing at the inaugural concert of the Manchester Bach Choir. The next day he wrote:

> A young singer, Miss Marjorie Robinson, had the courage to make her first appearance at a Manchester concert in two songs of Wolf. . . . She at once contrived to set a heart-felt mood, her general manner was fine, with dignified restraint and the proper impersonal air. Her singing showed much intelligence and a real instinct to mould a song phrase by phrase, giving point by the way, yet with an eye on the full arch of the music. To find a young singer getting anywhere near the secret of Wolf is a proper cause for satisfaction and congratulation.

Unlike some of the critical fraternity who gloried in pulling performances apart at the slightest opportunity, Neville was usually very sympathetic in his reviews of young artists. A couple of weeks after her Manchester debut, Marjorie Robinson was giving a performance at the Adelphi Cinema, Swinton, of songs by Charles Villiers Stanford, when she somehow contrived to sing the same verse twice. In his notice the following morning, 'N.C.' made little of her lapse: 'Stanford at his best could write a lyric as delicate in touch and as charming in sentiment as 'A Soft Day', which Miss Marjorie Robinson sung in sensitive style until she managed to forget her words momentarily.'

The Adelphi Cinema, Swinton, may have been a far cry from the French Restaurant of the Midland Hotel, but it was a transition Neville made frequently and with ease. The Midland was normally the scene of his meetings with the great international artists who visited Manchester in those days; here he dined with Schnabel,

Rubinstein, Horowitz (live or dead), Gerhardt and Rachmaninov, revelling in their presence and only occasionally seeking to ingratiate himself. There was nothing he liked better than to listen to their experiences, arguments and gossip, all the time storing the best anecdotes away for use in his own conversations. Some he would recount so often that they became his stock-in-trade. Schnabel, who once confided that he didn't think much of 'N.C.'s' notices but that 'Cricketer's' reports were wonderful, was a particular favourite. Everyone who ever dined with Neville must have heard (at least once) the story of how Schnabel, who was reputedly very close with his money, was once apprehended *en route* to a concert in Manchester travelling in a first-class compartment with only a second-class ticket. The great man was mortified when the vigilant guard, showing not the slightest interest in the identity of his passenger nor turning a hair at the terrible imprecations being hurled at him, threatened to put the by-now speechlesss virtuoso off the train at the next station unless he paid up. 'The great man unveiled,' Neville used to conclude. His own favourite 'Schnabel' tale involved none other than Albert Einstein. The great physicist enjoyed playing violin and piano recitals with Schnabel in his own study, but one evening he got rather out of time. Lifting his eyes momentarily from the keyboard Schnabel grunted: 'Albert, can't you count?'

No matter how much he enjoyed these meetings, Neville never lost sight of the dangers of over-fraternising. It would never do for the principal music critic of the *Manchester Guardian* to be thought to be in the pocket of a particular artist. To overcome this difficulty he made it a point of principle never to accept an invitation from artists until they were established figures and had already played in front of him. Thereafter, like W. C. Fields, he would never turn one down!

By a happy coincidence, most of the great artists of the day were people Neville enjoyed meeting, and *vice versa*. By the end of the 1932-33 season, Sir Hamilton Harty, whom 'N.C.' respected intermittently, had resigned, leaving the Hallé without a permanent conductor for nearly ten years. Though the vacuum may have done little for the playing standards of the orchestra, it gave Neville the chance to get acquainted with the string of visiting conductors who came to Manchester during this period. Dr (as he then was) Malcolm Sargent and Sir Thomas Beecham conducted the majority of Hallé concerts, but guests included Malko, Monteux, Boult, Coates, Heger, Szell, Schuricht, Ansermet, Weingartner and Lambert. Much though he may have welcomed the injection of fresh faces into what had become a stiflingly predictable programme, 'N.C.' soon realised that the absence of a central, guiding figure was having a disastrous effect on the orchestra's standards and hence its reputation.

By the end of the 1935-36 season, the number of performances had fallen from 75 in the palmy pre-Depression days to 37. The season was run at a loss of £98, and the Hallé Society could muster only 131 members. Conscious of this fall from grace, 'N.C.' was often unsparing in his criticism and as a result was rarely a popular figure with the Hallé establishment – players, conductors or administrators. At one stage in 1937, Beecham became so incensed by an 'N.C.' notice that he informed the Society that henceforth he would not 'conduct any concert to which Mr Neville Cardus was invited'. It was the first of several minor rifts between the two men and like the others it was quick to heal, particularly when Sir Thomas's attention was drawn to the fact that the *Guardian* had shown on a previous occasion that it was unwilling to compromise its independence by muzzling its principal critic. Nor was there any great hope of persuading Neville to pull his punches. The style had been established and the standards set.

'N.C.' was now something of an institution; he always insisted on having an end-seat in the old Free Trade Hall – impaired acoustics evidently counting for less than the opportunity to slip out if bored, or worse. It was not unusual for the seat to remain vacant during the second half of concerts. During a performance, he adopted a series of characteristic poses, many of which were to become instantly recognisable. He never spoke and took few notes; most of all, he hated being interrupted whilst preparing a notice.

Reading Neville's autobiographies, one could be forgiven for supposing that he and Beecham had been lifelong chums. The truth was rather different. Though Neville had been born only ten miles from, and ten years after, the mercurial knight, there the similarities ended. Beecham was born of solid entrepreneurial stock, his father being the inventor and first producer of the eponymous powders, whereas Neville's origins are anyone's guess. The two were not destined to meet until 1931, and then in Salzburg rather than Manchester. It was only thereafter that they struck up a friendship which was to last – with only a few ill-tempered interruptions – until Sir Thomas's death in 1961.

The relationship flourished during the 1930s when Beecham's engagements with the Hallé made him a frequent visitor to Manchester. It soon became the custom for Neville to join Sir Thomas after the performance in his suite at the Midland. Fortified by champagne, oysters and Beecham's unquenchable zest, they would discuss music until dawn. Sometimes it would seem that 'discussion' was hardly the correct word to describe the exchanges between them. As both were past-masters of the monologue, conversation often took the form of a series of long, rambling, reflective statements linked only by the most imperceptible and obscure of threads, with the outcome turning not on logic or technical expertise but on who had the most vivid imagination or the best line. Needless to say, Beecham usually won. Galling though he may have found this outcome, Neville could still draw solace from the fact that these sessions left him the proud possessor of an apparently inexhaustible stock of Beecham sayings. Many years later, having heard these *bon mots* more than once, some of Neville's best friends put it to him that they would only continue as his dining companions if he promised not to mention Beecham. He of course agreed and everything would go according to plan until suddenly a seemingly harmless remark gave him his chance. 'As Sir Thomas would say,' he began, and as often as not there then followed an hour or two of non-stop Beecham.

It was not by chance that Cardus and Beecham first met at Salzburg. Here, every August, the cream of Europe's musical and social worlds, together with a liberal sprinkling of instantly recognisable and very audible Americans, gathered to enjoy what had begun life as a modest meeting organised by the Mozart Stifftung, only to find itself transformed under the influence firstly of Richard Strauss and then Toscanini into one of the most prestigious events in the musical calendar. Beecham came to perform on and off the podium, while for Neville attendance at the Festival allowed him to pay homage to the cultural tradition he so loved and take a well-deserved holiday at the same time. There was probably no place on earth more suited to his tastes, a point he later confirmed in a *Guardian* column entitled 'Music at Salzburg':

We all have our own private ideas of heaven, which we change as our experiences of the world's good things get richer. At the moment, I can think of nothing more paradisaic than last week's music at Salzburg. The music itself has been only like one aspect or attribute, amongst others, of this lovely place; Mozart played by the Vienna Philharmonic Orchestra has not seemed a thing set apart, to which we may wish to escape from a rougher and less delightful world; on the contrary we have turned to the music as naturally as we have turned to the mountains, the pleasant old-world streets and stately squares, where there is nothing to be seen that is not pleasant.

Salzburg wasn't Neville's first experience of central European culture in its natural surrounds. On C. P. Scott's instructions, he had visited Vienna in 1924 'to contemplate Goethe in the snow', and to hear one of the most compelling operatic performances he ever attended – *Die Frau ohne Schatten*, with the composer himself conducting and a cast led by Lotte Lehmann. But it was his first experience of the grand festival, the international society élite and the highest of high life. The effect was dramatic. Suddenly many of the world's greatest artists – names that he had often conjured with in his columns but had never seen – were there in the flesh, either walking the streets or sitting in one of the many cafés. The Vienna Philharmonic, in Salzburg for their 'summer holidays', stayed in a hamlet just outside the town called Morzg. Some of the visitors came for the Festival; others because they felt it was an event one ought to attend. Douglas Fairbanks was often to be seen, as was Marlene Dietrich, resplendent in a green cape of such brilliance that no one could mistake her. Alice Astor, the wife of Hofmannsthal's son (who later committed suicide), always took a villa for the duration, but the majority were happy to stay in hotels, or to lodge in private accommodation as 'paying guests'. All over the town the local landladies could be heard boasting about their 'grafen' or their 'baronen'.

The English were always well represented – with the Astors, Cunards, and the likes of Victor Gollancz and Frederick Ashton to the fore; Sydney Beer once hired the Vienna Philharmonic and a small castle to entertain Lady Carnavon and Malcolm Sargent. Adrian Boult often brought a group of promising young musicians so that they could take in the atmosphere and see some of the great artists. After Toscanini took over from Richard Strauss, Americans came in ever-increasing numbers; some with little idea why, but all utterly convinced that Salzburg was the place to be. One night the

Prince of Wales caused great consternation by walking out of a performance of *Fidelio*; Schnabel was heard to mutter: 'I don't know why everyone is so upset. It isn't really necessary for the future King of England to know *Fidelio*.' For the shrinking number who felt their ignorance to be an impediment, a series of introductory lectures on the works being performed were provided by Frau Mitia Mayer-Lismann, whom Neville later portrayed as 'a greying, distinguished woman, who played examples from the opera's score at the piano, and who explained the involved libretto with charming lucidity'. The name of Mayer-Lismann was subsequently to play an important part in his life.

Neville himself often took friends along with him to the Festival. James Ramsbottom, alias Sydney Rowbotham, went in 1931, and later it was 'Milady' who accompanied him. Cricket permitting, he used to leave towards the end of August, travelling by train from Victoria like everyone else in those days. The last few hours of the journey would find him fretting, 'impatient as a child . . . standing in the corridors of the compartment of the train, leaning against the silver rail, and on the look-out for the first trace, afar off, of the turrets and domes which are Salzburg, standing in the meadows on two rocks, cloven by a river, and as unreal and as convincing as a mirage, a town suspended in the sky, not of this age or of any terrestrial substantiality.'[31]

Sightseeing and the normal practices of the tourist were not for Neville. On previous overseas visits, he had spent most of the day sitting in coffee-houses writing notices or articles, slowly puffing on a pipe but never inhaling, or walking through the parks and gardens feeding the ducks and squirrels. But Salzburg was no normal tourist centre. He attended the Festival as chief music critic of the *Manchester Guardian*, a position which then, more so than now, commanded respect and certain very practical privileges; it assured him entrance to as many performances as he wished to take in, an introduction to the great names, peace and quiet whenever he wished it (on the pretext of writing his notices), and as much of the surrounding social life as he wanted. And what is more, by the 1930s Neville had acquired enough self-confidence and guile to make the best of these advantages.

On arriving, he and his party checked in at the Stein (one of what was then a new breed of hotels by the river, not as famous as the Oesterreichhof, but nevertheless well appointed and very comfortable), and then proceeded to sample the pleasures of Salzburg. Though the emphasis was on relaxed informality and spontaneity, as is so often the case with prestigious events ritual and convention lent a predictability to the occasion. After an early bath, it was customary to go to the Café Bazaar for breakfast and then off to the first 'event' of the day, at the end of which everyone moved on to the Paterskeller. Richard Strauss always conducted in white flannels on Sunday, while his wife Pauline – somewhat unkindly nicknamed 'Die Schreier von Garmisch' – could usually be relied upon to make one or two tactless utterances every day. Clemens Krauss, Strauss's great friend and the librettist of *Capriccio*, gave a concert of (Johann) Strauss waltzes in the Mozarteum on Sunday mornings. The seats always creaked in the Festspielhaus and everyone rented cushions because they were so hard; performances of *Faust* in the Felsenreitschule were interrupted by rain as often as Test matches at Old Trafford. Among the artists who regularly performed were Furtwängler, Schalk, Weingartner, Walter, Kleiber, Busch and Klemperer. Beecham, too, was a major figure, though the orchestra never quite made up their minds whether he could be counted a truly serious artist.

Even the activities of 'loud-voiced harridans' and the 'strange doings of visitors from England and the United States, who buy the "native costume" and climb the mountains in handsome, expensive cars' couldn't upset Neville's enjoyment of Salzburg. As he reported to his *Guardian* readers, it was an all-embracing, captivating experience:

Music in Salzburg is only the bloom on the place, which at any time is an earthly paradise. The glorious sunshine has lighted Salzburg with a proper glow – the glow of romantic light opera. I have to remind myself from time to time that Salzburg is in Austria, and Austria is bankrupt and, according to our notions, afflicted with world depression at its most woeful and hopeless.

At the centre of everything, lending a unifying cultural and historical theme to the Festival, there were the great set-piece spectacles: *Jedermann* in the Cathedral Square, *Faust* in the Felsenreitschule, and the likes of *Fidelio*, *The Magic Flute*, *The Mastersingers* and *Der Rosenkavalier* in the Festspielhaus. No matter how familiar these great works may have been to Neville, in Salzburg they seemed to acquire a new dimension and meaning. It was a difference he attributed in part to atmosphere but mainly to the quality of the performers. In 1931, his notice extolled the virtues of the orchestra:

The performance of *Der Rosenkavalier* on Thursday was the finest I have ever heard, because it was framed by the Vienna Philharmonic Orchestra. We have much the same cast at Covent Garden – Lehmann, Mayr, and Margit Angerer; but we have never heard in England the right orchestra. I will go so far as to say that no orchestra in the world can play the Strauss of *Der Rosenkavalier* with half of the Vienna orchestra's lightness and swiftness of touch, its pride and verve of melody, its richness and refinement of harmony, and its freedom and felicity of rhythm. For years I have lived on memories of the Vienna Orchestra as I heard it in boyhood. I had begun lately to think that these memories, like all the memories of youth, were heightened and sweetened by time – the pathos of distance! But this week I find that I have not at all idealised the Vienna Orchestra; that, indeed, it is a more enchanting orchestra than on dark days in Manchester winters I have ever dreamed.

Five years later it was a production of *The Mastersingers* under Toscanini, with Lehmann as Eva, that prompted another sigh of admiration and wonder:

The performance of *Meistersinger* will remain in the mind for a lifetime, because of its beauty and dignity of proportion. The curve of the work was vast, yet none of the contained and varied energy, the multitudinous detail, was missed. The whole opera came to abounding life, until we forgot the illusion of art and entered the comprehensive and golden world of the work. Not all at once did we find this world easeful and sunny; Toscanini gave to the first act a certain rigidity; the Mastersingers were made to toe a strict line, and David in his explanation to Walter was allowed no time for a boyish appreciation of his own momentary authority over the knight and the scene. For a while I chafed under Toscanini's Latin clarity; I wanted the humour that expands and releases, not the wit that contracts and braces up. Probably the interpretation never did find the girth of a Richter's humour, that large mildness of laughter which has no use for the crack of the whip of an epigram.

But before Toscanini had finished with Act II, the miracle of recreation was complete. It would be impossible in words to convey the summer magic which fell over the Nürnberg scene; the tenderness of Sachs's first monologue; the steady burgeoning of beauty in the Sachs and Eva scene, 'Gut'n Abend, Meister'; the vividness of the orchestra in the cobbling song; the unbelievable control of the crescendo of the fight in the street, with the dominant musical motif in charge of all, the whole texture indeed clear and musical for the first time in living memory. Then the decrescendo, the watchman's horn and call, and the lovely modulation to the lyrical, the peaceful, and the miniature. The performance's shape and life-giving forms were never forced before us after Act I (in which Toscanini concentrated on clarity in the preliminary unfolding of the argument). To the end – where the banner of song was opened with a width and nobility that caused happiness and sadness, laughter and tears, to express one and the same pride in life – Toscanini held us like children listening to a tale told in the chimney corner, lighted by the glow of olden times.

At moments like this – moments when the magic of Salzburg seemed irreducible – Neville glimpsed and understood the profound insight in Thomas Carlyle's statement that 'music leads to the edge of the infinite and lets us for moments gaze into that'.

[XI]

There was to be little time for further revelations. In March 1938 Hitler decided to use Austria as the setting for another rehearsal of his own mad drama. After the *Anschluss*, Toscanini, Walter, Kleiber and Klemperer all withdrew from the Festival. When Neville left Salzburg that year he too sensed that it would be his last visit for many years. What he could not have realised was that a central chapter in his life was also drawing to a close. Back in England the gathering crisis had yet to disrupt the natural order of things. The Australians, this time under Bradman's leadership, had arrived in April to begin another battle for the Ashes. On 2 May at Worcester, Bradman marked the opening of hostilities with a double century – the third time in succession that he had performed this feat. That evening 'Cricketer' wrote:

THE "LUSTFUL TURK."

MANCHESTER CONSUL'S BREACH OF PROMISE.

TYPES IN COURT

THE PLAINTIFF (BEATRICE CARDUS)

THE DEFENDANT (MUSTAPHA KARSA)

THE MOTHER OF THE PLAINTIFF

THE SISTER OF PLAINTIFF

1a *above left*
Young Neville (aged four)
in his 'Sunday best'

1b *above right*
Ada Cardus –
Neville's mother

1c *left*
Ann (Grandmother),
Beatrice (Aunt),
Ada and other courtroom
characters in the case
of the 'Lustful Turk' –
as depicted in the
Daily Dispatch, April 1902

2a Neville *(far right)* and William Attewell with the 1st XI at Shrewsbury, 1913

2b Neville *(fourth from right, back row)* during his days as a cricket professional

3a Neville takes the field under the captaincy of his childhood idol,
J. T. Tyldesley

3b A *Manchester Guardian*
man in his prime

3c C. P. Scott towards the end of his time
as editor of the *Manchester Guardian*

4a *above left*
Edith Cardus in an
unusually formal pose

4b *above right*
Security, comfort
and relaxation

4c *right*
A spot of exercise
en route to Australia

5a Neville's Australian home:
West End, Crick Avenue, Sydney

5b Neville and Edith in Sydney

5c Enjoying a joke with Cary Grimmett

6a Discussing the score with Sir John Barbirolli

6b Sir John speaking at the Free Trade Hall on the occasion of the concert to celebrate Neville's fiftieth year with the *Guardian*

7a and **7b** Two studies showing Neville in reflective mood towards the end of his life

8 Nearing the end of the innings

He [Bradman] was generally expected to achieve this performance, granted that he himself felt in the mood. The Worcester-
shire captain, indeed, sensibly resigned himself to it and
decided to get it over as quickly and painlessly as may be, for
having won the toss on a thoroughly easy wicket he asked the
Australians to bat first, an invitation which was unanimously
accepted. The Worcestershire captain's resignation apparently
achieved a philosophy so profound that he declined the new
ball at 200. Probably he was right; a new ball costs money, and
Worcestershire are not a wealthy club and every little counts.

Much the same thing happened in their next match at Lord's, and
again no one seemed very surprised. 'Cricketer's' account was
suitably droll:

Splendid bowling and fielding, as good as any we could find in
the country at the present time, accounted today for five
Australian wickets for the poor total of 171. The good work was
ruined by Bradman, who is still not out 257. Several people
were heard to say that without Bradman the Australians might
not be so wonderful after all. Probably not; *Hamlet* without the
Prince would not be so wonderful and the Grande Armeé
without Napoleon might not have been exactly the force it was.

England's performance in the Test matches gave cause for
optimism until a second-innings collapse at Leeds gave Australia
victory and with it an extended lease of the Ashes. England won the
final Test at the Oval to square the series, but as injuries to Bradman
and Fingleton reduced Australia to nine men it was a pyrrhic victory.
But if a series of docile pitches deprived the series of much of its
potential excitement, it will nevertheless be remembered for three
legendary innings. At Trent Bridge on Monday 13 June, Stan
McCabe 'honoured the first Test with a great and noble innings'.
His efforts prompted Bradman to call the rest of his team to the
dressing-room balcony to witness a display the like of which they
might never see again. Neville's account was equal to the occasion:

Now came death and glory, brilliance wearing the dress of
culture. McCabe demolished the English attacks with
aristocratic politeness, good taste and reserve. Claude Duval

never took possession of a stage coach with more charm of manner than this; his boundaries were jewels and trinkets which he accepted as though dangling them in his hands. In half an hour after lunch he scored nearly fifty, unhurried but trenchant. He cut and glanced and drove, upright and lissom; his perfection of touch moved aesthetic sense; this was cricket of felicity, power and no covetousness, strength and no brutality, opportunism and no meanness, assault and no battery, dazzling strokes and no rhetoric; lovely, brave batsmanship giving joy to the connoisseur, and all done in a losing hour. One of the greatest innings ever seen anywhere in any period of the game's history. Moving cricket which swelled the heart. Not once but many times McCabe has come to Australia's aid in a crucial moment and has played gloriously when others have lost heart; he is in the line of Trumper, and no other batsman today has inherited Trumper's sword and cloak.

At Lord's on Friday 14 June, Walter Hammond came in to bat with England already 3 down for 31 paltry runs, and proceeded to score 210 before the close of play that day; a 'throne-room innings', 'Cricketer' called it the next morning. And finally at the Oval, beginning on Saturday 20 August and lasting until half-past two three playing days later, Len Hutton built an innings which for sheer concentration, determination and stamina may never be surpassed. He had been batting for over two days when a square cut off Fleetwood-Smith took his score to 336, thus beating the record Bradman had set at Leeds in 1930. 'Cricketer' revelled in the moment:

The scene which now occurred moved even the hardened critics. Thousands of happy people stood up and cheered. Somebody with a cornet began to play 'For he's a jolly good fellow' and the crowd took up the refrain in that evangelical tone which the British public invariably adopts when it lifts up its heart to rejoice in song. Moreover, the voices and the cornet did not keep together – but in the circumstances to say so is a piece of pedantic music criticism. Bradman shook hands with the hero, all the Australians shook hands with him, journeying to the wicket from the remoter parts of the Oval – all except tired Bill O'Reilly, who lay prone on the grass until he saw a man coming out with drinks when he got up at once and made for him, in a hurry.

Just a year later, with the exploits of Constantine, Headley and the other members of R. S. Grant's West Indian party still fresh in his memory, Neville found himself at Lord's on the fatal day Hitler's armies invaded Poland. The atmosphere of war was everywhere. Outside, aimless figures whose collective identity now seemed irrelevant played to empty stands, while overhead barrage-balloons lent a new dimension to conventional field settings. Inside, an air of quite unnatural urgency had overtaken the normal dusty calm; men in green aprons descended upon the Long Room, placing the treasured memorabilia in protective bags before moving them to safer surrounds. As he gazed out on to this scene, Neville's thoughts turned to the past and to the future. Barely twenty-five years ago, he had been 'Fred', an optimistic young man of dreams and ambition, but as yet little substance; now he was Neville, a man of international reputation, a husband, a member of a famous London Club, and the proud owner of suits made in Saville Row. (There was no truth in the rumour that Neville's wardrobe contained only one suit; in fact he had four, but they were all identical – double-breasted and made from grey flannel.)

But what now? The outbreak of war must lead to the disruption of his treasured life-style; it meant ration-books and air-raid sirens, black-outs and bombs, destruction and death. How would he fare without cricket and music? Would the *Manchester Guardian* still employ a cricket reporter and music critic, even at two for the price of one? All in all, the prospect which confronted him as he watched the last county championship match for seven seasons was as bleak as any performance of *Götterdämmerung* he'd ever seen.

4

Australia

'Now spurs the lated traveller apace
To gain the timely inn.'[1]

[I]

No one knew exactly why Neville decided to go to Australia, but few were surprised when he went. War-time England was no place for a cricket writer or a music critic. There was no first-class cricket, and even Neville would have been hard put to 'imagine' six years of competition as he had once 'imagined' the last day of a test match at Leeds. Orchestras and opera were similarly hard hit. Prompted by the fear of large-scale aerial bombardment, many public authorities prohibited assemblies of people in entertainment centres. One by one, his favourite arenas were taken out of service; Lord's was first to go, closely followed by the Free Trade Hall, which was requisitioned for use as a store. For one who had become accustomed to an uninterrupted round of cricket and music, these new conditions must have been difficult to bear. But Neville was wrong to suggest that music-making was almost non-existent during the 'phoney war'.[2] The executive of the Hallé Society met on 13 and 18 September 1939, and decided to organise a series of ten Sunday afternoon concerts at the Paramount Cinema in Oxford Street. Beecham conducted four of these, Sir Henry Wood and Malcolm Sargent three each.

Nor did these efforts to preserve some public music performances die with the heightening of hostilities in the summer of 1940. With Sargent as the principal inspiration and driving force, the Hallé organised a further twenty concerts during that winter; helped by a grant from the newly formed Council for the Encouragement of

Music and the Arts, they toured eleven nearby industrial centres. Neville's failure to recognise these efforts may have been more costly than he has imagined. To this day, there are many who look upon his departure as little short of cowardice, and in Manchester it is often cited as one reason why he was never given the Freedom of the City.

For the first few months of war Neville fretted in Manchester. 'As far as I was concerned,' he was later to write, 'I counted amongst the unemployed.' It was like being placed under house arrest for an offence of which he was only an innocent bystander. There was little for him to do at Cross Street, and Edith was fully occupied seeing to the evacuation of her pupils. So when in December 1939 a telegram arrived from Sir Keith Murdoch ('Lord Southcliffe' to friends and enemies alike) inviting him to cover a forthcoming Beecham tour of Australia for the *Melbourne Herald*, the response was immediate. By the beginning of 1940, Neville had packed, travelled and arrived. But once in Melbourne he soon discovered that it was a case of 'nor all that glisters, gold'. The main problem was the *Herald* itself: 'I couldn't write about music in an evening paper,' he protested (though eight years later his brief stay with the *Evening Standard* was to show that the lesson had not been learnt). Within six months of arriving in Melbourne he had upped and moved again, this time to Sydney where he took up a position with the *Sydney Morning Herald*. It was an association that was to last, on and off, for the best part of fifteen years.

When Neville decided to accept Sir Keith's invitation, he already knew something of the country that was to be his home for the next seven years. Covering the M.C.C. tour in 1936-37 had been an eye-opening experience. The warmth of the hospitality shown to him on that visit had come as a genuine surprise, as had been the discovery that Australia wasn't quite the philistine outpost he'd imagined. Of course there was nothing to compare with Salzburg, the Vienna Philharmonic or even the Hallé on its good days, but the country nevertheless had its share of competent artists, budding talent, enthusiastic institutions and a more appreciative attitude to music than he'd been led to expect. Moreover, the rise of Nazi Germany had led to a large influx of refugees from Central Europe whose experience of music matched his own and whose presence lent valuable support to the cause he was to lead. Finally, it would not have escaped Neville's attention that in Australia his views and opinions would command an influence greater even than that he had enjoyed in Manchester. There was simply no one else of his stature for thousands of miles. More than anything else, Neville loved holding court. (It was probably no coincidence that his disillusionment with Australia would come at about the time locals started to think of him less as a 'star' and more as 'one of us'.)

Like its Melbourne counterpart, the *Sydney Morning Herald* was at this time essentially a provincial newspaper. With air freight transport still in its infancy, the sheer size of the country ruled out a wider circulation. A few copies reached Melbourne, but no further. However, the areas it served – Sydney in particular – were the liveliest, least parochial and most culturally diverse in Australia. The city had its own orchestra and opera company and, to Neville's evident relief, provided enough music 'to keep me busy, three or four nights a week'. Many of the leading figures in the Australian music establishment lived and worked there. Bernard Heinze and Edgar Bainton were regular visitors, and Eugene Goossens was soon to take up a post at the Conservatorium. There was, in other words, the beginnings of exactly the kind of close-knit, energetic musical community that Neville thrived upon.

The move to Sydney warranted just one sentence in *Full Score*: 'Nearly broke, I flew one Saturday to Sydney, offered myself to the *Sydney Morning Herald*, and gladly agreed to the terms of five guineas a week.' Writing thirty years after the event, it may well have been that Neville could no longer remember the precise circumstances of his move to Sydney, though equally there may have been some he preferred to forget. Suffice it to say that the manner of his arrival did little to endear him to many of his new readers. For one thing the paper already had in Kenneth Wilkinson a critic and writer of some discernment and elegance. Wilkinson, who had a large gallery of admirers in the inner circle of local music-making, left within days of Neville's arrival in an atmosphere which was, to say the least, strained. Then there was the new critic's attitude towards the musical community he was now dependent on.

To the surprise and disappointment of many, the renowned Neville Cardus turned out on first acquaintance to be 'just one more sneering Pommy bastard come to hand down higher wisdom to the ignorant colonials'. This opinion was not a reflection on the 'irresistible excellence' of the Cardus style: on the contrary, Australians had always appreciated the richness of his allusions and references, and the absence of any trace of 'starched polysyllables'. The trouble stemmed from a basic difference of opinion over the purpose of music criticism. As well as taking a natural pride in their own achievements, the *Morning Herald*'s readers, few of whom had experienced European standards of performance, were innately suspicious of visiting eminences from the mother country. Neville, by contrast, was only too aware of the difference in standards of performance and appreciation between the hemispheres. As a critic he saw it as his purpose and duty to alert his new public to this difference and to suggest ways in which it could be overcome. Laudable though his intentions may have been, Neville became very unpopular because he failed to appreciate firstly the extent of his own influence and secondly the sensitivity of the public he was addressing. At one point relationships became so soured that Senator Lamp (Labour, Tasmania) felt obliged to ask the Australian parliament: 'How much longer are the people of Australia to be pestered with Neville Cardus?'

With criticisms ranging in tone from piously patronising to the downright scathing, it was little wonder that many readers rapidly concluded that their new critic viewed their musical landscape as an overgrown wasteland urgently in need of clearance, nor that most of his mail began 'Cardus, you bastard!' In those early days there is little doubt that Neville saw his mission as being to clear great swathes of an uncultivated wilderness to make way for richer material. Later, it is true, he sought to soften this impression. In *Full Score*, he described himself as 'a sort of gardener in the field of music, plucking out a weed here, or tending a delicate and promising growth there', and went so far as to point out that 'most of the weeds, to begin with, were English transplantations . . . notably a whole caterwaul of so-called "principal tenors" from Covent Garden Opera, quite unknown to me'. But by then the damage was done.

The strangest aspect of this episode was that Neville had not set out with the intention of making himself one of the most unpopular journalists in Australia. The early articles which so enraged his readers weren't fashioned as a statement of his intellectual superiority, nor were they intended to express his indignation at being forced to listen to the rape of great music. Insensitivity, not arrogance, was his failing. Part of the problem can be traced back to the man he had originally come to Australia to cover. As everyone knew, Sir Thomas Beecham was a brilliant eccentric with a very sharp tongue.

Wherever he went, the public expected spontaneous wit and outrageous comment and they were rarely disappointed. During his
stay in Sydney in 1940, the conductor was taken out on a launch to
view the harbour bridge. Looked at from a distance it presents an
impressive sight, but the Mayor of Sydney was determined that Sir
Thomas should appreciate the wonder at close hand, and so the
launch, swaying vigorously on a choppy sea, was instructed to take
up station immediately under the bridge. 'Now Sir Thomas,' asked
the proud dignitary, 'what d'you think of our bridge?' Craning his
neck as he glanced upward, Sir Thomas replied, 'I don't like it at all.
Why don't you have it removed?'

Now it was all very well Sir Thomas making wisecracks like that;
he could get away with them precisely because they were what was
expected of him. But this was not the case with Neville. Yet for the
first few months of his stay in Sydney, he seemed to many to be
behaving and writing as though he were Beecham. Artists of less
than first rank; young performers who had yet to establish themselves; even well intentioned amateurs; all felt the caustic edge of his
pen. At first the reaction was one of stunned surprise. So great was
the contrast with the urbane, sensitive 'N.C.' of the *Guardian* that it
was even rumoured that Neville had developed schizophrenic
tendencies on the way over. But once the initial shock had worn off,
readers began to take personal offence at the withering criticism
being meted out to local artists (undeserving though many of them
probably were!). Many readers never forgave Neville for these early
blasts even when, in later years, he 'tempered the wind to the shorn
lamb'.

Among the artists themselves, the feeling was that Neville was
indiscriminately employing critical standards more appropriate to
Salzburg than Sydney, with the result that his presence was damag-
ing rather than encouraging the local musical community. At one
point, officials of the Sydney Philharmonic Society (a typically
amateur group whose members presented the *Messiah*, *Elijah* and
the like) became so incensed at Neville's disparaging comments
about their concerts that they decided to beard the ogre in his den.
By all accounts neither party emerged from the meeting fully
satisfied, but it led to a clearer understanding of the issues at stake.
Thereafter, much of the ill-feeling that had threatened to jeopardise
Neville's stay in Sydney evaporated. Australians gradually came to
accept that at heart he was a kindly, sensitive soul, while he realised

that they weren't all uncultured 'ockers'. Just before his return to England, Neville confided to one of his colleagues that he had received a letter which began 'Dear Mr Cardus'. 'Time for me to move on', he observed wryly.

Throughout his career with the *Herald*, Neville kept himself very much to himself. Whenever possible, he would prepare his articles and reviews away from the paper's offices. Anywhere would do: even the General Post Office in Morton Place was pressed into service on one occasion. If there was no alternative to coming into the office, it was not to the Reporters' Room that he retired, but the end of the Classified Advertising counter in the main entrance hall. Very few of his fellow journalists saw much of Neville; almost no one claimed to *know* him. It was a peculiar custom at the *Herald* that the news editor was responsible for everything in the paper except the leading articles. While Neville submitted his copy to the sub-editors in the normal way, Angus McLachlan, the news editor at the time, recalls that there was an informal arrangement under which 'Neville's copy was not to be changed without reference to me'.

An isolated and apparently rather austere figure, more than once his remoteness created unforeseen difficulties with other con-tributors. On the occasion of Richard Strauss's eightieth birthday, for example, the *Herald*'s Saturday magazine published – without advising Neville – an impudent piece by a 'Lindsey Browne' on the 'five and ten cent store' aspects of the composer's work. Having never heard of the owner of this by-line, Neville wrote a scathing denunciation of the article in a letter to the *Herald*'s editor, H. A. McClure-Smith, who chose to publish it. To his credit, Neville subsequently let it be known that he would never have written such a letter if he'd been aware that 'Lindsey Browne' was in fact the *Herald*'s own second music critic – in Browne's own words (with tongue firmly in cheek), 'the hero who covered all the crummy little backroom events in 60-watt lighting while Neville peacocked it at all the chandeliered soirées!'

A different side of Neville's character emerged in a later incident involving the same Lindsey Browne. On this occasion:

The *Sydney Daily Telegraph*, always busily trying one-upmanship on the *Herald*, promoted a series of six Sunday night orchestra concerts. The orchestra was virtually the Sydney Symphony Orchestra, with Sir Frank Packer of the *Telegraph* paying the costs of hiring the players. The conductor was Maurice Abravanel, specially imported from Salt Lake City. Neville noticed the first concert in the series. Angus McLachlan asked me to review the second one – which I duly did without much in the way of relish, and my notice said as much. Two days later the *Telegraph*'s front-page columnist accused the *S.M.H.* of dirty politics by withholding the welcoming Cardus from the second concert, and sending along a minor-leaguer like me to knock it. . . . I erupted one of my higher dudgeons all over Angus McLachlan, said that in justice I must review all the remaining concerts in the *Telegraph*'s series. Angus demurred; I resigned. Meanwhile, so I learned later, Cardus was at that very moment trying to press much the same argument as mine on the editor, H. A. McClure-Smith. The upshot was that I reviewed the next concert in the series and after that we alternated.

It was nearly two years before Neville fully adjusted to his new surroundings. During that period he suffered greatly from loneliness (Edith was still in England) and insecurity, feelings which went a long way towards explaining the harsh and apparently insensitive tenor of some of his notices. By 1942, however, the worst was over. He and his public had more or less come to terms with each other, and soon legions of Australians, many of whom knew next to nothing about music, were responding to the encouragement of his columns. And the longer he'd stayed in Australia, the more he had come to appreciate both the country and its inhabitants. He learned not to patronise Australians (at least not too obviously!) and eventually managed to divine the mysteries of the Australian sense of humour to the point at which he could put it to good use in his own columns. When, for example, the daughter of an Australian politician included Schubert's 'Die Forelle' in her recital, Neville's notice suggested that she 'had changed it to an Australian schnapper, a toughish fish in home waters'.

Neville had also joined a circle of friends in whose company he could enjoy himself. The manuscripts which would eventually become *Ten Composers* and *Autobiography* were 'on the stocks'. As far as his public were concerned, the comments that had once caused outrage and offence were now taken as examples of his peculiarly waspish wit, and most readers were happy to accept that he always wanted his notices to be readable and could not resist a well-turned phrase, even at the risk of causing offence. Muriel Cohen, who became one of his closest friends, recalls how she once challenged the accuracy of some of the statements in *Full Score*. 'Ah yes,' chuckled Neville, 'but they read well.'

For many Australians, it was 'Enjoyment of Music', the hour-long introduction to familiar pieces and personal favourites put out by A.B.C. every Sunday evening that represented Neville's seminal contribution to their musical awakening. These programmes brought him into contact with a wider and more diverse audience than he had previously enjoyed with the *Herald*, or the *Guardian* for that matter. Simplicity and directness were the key to their success. Every week Neville selected works he loved, played as much of them as time permitted, and then discussed their qualities. At the time, the response was extraordinary. When Neville recalled how, ten minutes after one programme, he had received a phone-call from a gentleman in Alice Springs who had been overcome with enthusiasm for Mahler's music, for once there wasn't a hint of exaggeration in his account. Other admirers of the programme wrote direct to the *Herald*:

Bouquet for Cardus

While making still another appeal for more good music, conveniently timed, I feel I must speak in appreciation of the great work the Commission has already done. Probably I am only one of many to whom its programmes of classical and other music – not to mention the celebrity and symphony concerts – have opened up a new world of interest and delight.

But perhaps the most enjoyable and helpful of all is the Neville Cardus session on Sunday night, and one hopes the Commission will see fit to continue it indefinitely. Mr Cardus's phrasing and diction are music itself, and his comments so graphic that one lives and moves for the time being in the scenes and situations associated with the music, and the composer becomes a living presence. Notable in this respect was Wagner's *Tristan and Isolde*, and Gustav Mahler's work of more recent performance.

As Mr Cardus himself says, repetition is necessary to the fullest enjoyment of such music, and we hope the Commission

will continue our education by letting us have it – if under the
tuition of Mr Cardus, so much the better.

Mrs I. Curtis
Bundaberg, Queensland

   To this day many Australians can vividly recall his discussions of
such wide-ranging topics as the last quartets of Beethoven, *The
Marriage of Figaro*, *Der Rosenkavalier*, Mahler's *Das Lied von der Erde*
and his 9th Symphony, Toscanini and Furtwängler. As an introduction to these broadcasts, Neville frequently wrote a piece in the
A.B.C. weekly journal about the performer or piece he was going to
feature that week. To complete his education of the Australian musical
imagination, every Wednesday afternoon around six he presented a
fifteen-minute illustrated talk for children. Again he was amazed by
the quality of the response. After receiving outraged protests at his
initial decision to pitch the talk at the level of Humperdinck's *Hansel
and Gretel* overture and Elgar's *Nursery Suite*, he was obliged
thereafter to include more demanding pieces by Bach and Schubert.

[II]

By 1943 Neville had fully regained the confidence and respect of
Sydney's musical community. The more discerning of his audience
valued in particular the distinction he made between long-term
substance and merely ephemeral notability, while the average
listener welcomed his clear, intelligible elucidation and direction.
Without compromising his emphasis on the need to raise standards
of awareness and performance, he succeeded in bringing a greater
sense of balance and humour to his notices, which made them
popular with literally hundreds who had little interest in music.
According to legend, even race-horse trainers at the early morning
gallops were often overheard laughing at something he had written.
When the occasion demanded, however, Neville could still deliver
thunderous broadsides or wounding lances. Visiting artists who had
looked to the inaccessibility and backwardness of Sydney to provide
easy money for second-rate performances were a favourite target.
One such incident was recalled in *Full Score*:

   A visiting pianist, Paul Schramm ('world-famous', of course, in
   war-time Sydney) gave concerts in proliferous plenty. 'His
   concerts,' I wrote, 'are extremely difficult to fix in time and

space. In future, on sleepless nights, I shall cease vainly counting sheep going through a gate; I shall count recitals by Schramm, and when I have counted fifty-seven, the chances are that I'll be jerked into acute awakeness, and find myself at a Schramm recital.'[3]

Nor had his earlier brushes with the musical establishment made him any less inclined to highlight the weakness of home-grown talent. The difference was that now his observations were (nearly always) accepted in the constructive spirit in which they had (for the most part) been intended. Sir Bernard Heinze, for example, the leading Australian conductor of his day, received both generous and harsh treatment at Neville's hand. Angus McLachlan recalled how he saw these two gentlemen lunching together shortly after Neville had savaged one of Heinze's concerts. When his next concert a few weeks later received a much more generous review, McLachlan rang Neville and said, 'I know now who paid for that lunch I saw you having with Bernard.' Though the remark was delivered in jest, in fact it was not the only time there was to be a suspicion that Neville might be bought.

Now that he had come to terms with Australians and their sense of humour, Neville went about the daily business of writing his notices and articles with renewed enthusiasm. Pulling no punches, he wrote of one unfortunate performance of Beethoven's 5th Symphony that had happened to take place the day of the Melbourne Cup: 'At the first fence the second horn fell; at Becher's Brook the first trumpet and third trombone fell. . . . Result: 1st – Second flute; 2nd – Double bassoon; 3rd – Conductor. Also ran – Beethoven. . . .' With this robust denunciation of mediocrity he thus encouraged fellow critics to give up being merely 'polite guests' writing puffs in exchange for hospitality received. On another occasion, delighted by a cartoon in the *Sydney Bulletin* which depicted two street musicians, one of them saying: 'Look out, Bill, and tune up. 'Ere's Neville Cardus coming,' he immediately wrote a short, semi-satirical column entitled 'Correspondence' poking fun at the music profession, himself included:

Correspondence

To Hiram Boodle, Concert Agent

I need hardly warn you that dates between 27 February and 6

March will be useless for my Sydney recital, as they clash with the Test match, and it is most important for me to get a notice from Neville Cardus. Nobody else's opinion counts for anything with me. He knows what he is talking about, and tells the truth, and shames the devil.

PRISCILLA GLOTTIS

To Miss Priscilla Glottis

Thank you for your letter enclosing 26 tickets for your recital in the Conservatorium on 8 March. But I am sorry I must decline your invitation to lunch before your recital. If after you have read my notice you are still inclined to take me to lunch, I shall be delighted to accept.

NEVILLE CARDUS

To Hiram Boodle

Dear Hiram: The cigars are magnificent. Where on earth did you manage to get them? I have not yet finished the case of White Horse you sent me when old Blankovsky gave his recent recital.

NEVILLE CARDUS

To Hyacinth Jinks

Darling Hyacinth: I am ashamed that I haven't written to you for weeks; not even had time to ring you up about your perfectly wonderful recital last June. But such memories always keep, and I shall never forget your perfectly wonderful singing of 'One Fine Day', from *Bohème*. You made me feel I would never dare to sing in public again, and that is why I have let so many months go by before choosing 8 March for my recital in Sydney.

I hope you weren't upset by what Cardus said about you. Nobody takes the slighest notice of him.

PRISCILLA

My dear Cardus: I quite understand that you can't come to lunch with me before the concert, and, of course, I'll look forward to meeting you afterwards. I need hardly say that I didn't invite you in any way to influence your opinion. I was so anxious for you to honour my recital with your presence. Every artiste in Australia has benefited by your experienced criticism.

PRISCILLA GLOTTIS

One or two extracts from the notice: '. . . Possibly the most celebrated soprano ever born in Prahan. . . . She was extremely fortunate in her accompanist. . . . At her next recital Miss Glottis will be wise to choose another hall (in Teheran for preference).'

To Hyacinth Jinks

Dearest Hyacinth: It was so sweet of you to send me the cutting from the *Herald* with your most caustic comments on Cardus. Not that I had even read his notice. I don't take the slightest notice of a word he says.

I think we all ought to get together and send a letter to the editor of the *Sydney Morning Herald* protesting that a common cricket reporter should be sent to serious concerts.

YOUR DEVOTED PRISCILLA

From Priscilla Glottis's announcement for her next concert, to be given in Alice Springs, December 1948:

PRISCILLA GLOTTIS

World-renowned Soprano
(Prague, Teheran, Lisbon)

'Unique in purity. . . . Italian bel canto. . . . La Scala . . . unsullied by Wagnerian Sprechgesang. . . .' (*The Sun*, Sydney)
'. . . most . . . celebrated . . . soprano . . .' (Neville Cardus, *S.M.H.*)

It was in 1942, having found that even her capacity for improvisation couldn't relieve the unremitting gloom of war-time Lancashire, that Edith announced her intention of joining Neville in Sydney. Having taken this decision, she descended upon an unsuspecting estate agent's clerk at Kendall Milnes, handed over a key and the instruction: 'Sell the house and everything in it except the grand piano and the records.' With that she departed, and the next thing Neville heard was a brief communication stating her estimated time of arrival in Sydney. In fact Edith stayed in England only long enough to pack a trunk of her less valuable bits and pieces and deposit it with Marjorie Robinson for safe-keeping, before catching a train to London. Shortly afterwards, equipped only with a couple of bulging suitcases and a painted Molotov Cocktail, she embarked on a 'terrible banana boat' called the *Port Alma* which duly took its place in a convoy destined for the Antipodes via the Cape of Good Hope.

The prospect of his wife's imminent arrival threw Neville into some disarray. For a start, her presence caused all sorts of practical problems. While more conventional couples might have been expected to live together in a suitably appointed apartment, this would never have suited the Carduses. Ever since his arrival in Sydney Neville had been living in a small, rented flat (35, West End) in Crick Avenue, about a mile from the centre of the city. Here he lived an immaculately tidy bachelor existence, washing his own clothes and ironing his bedspread every morning.

The fact that 35, West End looked out on to the back of an adjoining apartment block would have been enough to discourage most potential tenants, but for Neville it proved a blessing in disguise. With just 'a suggestion of Rushcutter's Bay shining through the afternoon fall', he succeeded in preparing the manuscript of *Ten Composers* and *Autobiography*. Every day he devoted the hours from ten until five to writing, at first with great difficulty and dislike, but later, as the practice became established, with growing enthusiasm. The problem was 'that I had so far been a journalist, a music critic, drawing my honey from flowers to be found everywhere. It was a difficult matter, then, to sit down before blank paper, pads of it, with – so to say – nowhere, or worse still, everywhere, to go.' After much suffering, 'one day revelation was vouchsafed. The great thing I discovered, was the devotion, the wooing of the Muse. . . . I realised that the Muse will not respond if you court her only in her bountiful hours.'[4]

The lesson, once learnt, remained with him for the rest of his life. West End was Neville's monastic cell. Here he found seclusion and sanctuary. Few were allowed access; Neville never entertained there, and indeed very little food was consumed on the premises. Sometimes he took a light breakfast before seeking the Muse, but more often he was to be seen walking up Macleay Street (a major thoroughfare) with a packet of cornflakes in his hand, a habit which gave rise to some concern until it was discovered that he was on his way to have breakfast at a restaurant which either did not stock cornflakes or else failed to serve the particular brand he favoured.

Clearly, 35, West End was not a suitable residence for Edith. Not only was there nowhere near enough room for the lady and her effects, but, not to put too fine a point on it, Neville couldn't have survived the intrusion for more than a week. He had reached that stage in his life when he found it difficult to tolerate the physical presence of others, even his wife, for more than a few hours at a time. Day-time solitude and evening company, requirements which would become more pressing as the years went by, were already essential to his peace of mind. Thus the first requirement was to find a separate apartment for his wife. Fortunately, by now Neville had made some useful acquaintances, and with the help of some judicious string-pulling a suitable flat was found at 7, Elizabeth Street, only a mile from West End. There remained the more pressing problem of how to prevent Edith from disturbing his established routine.

Neville's apprehensiveness about his wife's arrival illustrates one of the stranger aspects of his character. Despite his genuine affection for Edith, the fact remains that he could at times be less than charitable towards her. It was one thing for friends to describe Edith as a 'strong woman, looking a little like J. B. Priestley, with a Yorkshire face and a strong personality', but when her own husband referred to her in public as one 'of the ugliest women you ever saw, with thick glasses, a fringe and tennis socks', the world had suddenly become a harsh and graceless place. All that can be said about comments like these is that they were never premeditated – Neville was often a victim of his own loquaciousness – and that Edith would probably have just laughed them off.

The lifestyle which Neville was so concerned to protect was based on a circle of close friends. There was Muriel Cohen whom he had first met in 1936 when she was a pianist at the Usher's Hotel in Sydney. As was his wont, Neville had objected to the presence of live music in the dining-room. Hurt and angry, Muriel Cohen immediately moved from light music to her classical repertoire. The effect on Neville was amazing. Standing up, he came over to the piano and bowed before offering his congratulations, so starting a friendship which was to last until his death nearly forty years later.* When Neville returned to Australia in 1940, they met again by chance on Albury Station, this time without a musical accompaniment. Other members of this circle of friends were Elizabeth Ogilvie, confined to a wheelchair from childhood, but a brilliant conversationalist; Isobel Henchman, widow of a high court judge and a very influential figure in Sydney 'society'; Ignaz Friedman, whom Neville once described as 'nearly the last great seigneur of the piano'; and Paula Horn from the A.B.C., who typed a great deal of the manuscripts of his books, and to whom the chapter entitled 'Australian Years' in *Full Score* is dedicated. (Shortly after the birth of Paula's first child, Neville came to offer his congratulations. Peering over the side of the cot, he was overheard to mutter, 'There! His first view of the grotesque.')

It was typical of Neville's love of routine that his week was organised around a set rota of dinner engagements. On Monday he visited Betty Ogilvie; on Tuesday he went up to Vaucluse to take sherry with Friedman; Friday was Paula's turn, and on Saturday he always ate with Muriel Cohen and her family. Sundays were spent alone. It soon became evident to all his hosts that as well as knowing when he wished to see them, Neville also had very clear ideas about the sort of evening he wanted. For a start, the right people had to be invited. He usually preferred female company, partly because they were more attractive and partly because he found them to be better listeners. Musicians, on the other hand, were to be avoided unless they were willing to play or sing Neville's own waltz, 'Love Me, Love Me'. The general feeling was that this was not a very distinguished piece, though Neville was very attached to it.† One evening Muriel Cohen's guests included a particularly attractive actress. Sure enough, a little later in the evening Neville invited her to sing 'Love Me, Love Me'. Unfortunately he had reckoned without her voice: the evening ended prematurely and in some embarrassment.

Normally Saturday evenings followed a more predictable course: 'I used to play the piano,' Mrs Cohen recalled, 'and Neville and my

* In *Full Score*, Neville claimed that he had arranged for roses to be sent to her room, but Muriel Cohen's version of the episode makes no reference to floral tributes.

† Although both the tune and the words were Neville's, he had enlisted Muriel Cohen's assistance with the harmonic structure, a little-known fact which helps to explain her embarrassment when Neville insisted on having it played.

husband talked cricket until well into the night. My casserole was adequate and my husband always had good wines. Neville always had trouble with his dentures; he used to say that there were only two stages in life – before dentures and after dentures. So the meal was always a casserole.' Those who first met Neville on these occasions were often struck by his conversational style. 'He never produced a revealing line,' one old friend recalled. 'He never made you want to talk about his inner life – about what really made him tick. He talked and while you replied he would be thinking of the next clever thing to say.'

Neville should have know better than to imagine that Edith would cramp his style. Within a few days of her arrival it was clear that she intended carrying on exactly where she had left off two years before. Neville organised a luncheon in her honour at the Normandie Restaurant, one of Sydney's best. All his friends were invited. (It was rumoured that he even went so far as to arrange for some of her luggage to be misplaced in order that she would be obliged to buy a more suitable outfit.) The occasion was a great success, but it didn't lessen Edith's determination to create her own way of life, and so it proved. As in Manchester, the Carduses came together only at the margins of their worlds. At Edith's insistence, they always had dinner together on Tuesdays, but otherwise they went their own ways. It took Sydney's fashionable circles a while to get used to this arrangement and for weeks the gossip columns were full of references to the Carduses' comings and goings. Neville probably revelled in this new-found notoriety, but not so Edith. After one particularly scurrilous reference to her husband's habit of lunching with 'attractive blondes', she decided that enough was enough. Scandalmongering was bad enough, but inaccuracy was inexcusable. As she pointed out in a strongly worded letter to the editor of the rag involved, Neville was equally frequently to be seen at another restaurant with attractive brunettes.

Edith's life-style bore very little resemblance to her husband's. While Neville seldom invited visitors to West End, she was forever entertaining young musicians and painters at Elizabeth Street. She loved company, and was always willing to offer advice, counsel and guidance. Armed with her unique brand of enthusiasm, Edith soon became a local celebrity. Within a year, she was directing performances of *Doctor's Dilemma* and Mauriac's *Asmodeé*, and addressing a public meeting on the need for a community hotel in the King's

Cross area where 'men and women may drink in pleasant surroundings' and organise 'communal activities such as co-operative stores, hotels, clubs, musical and dramatic entertainments, playgrounds, etc.' In her speech, Edith drew attention to the fact that 'limitations involved in the liquor trade compared unfavourably with conditions overseas . . . the brewing interests in England provided high-class entertainment in many road-houses.' Her special interest in painting was recognised in invitations to open various exhibitions; on 13 October 1943, for example, she opened an exhibition of paintings by women artists at the MacQuarie Galleries in Bligh Street.

Reporting the event, the *Bulletin* noted: 'Mrs Neville Cardus, who, it is said, ran an art gallery of her own in London, made the introductory remarks dealing with the emergence of women from the back to the front benches in life. She had a wit of her own and finished on quite an unexpected note.' Sadly, for it would undoubtedly have made for interesting reading, the reporter omitted to recall the substance of Edith's eyebrow-raising finale. Whatever the secret, it only added to the demand for her services. By the end of 1944 she had addressed the Dorcas Society on the Subject of 'Women's Fashions in a Changing World', presented a lunchtime lecture at the Public Library on 'Repertory Theatre in Britain', spoken to the United Association of Women on the subject of 'Female Emancipation' (in the course of which she confessed that her earlier support for the suffrage movement in Lancashire 'had not been worth it'), and finally, to prove her versatility, given an illuminating address entitled 'A Layman looks At Ballet'.

After a while some of her versatility must have rubbed off on Neville, for by the end of 1943 he too was performing 'guest' functions at a range of unlikely events. At the opening of the Contemporary Art Exhibition he created more of a stir than most of the exhibits by beginning his speech by stating: 'Frankly, I don't know what contemporary art is. I have never painted anything in my life. . . . It is always wise to ask a music critic to open an art exhibition because he can't find many faults when he doesn't understand the finer points.'

[III]

On 17 February 1944, Neville wrote to the General Manager of John Fairfax and Sons Ltd., who owned the *Sydney Morning Herald*, on the subject of money:

35, West End
Crick Avenue
Sydney

Dear Mr Henderson,

You will remember that when we arranged terms for my work as music critic on the *S.M.H.* I suggested a lower figure than the one named by yourself. At that time concerts in Sydney were more or less restricted to the months March–October, hence I was usually idle from November to March.

It is different now; perhaps I have myself added to my trials and labours. There is no close season in Sydney music any more. Each week I must reserve my evenings for you. And the point of having a music critic who is a specialist is that he ear-marks his time for you. It is not only the actual concerts he covers, but also the fact that he is there when you want him. In the last few days, in the height of summer – and what a summer – I have attended four concerts in eight days. Next week a 'Russian Festival' begins – and then comes the usual autumn and winter season.

All of which, as no doubt you have suspected, is leading to a request that the *S.M.H.* reconsiders my fees. I can't really see how I'm going to devote so much time to you at seven guineas weekly, less taxes, much as I enjoy working for a paper that in so many ways recalls the happy days spent on the *Manchester Guardian*.

Kind regards,
Yours sincerely,
Neville Cardus

It was typical of Neville that he generally preferred to let money matters take care of themselves. Only when there was no real alternative (either because he was hard-up or Edith was pushing him) would he show more than a passing interest in salaries and fees and pensions and expenses and the like. In the main he was more than happy to leave everything in the hands of his employers and publishers, trusting to their integrity and respect for him. When everything was going well it was a happy arrangement, but there were times when Neville proved to be his own worst enemy. How many famous figures today would suggest that they worked for fees lower than those originally offered? Towards the end of his career, with the spectre of a pensionless retirement looming ever more threateningly, Neville came to regret not having capitalised on his reputation and ability more assiduously. Suddenly all those years with the *Guardian* seemed to count for little.

But in Sydney in 1944 these clouds had yet to gather. His letter to Henderson sought to convey not deep dissatisfaction but a feeling that it was time for changing circumstances to be recognised and acknowledged. The reasonableness of Neville's position was immediately accepted and eight days later his fees were duly increased to twelve guineas a week, a response which Neville later described as 'both adequate and encouraging'. The next months were amongst the happiest he spent in Australia. Both professionally and personally he felt secure and appreciated. Edith was with him and he had an established and devoted circle of friends. At this time, too, he began to feel that his efforts to raise standards of musical performance and appreciation were bearing fruit. Everywhere, it seemed, people were responding to his message. Just as exciting was the emergence of a generation of native-born artists: pianists of the calibre of Muriel Cohen, Joyce Greer, Eileen Ralph and Joyce Hutchinson; singers like Marjorie Lawrence. True to his principles, Neville was often critical of their performances but he never ceased to admire their talents.

The happiness of these months served only to accentuate the difficulty of the decision soon to confront him. In Europe, the war was drawing to a close; peace brought with it the prospect of a return to those idyllic conditions he had lost in 1939. London would soon offer both a higher quality and wider range of musical events than Sydney could hope to provide, but a return might also mean more work in less congenial surrounds. Could he ever expect to recover the eminence and influence that had once been his? On 4 June he wrote again to the management of the *S.M.H.*, this time setting out his hopes for the future.

35, West End
Crick Avenue

Dear Mr Henderson,

Mr Fairfax has asked me to discuss with you my future
position with the *Herald*. I have had attractive offers to return to
England; but for a number of reasons – not the least of all
concerned with my health and the fact that I have been very
happy writing for the *Herald* – I'd like to explore all possible
avenues likely to lead to a long sojourn here with a status not
less than, comparatively speaking, I would enjoy overseas.

To make our conversations easy, I herewith state the
ideas I have in mind:

(i) to write exclusively on music for the *Herald*. This means
concert-notices, and any special article or leader on music
which, in my opinion, a situation may warrant;
(ii) opportunity to visit Melbourne on important first appearances of artists here; or first performances of important
works;
(iii) right to broadcast Sunday music sessions for the A.B.C.;
(iv) annual salary £1,200.

As to cricket, my present intention is *not* to write on the game
again – at least not regularly. But this is a point we can discuss
with the others.

Would Thursday morning be a good time to call on
you?

Yours sincerely,
Neville Cardus

At first sight, Neville's conditions don't seem unreasonable,
bearing in mind the prize on offer. From the tone of his reply,
Henderson thought likewise, though his reply did identify one
potential stumbling block.

6 June 1945

Dear Mr Cardus,

I have your letter of 4 June and shall be pleased to
discuss with you the matters you raise. We would welcome your

appointment to the permanent staff, and the only point you mention which I feel is likely to present any obstacle is that of broadcasting. However, it will be best to discuss the question fully when I see you.

Yours sincerely,
General Manager
John Fairfax & Sons

The two men met on Thursday 7 July and immediately found themselves substantially in agreement on most points, including Neville's reluctance to write regularly on cricket. But as Henderson had anticipated, the major sticking point proved to be Neville's insistence on being allowed complete freedom to broadcast. After a long discussion, the *Herald* made alternative suggestions which Neville agreed to 'take away' and consider. Nearly a month later, he wrote again to Henderson:

35, West End
Crick Avenue
1 July 1945

Dear Mr Henderson,

After long and careful thought I have been obliged to decline for the time being the offer you made me the other day, a generous offer which I deeply appreciate. But I cannot bring myself to give up the freedom to broadcast a serious musical session on a national network. This is not, I need hardly assure you, a matter of money. On the contrary, by taking the course I have in view, I shall lose in income. The fact is that I enjoy giving these broadcasts; moreover I know they are contributing to the musical culture of Australia in a permanent way.

I suggest, then, that we should leave arrangements as they are at present. I am exclusively your music critic, and at your call for articles and advice in any matter on which you may wish to consult me. Once again, I wish to express my appreciation of the offer you have made me; I shall do my best to deserve the appreciative spirit that inspired it.

Yours sincerely,
Neville Cardus

The tone of this letter scarcely reflected the seriousness of the message it conveyed. Neville had (more or less) decided that his future no longer lay in Australia, though the last paragraph suggested that for the time being he was determined to keep as many options open as possible.

For a long while there were few obvious signs of this change of heart. Life continued exactly as before, writing notices and the occasional article for the *Herald*, and broadcasting for the A.B.C. All his spare time was devoted to completing the manuscript which was to become *Autobiography*. Bearing in mind the sensitivity of the venture, it was hardly surprising that he contemplated the end product with caution and more than a little trepidation. Without revealing his intentions, Neville had gone to great lengths to gauge the reactions of his closest friends to the work as it progressed. It was to Angus McLachlan that he turned for an assessment of the Australian public's likely reaction to the news of his illegitimacy. 'At that moment,' McLachlan recalled, 'one or other of us (I like to think it was myself) remarked, "Sydney people have been saying 'that bastard Cardus' for so long that they might as well have the satisfaction of knowing it's true." '

The first indication of what was afoot came in discussions with the *Herald* over the forthcoming M.C.C. tour. Evidently Neville had been persuaded to cover 'one last series', and plans were already in hand to sell his reports to the English press. On 31 May 1946 Henderson wrote to Neville setting out the terms of the agreement under which he would follow the fortunes of Hammond's party:

Dear Mr Cardus,

This will confirm the arrangement made between us, whereby you will cover the forthcoming Test cricket matches for us at a fee of £500, plus whatever receipts we may obtain from the English sales of your service.

We are trying to place it with *The Times* and the *Manchester Guardian* for £500 sterling, and we shall advise you in due course of the results of our efforts.

Yours sincerely,
John Fairfax & Sons

Neville's reply, almost by return of post, while still studiously courteous nevertheless showed signs of a sudden stiffening of purpose. Not only was he now aware of his market value, but he was also unwilling to settle for less.

> 35, West End
> Crick Avenue
> 2 June 1946

My dear Mr Henderson,

Thank you very much indeed for your letter. But apparently I misunderstood one part of our conversation of Friday. My idea was to aim at £1,000 sterling from England: £500 from *The Times* and £500 from the *Guardian*. If this amount seems excessive to you, the point might be made that I have in the past declined £1,000 to visit Australia to cover Test matches – with expenses thrown in, voyage etc. from September to March.

Anyhow, there's no harm in aiming reasonably high; and I do feel that £500 is not enough for Neville Cardus on the Tests in the two great newspapers of England.

> Yours sincerely,
> Neville Cardus

I'm pretty certain the Express would go as far as £1,000.

It was most unlike Neville to take so close an interest in money matters, but with his career now at the crossroads he clearly felt it was time to take a stand. It was in this determined mood that he wrote to his old friend, Rupert Hart-Davis, on 5 November:

> 35, West End
> Crick Avenue

My dear Rupert,

I have just heard from Dunn in Melbourne who has sent me your address. Yes – I shall (for the last time) write on the Test matches – for the *Sydney Morning Herald*, and in England for *The Times* and the *Manchester Guardian*.

I hope next April to return to London. Whether I shall remain depends on what London may have to offer me in music. I have been able to make a decent livelihood in Australia purely and solely in music criticism, and every Sunday, an hour's broadcast, illustrating some composer or composition. In no sense have I been expected to 'write' or 'talk down' to my public.

In England, apparently, no paper will pay £1,200 a year for music alone – they continue to harp on my cricket; and I have no intention of returning to day-to-day journalism.

As you will probably know, I have temporarily left Cape – not for any adverse reason. I merely wanted a change. I am giving my *Autobiography* to Collins; they sold 11,000 of my *Ten Composers* in Australia! I am thrilled to hear that you are going into publishing yourself. I wish you every success; and if ever I can be of help, please let me know.

> With greetings and
> happy memories,
> Yours always,
> Neville Cardus

P.S. By the way, does Grant Richards still live at Henley? Give him my love if ever you see him. I have tried to do him justice in my Autobiography.

When, just over a month later, Neville wrote again to Hart-Davis, it was to thank him for offering to read the proofs of *Autobiography*, parts of which he felt were 'not so bad', and to reflect on the inadequacies of the M.C.C. team. Having decided to return to England, Neville could hardly wait to set sail!

> 35, West End
> Crick Avenue
> 7 December 1946

My dear Rupert,

I was delighted to hear from you and to read that you are as happy as anybody can be in this curious world. . . . It is tremendously kind of you to offer to read the proofs of my

Autobiography, and gladly I'll take advantage of your generosity. I have asked Collins to send you a copy. The book was finished more than a year ago and I haven't looked at it since. Parts of it are not so bad.

The Brisbane Test was full of misfortune for us. But the English team is much too weak in bowling, and not particularly accurate in the field. We *should* have the advantage in batting, though I still fear Bradman. My hopes rest on Wright if only he will bowl slow medium. But it will be difficult to win two games out of four and with the Australians free to connive after a draw, under the new time-limit procedure.

Write again soon – in fact immediately. And count the days for me between now and April.

Affectionately and always,
Neville

Much though he admired and enjoyed *Autobiography*, Hart-Davis found the task of checking its proofs to be much more demanding than he'd anticipated. In part the fault lay with the poor quality of the galleys he received from Collins, but not all the mistakes were the fault of the compositors. Neville's penchant for the vivid phrase often led him to employ words which he either didn't fully understand or else misspelt. When Neville wrote to Hart-Davis for the last time before embarking for England, it was to recognise the latter's contribution to the success of the book. Again the mood of the letter is one of barely suppressed excitement at the prospect of coming back to England, though at the same time it is clear that he was coming under great pressure to delay his departure:

35, West End
Crick Avenue
14 March 1947

My dear Rupert,

Your letter of 4 March has made me very happy, first because of your generous praise of the book, but not less for the devoted way you have gone through the proofs. This is one of those things that cannot be reckoned in thanks by word of pen. You have removed loads of anxiety from my head. The page-proofs sent out to me contained incalculable errors, misprints and so on. And no writer is able to read his own proofs; he becomes afflicted with blind spots. I would never have spotted 'beneath the pale'. As for 'caravanserai', I can only plead, like Dr Johnson, 'pure ignorance'. I am also told that on page 27 'Zuave' should read 'Zouave'. . . . Feebly but fervently I say 'Thank you, Rupert, thank you.' My regret is that I am not publishing it with you. . . .

I had booked to return to London by the *Orion* sailing from here on 12 April, but severe pressure is being put on me to stay for at least half of the new music season. I am definitely booked to return on 26 July; but if a decent opportunity occurs before then, I'll take it.

I hope you are all weathering the terrific blizzards. Here we are at the moment gasping for breath in awful airless heat and humidity. Bless you.

My love to you and to all,
Neville

Though in the event he managed to leave in early June, the last months of Neville's domicile passed unbearably slowly. Sensing this mood, the *Herald* sought only to delay the inevitable. Apart from the odd query about taxes, no correspondence passed between the paper and its music critic; nothing more was said of the earlier proposals. Everyone seemed to take it for granted that Neville would be back before long, the only question was 'when?' Local gossip columnist 'Granny' summed up the mood when he wrote:

Neville Cardus has put his name down on the passenger list of the 'Orion', due to leave for England next month.

He may not go by that ship. He may not go at all – but if he does, it will merely be for a few months' holiday. Cardus has grown too fond of Australia to leave it for good.

As an oracle 'Granny' was no match for his Delphic predecessor. Neville duly returned to England that summer, and thereafter his visits to Australia were never more than working holidays.

5
Rediscovery

*'Leaf after golden leaf
drops from the tall acacia.
The summer smiles astonished and weary,
into the garden's dying dream.'*[1]

[I]

Neville was fifty-eight when he returned to England in the late spring of 1947. He had been away for more than seven years, and in that time a war had been fought and won. Manchester and London, the cities he knew best, now bore all the signs of the struggle. Buildings he had once treasured now lay devastated; the Free Trade Hall, where he had attended his first concert, had been engulfed in a fire blitz on the night of 22 December 1940 and left with only its outer walls standing; the Queen's Hall had been destroyed on 11 May 1941. Cricket had generally fared rather better. Though bombs had fallen all around, Lord's itself had suffered only minor indignities: an incendiary bomb had caused a fire in the Secretary's House, the Grand Stand and on the roof of the Pavilion, while the cables of an errant barrage balloon had had the temerity to dislodge Father Time; otherwise nothing had changed. In a dusty vault somewhere in England 'W.G.' had chaffed and fretted and fumed, but had lived to re-occupy his plinth overlooking the sacred turf.

Others had been less fortunate. Hedley Verity, Maurice Turnbull and Kenneth Farnes, each of whom had at some time fired 'Cricketer's' imagination had all been killed in action. One of Neville's boyhood heroes, A. C. MacLaren, had died in November 1944; W. P. Crozier, 'Cricketer's' mentor, had published his last short leader on April 14 1944, and died two days later. James Agate had died on the very evening of Neville's return.

Elsewhere the prospects awaiting Neville on his return were less depressing. On arrival, he went directly to the National Liberal Club, where he found Frank, the head porter, and a bundle of mail. (Only the main staircase was missing, a fault that post-war recovery would duly rectify.) Accommodation was the first problem. Neville never really had too much time for 'homes'; in fact he rather despised the 'Englishman and his castle' mentality, smacking as it did of a blinkered insularity which denied the possibility that the one redeeming feature of humanity might be its infinite variety. Apart from Edith, who was still in Sydney and in any case well capable of looking after herself, and his mother, who was presumably the subject of other arrangements, he had no one to house, to rear, to feed or to protect. He never looked upon a home as a place to entertain; restaurants and clubs were much better equipped in his view to satisfy this need, and they also offered at least the prospect of conversation. What he most needed was a base, a professional address and a sanctuary to which he could retreat in search of peace and solitude – states of mind which he had yet to equate with loneliness. The National Liberal Club, which he already knew and enjoyed, was the ideal solution and it became his 'home' for nearly twenty years.

At first sight, the world he had returned to 'was a place of pathetically visible war wounds, dismantled buildings and persistent rationing . . . [of] obviously undernourished girls and youths'. All this was a far cry from the healthy, unscarred existence he had left in Sydney. Worse still, London seemed to be lapsing into 'the provincialism' of down-under. The privileges of pre-war London which he had so much enjoyed – the theatre, the concerts, the operas, international artists by the score – all these seemed at first sight to have disappeared. In their place he found ugliness and austerity. Those who had lived through the years of blitz and bombs were thankful to be alive, and happy that the cost of victory had not been still higher, but this was not a reaction Neville could share. At this moment he found himself an outsider; it was not his moment of triumph. 'My exile in Australia had disqualified me. I could not share the privilege and honour of being one of the immortal islanded multitude that, through darkness and despair and hell, had done its best to salvage, if only temporarily, a civilised way of life.'[2]

Happily this feeling of exclusion soon passed. Once he had settled down and rediscovered his bearings, the pleasures of being home quickly rekindled his optimism. The more he went out, the more he found that England was not in such desperate straits as he had feared. The summer of 1947 found Compton and Edrich indulging in an orgy of run-getting the like of which had never been even approached before or since. In Compton, Neville found a 'symbol of peaceful summer rejuvenation'. 'The London crowds at Lord's,' he wrote, 'the ground packed at noon, identified their war-weary souls with the image of happy, recuperative youth.' And when, late one afternoon at Lord's, a fellow spectator from East London informed him, in no uncertain terms, that 'Milton was a bloody great poet', Neville's joy was boundless.

Refreshed in mind and spirit, he began to think about his own future. Music was one source of hope. If Hammond's tour of 1946–7 had left nobody in any doubt about the weakness of English cricket, the country's musical condition was surprisingly healthy. In the face of war, danger, damage and death, more and more had sought solace, comfort and entertainment in music. Malcolm Sargent's contributions towards satisfying this new demand had been widely and gratefully acknowledged, but in addition Adrian Boult had stayed to continue his work with the BBC Symphony Orchestra, the Promenade tradition had been maintained, and countless other artists had gone on performing wherever and whenever they could. Both during and immediately after the war, suitable venues for concerts, operas and recitals were hard to come by, but there was no shortage of performers. The arrival of peace in 1945 found London with three major orchestras – the L.S.O., L.P.O., and the BBC Symphony; and within the next eighteen months two more were to be founded. In late 1945, Walter Legge founded the Philharmonia, and the following year Sir Thomas Beecham formed his second orchestra, the Royal Philharmonic. Nor was this recrudescence of musical activity confined to the capital. Edinburgh staged its first International Festival in 1947, and Leeds, Harrogate and Cheltenham had similar, if less ambitious, plans. But of all the changes that awaited him, it was the Manchester 'revolution' that most intrigued and excited Neville. As long ago as 1926, Sam Langford had drawn the attention of M.G. readers to the promise of John Barbirolli. After hearing 'Giovanni Battista', as Barbirolli had been christened and was known to his friends, conduct a performance of *Madam Butterfly*, he had written: 'What Mr Barbirolli may do with other masters remains to be seen. In Puccini at least he is an absolute master.' Neville's deputy and successor, Granville Hill, was similarly fulsome in his praise of a concert Barbirolli gave in Manchester in 1933. 'After the Purcell suite', he had written, 'the conducting became greatly broadened and the two symphonies [Mozart 40 and Franck] were matched by an interpretation that was as compelling in its range as in its intensity of feeling.' Though, for one reason or another, Neville's early impressions of Barbirolli were not committed to print, there is no doubt that he had also held the young conductor's abilities in the highest regard. But from 1936, when he had moved to New York as Toscanini's successor, English audiences had heard little of Barbirolli.

Meanwhile the Hallé had continued to slip further from the peaks of excellence it had occupied under Richter. Without a permanent conductor and beset by financial difficulties, it had floundered from crisis to crisis, at every turn losing more self-respect and public admiration. By 1939, the once-mighty ensemble was in danger of becoming little more than a provincial hack-band, capable of occasional excellence but generally content to stagnate in 'the appallingly limited rut into which they had increasingly become fixed since Harty's day.'³ In the event, it was to take a world war to revitalise both the players and their administrators. Contrary to Neville's expectations, public interest in music had flourished after 1939. New audiences listened to music rarely played in peace time; the Royal Philharmonic Society now even included English music in their programme. During the darkest hours of 1942 the Hallé, 'which in peace time would have been scattered to the winds of seaside promenades', found itself confronting the busiest summer in its history. 'In three weeks of May 1942 it played to 40,000 people. The next month it visited London for the first time since Harty's day and its two concerts attracted 10,000 people to the Royal Albert Hall.'⁴

Neville of course missed all these occasions, just as he missed an invitation to write new concert programme notes for the Hallé when a paper shortage rendered Newman's lengthy original set unusable. Encouraged by their orchestra's unexpected popularity, but at the same time constrained by the terms of their 1934 pact with the BBC, the Hallé committee resolved to grasp the nettle they had for so long avoided. On 25 January 1943, a telegram was sent to Barbirolli asking whether he would be interested in becoming the Hallé's permanent conductor. After extended negotiations and a misunderstanding about his American 'call-up' status, Barbirolli's appointment was confirmed on 19 April. 'Now the great adventure began,'

Michael Kennedy wrote. 'Henceforward only a third of the orchestra's annual schedule would take place in Manchester.'[5]

The first step involved little less than a total rebuilding programme. When Barbirolli arrived in Manchester on 2 June 1943 he was immediately faced with the task of recruiting and training a virtually new orchestra in a month. Yet after the final rehearsal for the Hallé's first concert under their new conductor, the *Yorkshire Post* commented: 'There can be no doubt that a miracle has been achieved.' Barbirolli's first concert in Manchester took place on 15 August before an audience of 6,000 at Belle Vue. Hill's notice the following morning speaks for itself:

> The orchestra playing was indeed finer than any we have heard in Manchester for many years . . . the period during which the orchestra might claim indulgence because its members have not been playing together long enough will be passed very much sooner than expected. . . . Mr Barbirolli conducted superbly, his qualities of leadership impressing in equal degree players and audience.[6]

Twelve thousand miles away, Neville had kept fully abreast of these dramatic developments. The pseudonym 'N.C.' may have been abandoned for ever, but Neville's emotional attachment to the orchestra that had first awakened his musical imagination never faltered. After the successful inauguration of the Barbirolli era, the Hallé committee had turned its attention to the question of how to secure the orchestra's future. As always, money was at the root of the problem. Ever since anyone could remember, the Hallé's finances had been at best unpredictable; now rising costs, a larger complement of players and a more ambitious concert programme threatened to render the position untenable.

Whereas other regional centres – Birmingham and Liverpool, for example – had taken the view that their orchestras were a civic amenity and hence worthy of subsidy, Manchester and the Hallé had never been able to reach such an agreement. The City Council had never made a habit of handing out large grants or subsidies to an institution which some of its members saw as catering basically for only a small and relatively privileged section of the local community. Short-sighted, narrow-minded, parsimonious? Maybe, but then it should also be remembered that the Hallé was not a *municipal* orchestra, and its Committee had always fiercely resisted any challenge to its historic independence.

Neville's attitude had never been in question; in his eyes the Council's unwillingness to subsidise one of Manchester's greatest adornments was just another example of their general philistinism. Mindful perhaps that the protracted debate was about to enter yet another stage, Neville had used the first issue of the *Hallé* in August 1946 as an opportunity to weigh in with another diatribe on municipal meanness. Noting that Sydney had recently given £30,000 to its orchestra, he asked: 'What is Manchester doing to deserve this great Hallé Orchestra? What is the city doing to guarantee continuance of these rare delights?' The attack may have had some effect, for, almost exactly as Neville returned to London, the Manchester City Council announced that the Hallé had been voted grants and guarantees to the value of £15,000.

The Hallé and their new conductor; the new Edinburgh Festival; Compton and Edrich in full swing; Gielgud, Peggy Ashcroft and Edith Evans in the West End. With so many distractions at hand, Neville could have been forgiven for forgetting that the main purposes of this first post-war visit were to be present at the publication of *Autobiography* and, with half an eye to the future, to look out for likely sources of employment if (or when) he decided to return to England for good. The *Guardian* had nothing to offer; 'N.C.' had been replaced by 'Grannie' Hill, and Neville was determined that 'Cricketer' should not be resurrected. Elsewhere there were a few vague possibilities but nothing by way of firm offers. Not that Neville was at all perturbed: for the time being he was more concerned with rediscovering London and looking up old friends. Whilst preparations were going ahead for the publication of *Autobiography*, he took the opportunity to canvas the idea of an 'omnibus' edition of his pre-war notices and reports. First reactions to the proposal were very encouraging. On 26 July he wrote to his old friend Rupert Hart-Davis:

> National Liberal Club
> Whitehall Place SW1

My dear Rupert,

Nothing would give me warmer pleasure than to know that you would soon be publishing an Omnibus book of my stuff. And I don't see why the thing shouldn't be done if we use a little diplomacy with Cape and Collins! Let's talk it over without loss of time.

Love always,
Neville

It was typical of Neville's naivety that he never foresaw the possibility that the two claimants on his literary output might not respond to 'a little diplomacy'. Collins were to prove particularly difficult, perhaps because they already had an option on a second volume of his autobiography. But by the time he next wrote to Hart-Davis, in early autumn, this ingenuous optimism had given way to a mood of anger and frustration. Nothing had been finalised and now he had been recalled to Sydney to help the Australian publication of *Autobiography*: suddenly the visit to London seemed to have been a waste of time.

National Liberal Club

My dear Rupert,

God forgive me – God forgive us.
We've wasted ourselves. I am suddenly summoned back to Sydney. I leave on Sunday. But I'm returning in April – for good.
Nothing has been done about the cricket book. Collins wants them, Cape wants them. I'm sick of all the negotiations. Write to my Sydney address. . . .

Bless you,
Ever,
Neville

[II]

Back in Australia, word soon got out that Neville Cardus was on his way. For one newspaper, his arrival was seen as a challenge: 'We'll have to start brushing up our music again,' it announced, 'Neville Cardus will be back with us in a few weeks.' Others contemplated his return with greater equanimity:

Many 'fans' will welcome the announcement that Neville

Cardus is to resume his 'Enjoyment of Music' session on Sundays. . . . Mr Cardus means to concentrate on many neglected works, and performances by the best artists, particularly those who have been in Australia. He will also deal with chamber music. Tchaikovsky's Trio in A Minor is listed for his first programme.

Very few of Neville's friends and admirers had any idea that he had already decided to sever his connections with Australia as soon as decently possible. Even those who were aware of his intentions tended to take everything Neville said with a pinch of salt. 'After all,' one friend noted, 'when in Australia he longs to be in London, and when in London he wishes he could be back in Australia.' When the truth finally emerged, the reaction was a combination of sadness and disbelief. No one really believed that, sooner or later, he wouldn't change his mind. But in the first months of 1948, Neville himself had doubts about his feelings towards Australia and Australians. Despite the success of *Autobiography* 'down under', he couldn't wait to get back to England. It was in this mood that he wrote to Rupert Hart-Davis on 6 March:

> Hotel Windsor
> Melbourne

My dear Rupert,

> Greetings – and auf wiedersehen! God, I shall be glad to get back, and to hear intelligent voices again! Meet me as soon as you possibly can, after April 23. . . . I hope you've wintered well. I am absolutely cured and ready for work! Most of all, I am aching for good talk and plenty of laughter with you.

> Ever,
> Neville

The chance to return to England came in the form of an invitation from several English papers to cover the 1948 Test series. News of his imminent departure was conveyed to the Australian public in a small article by 'Jim MacDougall' in the *Morning Herald*:

Neville Cardus (my double) is going back to England again in March to do the Tests.

He got a cable at the weekend from Lord Beaverbrook, offering him fifty guineas a week (and expenses) to write for the *Sunday Express*.

Neville had to turn it down because he was already tied up with London's *Sunday Times*.

Needing no second bidding, Neville hastily booked a passage on the *Orion*, and found to his surprise and pleasure that he would be travelling in the company of Bradman and the rest of the Australian party. When the ship docked on 23 April Neville went directly to the National Liberal Club. For the first time in months he felt genuinely happy. The long sea passage had proved mentally and physically envigorating; now he was back in England, surrounded by the company he most respected and enjoyed, close to his publishers (if only they could be persuaded to fit in with his plans), and with the prospect of a full summer of cricket, music and good living set out before him. Suddenly he felt that it was only a matter of time before his life slipped back into its idyllic pre-war routine.

Then, just as suddenly, everything started to go wrong. Soon he began to realise that seven years away from home had left him with dangerously inflated expectations of the 'old country'. Though he had spent the previous summer in England, for most of the time he had been too preoccupied with his own world to appreciate the full effects of war. He was taken aback by a city and a country in which food and clothes were still rationed and fuel was at a premium. But more than anything else it was the difficulties Neville encountered in finding suitable work that brought him face-to-face with the realities of post-war austerity. Neville had returned to England with the firm intention of devoting the whole of his energies and resources to music. Cricket would be allowed to occupy his pen only 'as an occasional holiday from music'. Admirable though these intentions may have been in theory, in reality they were simply impractical. It was typical of Neville that he had given little thought to the possibility that things might not work out as he had planned. For the next few months he was to be the victim of his own naivety.

At about the same time as the *Sunday Times* had asked Neville to cover the 'Ashes' series, word had also got out that the same paper's principal music critic was confidently expected to use the occasion of his eightieth birthday to announce his retirement. Neville's version of the story was that he had been given to understand, privately but unambiguously, that the post would be his. As was his wont, Neville found the greatest difficulty in keeping the arrangement a secret, and before long what had started life as a tentative suggestion had become a foregone conclusion. In Sydney, newspapers carried the news under the headline: 'Big plum for Cardus.'

> Neville Cardus, who keeps travelling backward and forward between England and Australia with something of the air of an angular metronome, will soon make England his permanent home. He'll take over the job of one of the most distinguished music critics in the world – Ernest Newman, of the *Sunday Times*. Before he returns for good, Mr Cardus will do seven farewell broadcasts on music for the A.B.C.

With the benefit of hindsight, it seems more than likely that the *Sunday Times* had dangled the carrot of music criticism as an added inducement to Neville to accept their cricket reporting proposal. Whatever the case, only Neville could have believed that the incumbent music critic – none other than his old sparring partner, Ernest Newman – would take kindly to the news that Cardus of all people was to succeed him! Once again, Neville's ingenuousness was to cost him dear. In *Full Score*, he recounted how

> Newman, of course, did not abdicate, so when the 1948 season was ended I was left without serious occupation in music criticism. The *Sunday Times* was prepared to continue to pay me a generous salary, but I was remarkably switched to the now defunct *Sunday Chronicle* as a weekly columnist. I suggested to Hadley that, as Newman did not attend concerts regularly, I might be graciously allowed to have some space in the *Sunday Times* every week to cover the events not covered by Newman. I then received a letter from Hadley informing me that Newman had written to him, saying that he had heard of a rumour going around to the effect that he was about to retire and to be replaced by a person 'now engaged on the staff of the *Sunday Times*'. Obviously the 'rumour' had reference to myself so to quieten anxieties in my revered Ernest's mind, I sent in my resignation to Hadley.

It is a measure of the extent to which Neville was aggrieved by this incident that over twenty years later his narrative still carried a trace of bitterness. But worse was to follow. As soon as word spread around Fleet Street that Neville was still 'on the market', others moved in to snap up his services. Within a few weeks, he had been engaged 'at a colossal salary' by Lord Beaverbrook as music critic of the *Evening Standard*. Neville had the gravest reservations about the appointment from the start; in *Full Score* he tells how he argued with Beaverbrook that the *Evening Standard* 'would find my way of writing about music, and my profusion of words every day rather an embarrassment'. Whether Beaverbrook could not be denied, or whether Neville chose to soft-pedal his reservations, the new partnership was soon being advertised:

NEVILLE CARDUS ON MONDAY

Neville Cardus, the great descriptive reporter, has joined the staff of the *Evening Standard*. In future he will write regularly and exclusively for this newspaper.

Cardus is the foremost music critic in this country. Now he is to write about music for the *Evening Standard*. He will take the whole music world as his province; he will write with complete freedom about music and musicians, concerts, composers, orchestras and performers.

His first article will appear in the *Evening Standard* on MONDAY.

It proved to be a short-lived attachment. 'Complete freedom' in Neville's language meant returning to those halcyon pre-war days when he could write a full column in anticipation of a great event, one about the event itself and one on its significance. The *Standard*'s sub-editor had different views. With neither party prepared to compromise, Neville's resignation was inevitable. Though he could not have realised it at the time, this episode was a foretaste of the running battles with sub-editors which were to blight his final years as a journalist. The trouble was that he never fully came to terms with the post-war conditions under which newspapers traded and journalists worked; he could never accept that 'lack of space' was a sufficient reason for depriving readers of the benefits of his particular insight into music. Nor could he bring himself to heed Beaverbrook's advice: 'Never resign: wait to be sacked.' In Edith's absence, there was something in Neville's character which led him to issue resignation threats almost at the drop of a hat. 'Neville,' one of his closest friends recalled, 'was always resigning.'

Coming so soon after the *Sunday Times* débâcle, this fresh disappointment left Neville a chastened man. Nothing, it seemed, had worked out as he had anticipated. Instead of optimism, promise and inspiration, he had found austerity; instead of making a triumphant re-entry into the scene of past triumphs, he had faced difficulties and obstacles at every turn. The one consolation was that receipts from sales of *Autobiography* meant that for the time being he had no financial worries, though, as he told Hart-Davis, future prospects were much less rosy:

> 73, Lyall Mews West
> London SW1
> 4 October 1948

My dear Rupert,

   The Essential book is born to sorrow. . . . Collins won't budge, won't give a chapter. And Longmans are bringing out a new edition of *Cricket*. Let us let the thing perish.

> Ever,
> Neville

Thus it was in a mood of frustration and anger that Neville returned to Australia at the end of 1948. Just before leaving, he told an old friend that he had been wrong about Sydney; at least there he could be assured of an appreciative audience for his music criticisms. Despite all his previous reservations, he was now resolved to settle in Australia. But barely a month after docking in Sydney, he had changed his mind again. 'I am not happy here,' he told Hart-Davis, 'The spell – whatever it was – is broken. It is a crude place, God wot. We'll meet again at Lord's, soon, very soon.' Earlier in the same letter, in the course of setting out his reactions to an Introduction which Hart-Davis had prepared for the anticipated *Essential Neville Cardus*, Neville revealed a little of his self-consciousness. Notwithstanding all the other problems on his mind, he was concerned about being described as 'small'.

34, West End
Crick Avenue
5 January 1949

My dear Rupert,

I am more than satisfied and pleased with your
introduction to the 'Essential' – you almost persuade me that it
has been a labour of love. You have 'gone into me' very cleverly
and sympathetically, and as a piece of writing and craftsman-
ship the whole introduction is first class.

May I suggest one or two alterations or emendations –
I'd like you to omit in the first paragraph from 'All that Neville
ever learnt' to 'in an orchestra' . . . the last sentence in the
paragraph in fact. After all, we have had this revelation in the
Autobiography, and I don't wish it to be overdone.

Section V, first sentence: 'Small'? Surely you wouldn't
call me 'Small'. . . . Insubstantial, if you like!

With the 'spell' broken, it was only a matter of time before Neville
began to plan his return to England. He was now certain that
Australia was not the answer to his problems; at least in London he
would listen to good music, even if no one wanted to read his
notices! In the past, the major obstacle to leaving Australia for good
had been Edith's wish to stay. Six months apart was as much as their
flexible partnership could tolerate. But in 1949 this last barrier was
removed. Finding the heat and humidity too much even for her
considerable reserves of stamina, Edith decided that the time had
come to return home. Once the dye had been cast, the necessary
arrangements were made without further delay. Moving Edith and
her extensive luggage was a substantial operation, but a passage was
booked on the *Orcades* sailing on 19 June. The next problem was to
find somewhere for her to live in England. With his initial inquiries
meeting with no success at all, Neville was beginning to despair
when an old friend, Harold Holt, told him of a basement flat in
Bickenhall Mansions, just off Baker Street, which was about to fall
vacant. It was the perfect answer, and again arrangements were
made forthwith.

As the winding-up of his affairs in Australia was well-advanced,
Neville was able to leave in mid-April. Edith, however, was not to be
rushed and followed at her own pace. The news of her departure
had been received by the Sydney *cognoscenti* with genuine sadness,

and several farewell parties were held in her honour. The last of these took place at the Vaucluse home of Neville's old friend, Betty Ogilvie, just two days before the *Orcades* sailed.

As always, the prospect of England filled Neville with excitement. Though he had no job to go to, there were any number of minor matters to be settled. Publishers, for example, were causing problems again and needed firm handling. Unfortunately, Neville was quite incapable of applying himself to detail. In business as in writing his mind worked in broad brushstrokes. If he, Neville Cardus, wanted his own work to be published, and Rupert Hart-Davis wanted to publish it, what could be simpler? What if Jonathan Cape or Billy Collins or anyone else had other plans? They were his works, after all. In fact the immediate post-war years saw the publication of several Cardus books. As well as four impressions of *Ten Composers* (Jonathan Cape), and the publication and three reprints of *Autobiography* (Collins), Cape also brought out Hart-Davis's *The Essential Neville Cardus* while Hart-Davis himself brought out new editions of *Days in the Sun*, *The Summer Game*, *Good Days* and *Australian Summer*. But these successes were not uppermost in Neville's mind in the summer of 1949. Instead, his thoughts continually turned to the petty wrangling that inevitably preceded each new publication, and which seemed about to break out again.

Collins had asked him for another volume of autobiography, a request he had been more than happy to accept. The manuscript had been completed, but now a disagreement had arisen over the title of the new book. Equally typical of Neville was the fact that, within a few days, half Sydney seemed to be aware of his difficulties. One Sydney paper carried the following notice:

Neville Cardus and his publishers cannot see eye to eye about the choice of a title for the second volume of his autobiography. His own suggestion, *Remembered Pleasures*, meets with the publishers' opposition as they fear it may mislead readers to expect a series of essays. Their counter proposal, *Second Innings*, strikes a slightly discordant note in Cardus's ears. Anyway Cardus is off to England and doubtless the argument will have a harmonious conclusion.

Whether Neville viewed the prospect of his forthcoming meeting with his publishers in St James's Place with such equanimity is very doubtful indeed. While he loved conversation and discussion, detailed business discussions and haggling over contracts were not his forte. If there was no way of avoiding an argument, he usually preferred to conduct proceedings through the more detached medium of the letter. Only after the event did he sometimes come to regret not having fought his corner more vigorously. It was thus no surprise that when his second autobiographical volume came out in 1950, it bore the title *Second Innings*.

Once back in England, Neville found to his surprise and relief that many of his fears had been misplaced. Indeed, publishers apart, his fortunes seemed to have taken a distinct turn for the better. The immediate problem – accommodation for Edith – had been solved thanks to Harold Holt's timely suggestion. 112, Bickenhall Mansions proved to be near enough to the National Liberal Club in Whitehall Place to allow him to call in regularly and large enough to meet even Edith's insatiable demand for space. The one aspect of Edith's character that continually amazed and slightly irritated her impeccably tidy husband was her capacity for hoarding. At first sight, the flat looked as though nothing had been thrown away for years. Paints, brushes and canvases (many used several times) competed for space with all manner of bric-à-brac. When she let slip that there were several more packing cases in Manchester waiting to be collected, Neville decided that 'enough was enough'. 'I wouldn't be seen dead with them,' he was heard to mutter, and the offending objects were discreetly mislaid. If Edith ever noticed their disappearance she said nothing, doubtless reassured by the knowledge that the losses had already been replaced.

The success of *Autobiography* had done much to revive Neville's spirits. Encouraged by the critics, the romantic theme, set out in rich, colourful prose, had caught the imagination of a war-ravaged public. One congratulatory letter had given him special pleasure. Writing from his home in Wiltshire, Siegfried Sassoon was fulsome in his praise for the book:

> Heytesbury House
> Wiltshire

Dear Cardus,

     There are several reasons why I should write to you about your *Autobiography*, which I have been reading with the fullest enjoyment. One is that I *want* to! Another is that, having been born in 1886, you cover my period of human experience. Utterly different though our early environment and upbringing were, I have shared many of your enthusiasms and admirations – notably in cricket history. So you must bear with me awhile when I tell you that, fifty years ago, I watched MacLaren (in that I.Z. bordered sweater) at Canterbury – he made 244 – and Shrewsbury (in '98) – 77 not out wearing a pale pink shirt. MacLaren appealed to me as he did to you – something god-like about him and the genius of his batsmanship . . . the thought of his later years is saddening – (the Test match incident you describe is so moving – almost tragic). I agree with you – as in most things – about the disappearance of character from the players. How flavourless their personalities have become, in most counties! – amateurs and pros alike (and alike they are now). An old county cricketer once told me a story which may amuse you. W. H. Patterson (a great Kent batsman in my boyhood), arriving at Lord's, encountered Tom Wass and said, 'Good morning, Wass, and how are you, and how is Mrs Wass?' Answer. 'And what the bloody hell's Mrs Wass to you?' Where are our Wasses and Lockwoods and Brearleys now? By the way, after reading your Woolley pages, sleuthlike, I looked the match up, and deduced that the account (given you by Brearley?) had improved in the telling. I could read your cricket reminiscences forever. But there is so much of you – as Stevenson said of Meredith – you illuminate all your subjects – music most, of course – and the *writing* in your first part, makes me, as one autobiographer to another, glow with satisfaction. . . .

    I don't suppose you are ever likely to be near here – (Bath is only 22 miles away). But if you are, it would be nice to have a talk; and my cricket ground and village team are a refreshing experience on a fine Saturday afternoon. (*Natural* county cricket, quite unselfconscious in spite of my presiding presence.) You are busy, and I am idle and solitary. So don't irk yourself to reply lengthily to this tribute. The humanity of your book has warmed my heart and nourished my mind.

Yours sincerely,
Siegfried Sassoon

Unlike Sassoon, the majority of readers never dreamt of questioning the absolute accuracy of the narrative; those who did, generally found themselves confronted with the deadest of dead bats. After one review had called attention to one or two apparent inaccuracies, Neville wrote to Rupert Hart-Davis: 'But frankly, Rupert, I don't think a rejoinder is called for; the review is good and generous on the whole. A difference of opinion about what constituted a slum in the reign of Queen Victoria, or about my first visit to London doesn't justify the breaking of a failsafe guiding principle: Never reply to critics.'

Although he still had to find a full-time job, the gradual reconstruction of his personal and social life made this seem less and less of a problem. With Edith back to sustain and support him in her own inimitable way, the future became a much less daunting proposition. And as a public figure it was only a matter of time before he found himself at the centre of a wide circle of acquaintances, though to this day there are some who feel that Neville's choice of 'friends' at this time showed him to be a poor judge of character; that in his desire to be surrounded by kindred spirits he attracted more than his fair share of 'hangers-on'. Perceptive though this observation was to prove, Neville's vulnerability had the effect of inspiring even greater affection and loyalty from his true friends. Of the many people Neville met at this time, two in particular – Else Mayer-Lismann and Margaret Hughes – were to remain the closest of friends for the rest of his life, each in her own way providing the sort of stimulation and company he thrived upon.

Having come to terms with the fact that his return to music criticism in London wasn't going to be as easy as he'd hoped, Neville settled down to enjoy himself. If he couldn't write about music, there was nothing to stop him listening to it, and in the late 1940s London was the place to be. Profiting from the chaos and destruction of post-war Europe, the city found itself regularly playing host to the likes of Bruno Walter, Krips, Klemperer, Rubinstein, Flagstadt and even Richard Strauss. Nor was there any shortage of home-grown talent. With five major orchestras and conductors of the stature of Boult, Beecham and Sargent regularly in action, the capital offered a programme of concerts as varied in content and rich in quality as anywhere in Europe. It was at this time too that Neville fell under the spell of Kathleen Ferrier, the Lancashire-born singer for whom he was soon to have the greatest admiration and affection. He had first heard her sing in a performance of Mahler's *Das Lied von der Erde*, given by Bruno Walter at the 1947 Edinburgh Festival. On that occasion, as Neville was to recall in his obituary notice,

> she could not finish the repeated enunciations of the word 'Ewig' at the end, she dissolved into tears, her voice dying to a gulp of silence. Afterwards, in the artists' room, I met her, and as though she had known me a lifetime she said, 'What an idiot I've made of myself. And what will Dr Walter think of me?' I told her I thought she need not worry; and presently Dr Walter entered. She went to him and apologised for her inability to sing on to the end. 'My dear,' he replied, taking her by each of her hands, 'if we had been all as great artists as you, we should all have wept – orchestra, audience, myself – we should all have wept.'

When, later in 1949, Barbirolli brought his 'new Hallé' to London and even hardened London critics were obliged to agree with Richard Capell when he concluded that 'the famous orchestra can, in its long history, never have played better', Neville's happiness was complete. While unemployment may have had its drawbacks, nevertheless for the time being he was more than content to sit back and let life take its natural course.

It was probably no accident either that Neville's reappearance in London coincided with the beginning of the Test series against New Zealand. Though this series proved to be relatively dull – all four matches were drawn – nevertheless there were many moments to savour. At Lord's Martin Donelly, a left-handed opening batsman of classical elegance, scored 206 and Denis Compton and Jack Robertson replied with centuries for England. That summer, too, Lord's found itself at the centre of the struggle for the County Championship with Middlesex and Yorkshire contesting, and finally sharing, the honours; and as always there were a host of traditional fixtures like the Gentlemen v. Players, the Varsity match, and the schools' matches, all of which Neville greatly enjoyed.

But the headquarters of cricket was also destined to be the source of one of his biggest disappointments. No matter how closely he may have become associated with the game in the minds of cricket-lovers the world over, Neville had yet to become a member of the M.C.C., the game's controlling body and of course a highly prestigious social institution. In practice, this meant that he could only venture into that most sacred of shrines, the Pavilion at Lord's, at the invitation of a member, and then only on certain occasions; otherwise he was confined to the Press Box or those areas of the ground set aside for the general public. Though to many both inside and outside the Club this seemed an undesirable, unfortunate situation which should be remedied without delay, there were powerful voices within the Club who thought otherwise. Thus when the question of Neville's membership was raised, it soon became clear that the Committee remained to be convinced that he was a suitable candidate.

Rupert Hart-Davis was alerted to this opposition in a letter from a much-respected member of the Club which says as much about establishment morality as about Neville's pedigree and character:

> Finndale House
> Grundisburgh
> Suffolk
> 18 March 1949

Dear Rupert Hart-Davis,

There was a meeting of the M.C.C. Committee a day or two ago & I did some mild lobbying in the matter of Neville Cardus. I am afraid the suggestion would have no chance of going through if it were proposed. The obstacles are (1) Precedent – that hoary old stick-in-the-mud. You can only jump the queue if you are a distinguished cricketer or a great servant of the state, e.g. Lord Montgomery. Playing members get precedence over those who are entered and wait their turn, but I imagine N.C's playing days are over. (2) Some of them admit that N.C. has written well about the game (though I doubt whether all of them realise how much better he is than all the other writers) but they say he has been very well paid for it, & that is adequate recognition. (3) There is some feeling against him as a man, partly I gathered because he said in his autobiography that his aunt (or even his mother) was a harlot. Now though you might look at the members & even the Committee of the M.C.C. for a long time before their individ-ual & collective resemblance to Sir Galahad actually hit you in the eye, we look upon the club as Mr Squeers did upon Dotheboys Hall, i.e. as the right shop for morals, & we take a grave view of reflections cast upon an aunt. That at all events is how I construe the pursed lip & the raised eyebrow which mention of the book was apt to produce. So there, I fear, it is. If you say we are a lot of pompous old snobs, my defence will not be an indignant denial, but merely to ask what committee which runs anything so ancient & traditional & genteel is not!

Yours ever,
George*

Happy though he might have been, Neville could never quite shake off the feeling that all this leisure wasn't good for him. Sitting outside the Tavern at Lord's or in the Albert Hall, he began to wonder whether too long a period of leisure mightn't sap his creative talents and blunt his ability to write. On 30 September he told Margaret Hughes, 'Last week I was worried in conscience because of my inability to get down to any sustained stretch of writing; I was apparently "run dry", extinct.' It was a prospect too awful to contemplate. What he clearly needed was a period of self-imposed discipline, of rigorous mental exercise, and of honest introspection. Most of all, he needed to recreate the sense of purpose and the application of his younger days.

A week later, however, all was well again. He explained to Margaret Hughes how 'I hit upon this idea of a daily task – to produce so many words for you, free of the responsibility even to write well, so long as I wrote something. I am most thankful to have escaped the obsession of Lord's and the cricket season; a bad habit.' In typical fashion, Neville then began to quote the views of other literary figures who had discovered the virtues of discipline: ' "Success in life," said Walter Pater, "depends much on our capacity *not* to form habits"; and I suppose Goethe means the same when, in *Faust*, he urges us to renew ourselves day by day.' Goethe and *Faust*, Goethe and *Faust*; the names crop up time and time again in Neville's writings. Apart from the fact that *Faust* had been one of the first 'serious books' he had read, Neville had to confess that he couldn't 'rationally account for the persistent hold on me of *Faust* and Goethe. He is not, in my view a poetic genius.' Nor, as he later

* Neville was eventually elected to membership in 1958.

admitted to Margaret Hughes, had the influence been entirely beneficial.

> Goethe was responsible, I suppose, for certain directions taken by me in my twenties – directions which you would certainly not have liked. He made a snob of me in my choice of ways of living, in persuading me that pleasure of all sorts must submit to degree and severe selection . . . that there should be a certain aristocracy, fastidiousness and aloofness in all our reactions.

Snob he may have been, but here, as in so much of his autobiographical writing, Neville's recollections are tinged with an element of wishful thinking which should alert the reader against taking too much too seriously.

The impact of Neville's new regime was as striking as it was immediate. Only a week after he had first voiced his fears to Margaret Hughes, he revealed that 'maybe part of the satisfaction I feel is as much moral as creative' – and then noted in his own informal diary: 'I didn't intend to write again today. I have performed my disciplinary act; why then do I not go out into the warm afternoon? And the point is . . . I am itching to write; my mind is seething; my consciousness as writer is like a lake that has been suddenly stirred to motion after months of stagnant stillness.' It was a mood of optimism that augured well for the future.

[III]

In 1950 Granville Hill announced his retirement as principal music critic of the *Guardian*. The choice of Colin Mason as his successor, in preference to Hill's deputy, the tried and trusted J. H. Eliot, raised more than a few eyebrows amongst the Mancunian musical establishment. Less than thirty years old and a relative newcomer to the 'priesthood', Mason was known to take a distinctly independent approach to the business of musical criticism. Perhaps wary of the impact of this 'young Turk', at the same time the *Guardian* asked Neville to return as its London music critic. Once again, it seemed, the fates had smiled upon him. The fact that the appointment carried 'much the same salary the paper had paid me in 1939' did not prevent him from accepting the offer on the spot.

With a regular salary and a ready outlet for his critical and literary talents restored, Neville could hardly wait to get back into harness. 'N.C.' might have disappeared, but now 'Neville Cardus' found himself as close to the 'happy isles' of his youth as he could have expected. Free to live and work as he wanted, blessed with reasonable health and a comfortable bank balance, 'I cannot imagine any essential change that might not leave me poorer. I would enjoy conducting an orchestra but not at the price of an ability to write; I couldn't put up with work that is mainly reproductive.' As an afterthought, he added:

> Small matters, maybe, I would alter in my lot and physical make-up: I could wish that all my life I had seen well with my own eyes (though there is magic in spectacles); better still, I would have preferred to retain to the end my own teeth. I could wish to have lived in my prime in London and Vienna of the 'eighties and 'nineties. All in all though, I am very content. . . . I am grateful. I have lived to the full of my capacity.

As the *Guardian*'s London music critic, Neville had been given virtual *carte blanche* to report those of the capital's musical events which he felt warranted his presence. In addition, he had been invited to contribute a regular notice on a broader topic, again of his choice. The *Music Surveys*, as these articles were entitled, were conceived specifically with Neville's preference for the 'broad-brush' approach to writing and criticism in mind. They afforded him a licence to muse and argue which wouldn't have seemed ungenerous in his hey-day; in the harsher, tighter regime of the '50s and '60s, it was unusual to the point of being an anachronism. Statisticians may argue, correctly, that word-for-word the *Surveys* never matched 'N.C.'s' seemingly endless pre-war notices, but this is to miss their real significance. The *Surveys* were probably the last relic of those pre-war palmy times when no one doubted that true musical appreciation depended as much on guidance beforehand as on critical assessment afterwards. The listener needed to be introduced to the work, to the composer, to the performer and to the tradition; then, and only then, would he be able to understand how music was related to the rest of human experience.

In the late 1940s Neville had begun to despair for the survival of that tradition. After Sydney, where he had wielded enormous influence over musical tastes, London had proved to be a grave disappointment. Unemployed, without a pulpit, he had felt himself to be impotent and outmoded, and that it would be only a matter of time before he went the way of the dinosaur – the only difference being that unlike that old monster, he was only too aware of the fate awaiting him. This sensitivity largely explains the excitement and relief with which he greeted the news of his new appointment; excitement at the nature and potential of the post, relief at the news that he had yet to be consigned to Fleet Street's scrap heap.

There were those who felt that the *Surveys* only succeeded in delaying the inevitable, and that it would have been better both for Neville and English journalism if he had been forced to come to terms with reality at a point in his career when he could possibly have adjusted to changing circumstances. *Guardian* readers would have been deprived of glimpses of 'N.C.' in all his glory, but Neville himself would have been spared some of the disillusionment of later years. But in 1950 nothing could have been further from Neville's mind. After a long wait, he had suddenly been offered the chance to establish himself as a major force in English music criticism. At first he found great difficulty in adjusting to working in London. As 'N.C.' his had been *the* voice of authority, the only opinion Manchester readers had taken notice of, but in London he found himself in competition with other established critics for a wider and possibly more discerning audience. But these were passing problems and soon it became clear that the *Surveys* were to prove an admirable outlet for a quarter of a century's wisdom and experience. They gave him the chance to roam at will over the musical landscape, stopping off here and there to reflect or recall, all with impunity. If the *Surveys* rarely attempted to break new ground, then it has to be said that a man in his mid-sixties was hardly likely to change the habits of a lifetime; and nor would the majority of his readers have wished him to do so.

The subjects he covered were a typically Cardusian mixture of the specific, the general and the abstract, ranging fom 'Chopin and Pianists' through 'Period Music' to 'Relative Values'. The name of Gustav Mahler was to crop up frequently in these pieces. Following in the footsteps of his predecessor at the *M.G.*, Samuel Langford, Neville had long been a champion of Mahler's music, and by the beginning of the 1950s there were signs that his message was getting home. The *Surveys* were an ideal means of furthering this evangelical mission. In October 1952 *Guardian* readers found themselves presented with a piece entitled 'Mahler's Growing Influence' in which Neville noted: 'The best brains in actual music-making nowadays are attending diligently to Mahler. In this country, though in large numbers we still fight shy of original Mahler, we readily take to him if and when he is diluted by – well So-and-So, and Never Mind.'

In February 1954 he returned to the same theme in an article specifically devoted to Mahler's 9th Symphony, in which he assessed the qualities that made the composer so exceptional: 'No composer has associated as unambiguously as Mahler certain conditions of mind and feeling – known as 'ideas' in music – with a more easily recognised set of symbols. . . . He not only wore his heart on his sleeve; he exposed lungs and liver.' Having identified the genius of Mahler, Neville was determined that his readers should not be left on their own to understand and appreciate how these qualities were expressed in his music. Again, the *Surveys* were an obvious channel for advice; in May 1955 he wrote a piece entitled 'Misunderstanding Mahler', and lest anyone was in any doubt as to the extent of the challenge presented by the composer's music, a later *Survey* (February 1957) bore the heading, 'The Mahler Problem'.

In less serious moments, Neville took great pleasure in indulging his distinctive sense of humour. In March 1957, for example, he couldn't resist drawing his readers' attention to the anniversary of the death of a much-loved Austrian performer – 'it is thirty-two years since Erich Hartleibig died in Vienna at the age of forty-four, poisoned by eating an overripe *Saltzgurke*' – while six years later he chose to cast himself in the role of a tutor in a letter which took the form of an end-of-year report:

14 March 1963

Dear Cuthbert,

You have just completed your first year as a music critic of 'The Filibuster' and I now send you my report on your work to date. I was taking a risk when I recommended you for the job; for you were labouring under the disadvantage of a late start. After all, twenty-six is a fairly advanced age to begin music criticism. But obviously you have been extremely diligent in your studies and have more or less got over a by-no-means inconsiderable handicap . . . you are fortunate, dear Cuthbert, to be engaged in a profession in which you can get away with nearly everything. . . . You complain that there are bouquets for performers, none for critics. Not even letters of thanks (with cigars attached) from artists you have praised and put on the map. Only complaints. Ah, dear boy, you are still in the green leaf. For many more years than I care to count I have . . . been waiting for the morning post to bring me a letter couched in some such terms as this:

'I have just read your notice of my recital last night. It bears out what I have long suspected, that you are even less qualified than your colleagues to criticise great artists. Obviously you are tone-deaf, for you say in your notice that I was in good voice. As a fact I was suffering from acute laryngitis. You wrote that my intonation was perfect. Anyone with half an ear could have told you that often I was a quarter note flat. You even praised the pianist who accompanied me. He was lousy.'

When, dear Cuthbert, I receive a letter of this kind from a performer of any kind, from a performer of any sort, I shall know that the kingdom of heaven is at hand.

Yours,
Neville Cardus

Compared with the demands made of 'Cricketer' and 'N.C.', Neville's post-war responsibilities were relatively untaxing. On average he wrote between twenty-five and thirty notices a year, including five or six *Surveys*. London was now his home and his parish. Most of the performances he reviewed were given within a mile or two of the National Liberal Club. With the opening of the Royal Festival Hall in 1951, the capital acquired an auditorium which, for all its notoriously 'dry' acoustic, was a great improvement on existing facilities. The recording business was also going through an extraordinarily innovative period, with Walter Legge at EMI producing a series of new interpretations of a quality hitherto only dreamed about. Though he and Neville had met on many occasions before the war, theirs had always been an uncertain relationship. Neville never could quite make up his mind about Legge;

sometimes they got on famously, but on other occasions Neville let it be known that Legge was one of his 'pet aversions'.

Oxford was the scene of one of their most memorable encounters. Having just discovered that his contributions to the works of Hugo Wolf were well represented in the Holywell Rooms, Legge was in fine form. In the evening, he and Neville met up with Sir James Colyer-Fergusson and Dennis Rowbotham (an old friend from Manchester) for dinner; afterwards, with Rowbotham providing a piano accompaniment, Legge treated the party to a solo perform-ance (in Italian) of Verdi's *Falstaff* – falsetto and all!

As befitted a critic of his status, Neville tended to reserve his appearances for the big occasions – or at least the ones he knew he was most likely to enjoy. It soon became clear that seven years in Australia had done little to change his pre-war preference for the central European romantic tradition, and by and large his favourite artists were drawn from the same background. The one major exception was Toscanini. When the Italian conductor came to London in September 1952, for his first post-war concert, Neville marked the occasion by writing an introductory piece entitled 'Toscanini in London' which reminded his readers of the Maestro's place in musical history, and followed it up with long notices on both of his concerts. Among the more familiar visitors to London, Neville was particularly fond of Krips and Kempe, while Boult (particularly when Elgar was in the programme), Barbirolli and of course Beecham remained his favourite English conductors. He greatly admired, but at the same time slightly distrusted, Sir Malcolm Sargent; in his view sartorial elegance and buttonholes didn't make for great music. 'The freshest carnation can hardly live up to him,' Neville once wrote.

Now nearing the end of his career, Sir Thomas Beecham nevertheless retained his hold over Neville's personal and pro-fessional affections. It was a measure of the depth of this relationship that both men felt able to state, frankly and openly, their criticisms of the other. Beecham had frequently objected to 'N.C.'s' notices of his concerts, while Neville always believed that Toscanini's was the more substantial and profound musical influence. In *Autobiography*, he wrote: 'I suggest we must for convenience's sake call a man a genius if we cannot explain how he came to be what he is unless aided by some personal force hard to define. Toscanini, to a large extent, can be accounted for without reference to the inexplicable and the indefinable; he would have been great without his genius. Not so Beecham.'[7]

Yet in his own way Beecham was incomparable. In Neville's view, he had a greater range than any other living conductor, a natural feeling for style and an immense personal magnetism. Toscanini was 'the experienced and wise vintner, but Beecham personally flavours the wine like the connoisseur of cellarage'. But, as Neville would have been the first to acknowledge, versatility doesn't necessarily equate with genius. He often made the point that Sir Thomas was not 'a long-distance conductor. His happiest gifts were for improvisation and wit; neither will fill the space of an epic or symphonic enlargement.' It followed therefore that

he was more successful with the concentrated energy of Strauss's *Salome* and *Elektra* than with *Rosenkavalier*, which he presented brilliantly and enthusiastically, missing very much the note of the Marschallin's reflective pathos. So in *Meistersinger*, he revelled in the pageantry, the lyrical impulse of Walther and Eva, the spriteliness of the Apprentices; but he had no time for the introspective communings of Hans Sachs.

Above all, Neville retained a lasting sense of gratitude to Beecham for the way in which he raised standards of performance and appreciation in Britain. As he acknowledged in a tribute written on the occasion of the conductor's seventy-fifth birthday,

Many of us today are still in debt to Sir Thomas; he led us out of the Teutonic captivity. He showed us other and more sensitive worlds. . . . Sometimes his tongue is cruel simply because he cannot resist the crack or snap of his own wit. At a certain concert, a pianist played abominably, with Sir Thomas conducting. At the end of the performance the piano men came to the platform to move the instrument away. 'I don't think,' said Sir Thomas, 'I don't think that you need to waste energy on this occasion. Just leave the instrument alone for a few minutes longer and I fancy it will slink off on its own accord.[8]

Despite Neville's great regard for Beecham, he would have been the first to concede that by the mid '50s his old friend was rapidly approaching the twilight of his career. Though still capable of brilliance, Sir Thomas could no longer sustain the incandescent spirit that had excited concert- and opera-goers the world over for nearly half a century. One by one, Neville realised with growing sadness, the great pre-war figures whose performances had called forth some of his finest notices were leaving the stage. But the effect on his own mood was cumulative rather than instant; as yet there was plenty to enjoy and savour about London's musical offering.

Of all the regular visitors to the capital during the '50s and '60s it was two German conductors who came closest to filling the void created by the retirement or death of his old favourites. Herbert von Karajan and Otto Klemperer may have had little in common either on or off the podium, but they shared an ability to stimulate Neville's critical faculties. No one, least of all Neville, would have considered denying Karajan's exceptional abilities. Since making a series of historic recordings with the Philharmonia for Legge, he had returned to London with both the Vienna and the Berlin Philharmonic orchestras to, usually, a rapturous reception from audience and critics alike. Neville acknowledged that Karajan at his best scaled 'Olympian Heights' and his 'mastery over instrumental forces [was] complete and comprehensive'.

Yet for all that, there was one respect in which Neville believed him to be inferior to Klemperer. Whenever he criticised a Karajan concert, it was always on the grounds of uneven or idiosyncratic interpretation. After a concert at the Edinburgh Festival in 1961, for example, he concluded: 'As a music-maker, he frankly leaves my ears and musical imagination unsatisfied.' By contrast, Klemperer could do little wrong. Throughout the '50s and '60s Neville's columns rang with his praises. 'Klemperer is really remarkable,' he concluded in February 1960. 'His concert on Monday was of a greatness of style the like of which we have not heard in London recently.' Four months later, he credited Klemperer with having presided over 'the greatest performance of our time'.

Beneath these tributes there lay an affinity between artist and critic of unusual duration and depth. Klemperer had first come to Neville's notice at Salzburg in the early '30s. Twenty-five years later he had assumed a significance that extended far beyond his individual performances. While others may have looked upon him as a relic of a bygone age, to Neville he was perhaps the last surviving exponent of what Bruno Walter once described as 'music of spiritual meaning'. In Klemperer's performances, Neville sensed the

existence of a simple but universal message; an insight etched in
shadings of light and dark at once delicate and profound; an insight
that transcended convention, tradition and artifice; an insight
sustained by a rare combination of intellectual power and emotional
depth; an insight that 'grasped the spirit that ran through the score'.
The coincidence of these qualities explained Klemperer's genius.

'One night at the Festival Hall,' Neville was later to recall,

> he [Klemperer] took his seat, unable to stand erect, and without
> a baton waved into motion the *Nachtmusik* of Mozart. And
> having given this music freedom, will and flow, I felt he could
> have left the conductor's seat and joined the audience while
> every note went on its pre-determined way. Here is, perhaps,
> Klemperer's secret: he can liberate music, seeing and hearing
> the end in the beginning, theme and tempo one and
> inseparable.[9]

Only one element of the 'essential' Neville was missing from this
passage, but his readers were not to be disappointed for long.
Towards the end of the notice came the inevitable reference: 'He is
Goethean, a Faustian usually accompanied by a Mephisto.'

Though he had little time for formalised religion, Neville was in
his own way a very spiritual person, and it was this that enabled him
to perceive the inner depth of Klemperer's performances. And if his
own ability to grasp and illuminate the essence of music lacked
Klemperer's profundity, then he enjoyed by way of compensation a
sense of humour that is often missing in German personalities.
From Dickens in particular he had gained an ability to see the irony
in life, to appreciate the trivial as well as the profound, the profane as
well as the sacred; and bearing in mind the high seriousness of his
profession, perhaps most important of all he had learnt to laugh at
himself.

After his expulsion from Nazi Germany, Klemperer had moved to
the United States, eventually taking up American citizenship. There
he had suffered a series of set-backs (including a brain tumour, a
broken pelvis and near immolation when his bed-clothes caught
fire), which might have persuaded a lesser man that the gods were
against him. But not Klemperer. By the mid-'50s, largely as a result
of his work with Walter Legge, he had re-established himself
amongst the foremost international conductors. It was about this

time that Neville got the idea that, as one of the greatest exponents of Mahler's music, Klemperer should be invited to write the composer's memoirs. The two men discussed the idea when they met at the Hyde Park Hotel in October 1956. Neville described the meeting in a piece entitled 'A Lunch with Klemperer'. Following German custom the two referred to each other throughout by their surnames. Klemperer, it transpired, said very little else. When Neville recalled that 'Klemperer did not talk until I began – in fact he mostly listened' no one was very surprised.

In the event Klemperer responded enthusiastically to the Mahler idea (partly because it had been at the back of his mind for some time), and several more meetings followed. One of these took the form of a dinner party given by Else Mayer-Lismann at her home in Chelsea. For any number of reasons entertaining Klemperer wasn't the easiest of tasks; it was only after much thought and consultation that it was agreed that the menu would consist of soup, schnitzel and a sweet (prunes) to finish. On the evening in question, as was his wont, Neville arrived a little early and waited in the lobby for the great man to arrive. At the appointed hour Klemperer arrived in a chauffeur-driven limousine provided by Walter Legge, accompanied by Hilda, his companion-cum-assistant. With some difficulty he negotiated the lift, hobbled into Else's flat, and almost fell into a chair. After a while he recovered sufficiently to accept a glass of sherry, which unfortunately he succeeded only in upsetting all over the carpet. Dinner was duly served: first the soup which Klemperer consumed to the accompaniment of a terrible spluttering sound; then the schnitzel which he found very difficult to eat because he wouldn't allow anyone to help him cut the meat up.

After the meal Klemperer turned to Hilda and asked to be handed the draft of the Mahler memoirs. Though these were in German, he insisted on reading them aloud, and in full. At ten-thirty the door bell rang to announce the return of the chauffeur. Klemperer, however, refused to move; the atmosphere, he had decided, was *gemütlich* and he wished to stay a little longer. Tea was provided. Klemperer accepted a cup and promptly forgot about it. Turning to Hilda again, he asked her to pass him a second bundle of papers. These, it transpired, contained a short story about an old man who had followed a prostitute up many flights of stairs in a block of flats, only to discover, when they finally reached her door, that she wasn't in the right mood. Again, Klemperer insisted on reading the entire draft. At this point Neville, who had been surprisingly quiet, burst out laughing, though in all probability he hadn't understood very much of Klemperer's text. Whatever the case, his outburst proved unfortunate in the extreme as the story was supposed to have had a tragic ring to it. Failing completely to see the funny side of the situation, Klemperer became very irritated, summoned the chauffeur and departed in a huff.

Along with Karajan and Klemperer, Claudio Arrau and Clifford Curzon were probably Neville's favourite artistes. The piano was the only instrument he had ever played, and looking back over his life this seems to have had an important influence on his musical preferences. Schnabel, Rachmaninov, Backhaus, Rubinstein, Horowitz, Gieseking, Rosenthal, Cortot; these had been the gods in his early days. Muriel Cohen, Pina Salzman and Ignaz Friedman had been among his closest friends in Australia. And now Arrau and Curzon. As both made regular appearances in London, Neville had plenty of opportunities to compare and contrast their styles and techniques. After one of Arrau's recitals, Neville wrote a notice entitled 'Virtuoso Without Vanity', in which he described the Chilean-born artist as a 'masterful pianist, comprehensive of technique and extremely musical', and later he told Robin Daniels, 'If I want to hear either the D-minor or the B-flat concerto of Brahms, if I want to hear Beethoven in all his stature – I go to Arrau.'[10]

Clifford Curzon was arguably the last pianist to achieve truly international status during Neville's working life. Ashkenazy and Barenboim were still at the start of their careers, though he was well aware of their exceptional promise. As early as 1955 he had written of 'Master Barenboim', then only thirteen, that he was 'obviously naturally musical with supple fingers which already touch the keyboard instinctively'. But with Curzon, Neville knew he was dealing with a proven product. Add to this the fact that the English pianist was one of the greatest exponents of the works of Mozart and Schubert, composers whose piano music Neville was particularly fond of, and it is easy to understand why he later said of Curzon: 'He is the kind of pianist I would like to be.' As Curzon lived in London, the two met frequently and became close friends (fittingly, it was Curzon who played at Neville's Memorial Service). It was a performance of a Mozart concerto in Edinburgh in 1961 which had convinced Neville that his friend was the greatest Mozart pianist of his day. In his notice of that concert, Neville wrote of Curzon: 'He led us to the heart and into the fine-textured intelligence of the B-flat concerto. Frankly I find it almost impossible to write of this interpretation of Mr Curzon's. It mingled perfection of touch with felicity of phrasing. Each note had a glow and was like a pulse-beat or a star in the sky.'

One of the criticisms most frequently levelled at Neville, particularly at this relatively late stage of his career, was that he disliked and hence largely neglected 'new music'. It was an accusation that Neville found more than a little galling. As he told Robin Daniels, 'They call me "square" because I don't acknowledge Stockhausen as the greatest composer of all time! Decades ago, I was fighting for Stravinsky and Debussy and Sibelius and Vaughan Williams, and for a lot of composers who are not nowadays considered to be modern.'[11] Nor was it self-evident that old age had rendered Neville a reactionary 'fuddy-duddy'. A brief glance through his notices during the '50s and '60s shows that he was present at first performances of works by Wordsworth, Bliss, Alwyn and Karl Hartmann, and in each case, whilst not suggesting that the piece automatically stamped its composer as Beethoven's equal, his assessment was balanced and fair. Pushing the argument one step further, his critics might justly retort that though these were new works, they were nevertheless cast very firmly in a traditional mould. The acid test of Cardus's receptiveness to change, they could claim, was his treatment of composers whose music reflected a desire to shake off the last vestiges of tonality and diatonic harmony. On this point Neville's record is more difficult to defend. Though he attended concerts of 'contemporary music', his reviews were unambiguously hostile. After a performance in 1954 of Oliver Messiaen's relatively conventional *Turangalila*, he wrote:

This so-called symphony is drearily repetitive, and its 'modernisms' are even more naive and adolescent than yesterday's ... the general impression in fact was of an elaborate dance orchestra playing in a sophisticated night club, where undivided attention to the music was hard to come by because of perpetual banging of doors, dropping of trays and popping of enormous corks.[12]

Three years later, as if to test the water again, he went to a performance of works by Varese, Antheil and Jolivet – a 'Concert for

Breakdown Gang and Furniture Remover', as he dubbed it. Obviously determined to avoid jumping to conclusions, he then went to hear Roberto Gerhard's *Collages*. The verdict was never in doubt, but the ensuing notice perfectly illustrates his contention that a critic must always retain his sense of humour.

> While the orchestra 'doodled', not atonally, but subtonally, the soloists (the loudspeakers) chattered like falling crockery, rattled like an electric drill, reproduced sounds of water going down the kitchen sink and screamed like a jet plane. Other noises were harder to name, but at one point in the racket someone was playing 'Collages'. Towards the end of the piece, the orchestra suddenly downed instruments, while a loudspeaker played a coloratura gargle. This, I take it, was the cadenza.[13]

In 1965, at the age of seventy-six, Neville attended a performance at the Royal Festival Hall of *Pli Selon Pli* by Pierre Boulez, with the composer himself conducting. Assuming that Neville wasn't under the critic's equivalent of a three-line whip, it was a brave, if futile, gesture. At some stage in his life, every music critic has to face the unpalatable fact that the older a man becomes and the healthier his appetite for life, the larger is the aesthetic barrier he can no longer cross. The effect of Boulez's music was to provoke Neville into formulating a carefully reasoned statement of his attitude towards works of this kind. It wasn't just a question of disliking horrible noises, nor of feeling that the composer was using 'a different language from the one that I – and any other critic of my age – was brought up to understand'. As his review of the Boulez concert makes clear, Neville's reservations sprang from the even more fundamental conviction that what passes as contemporary 'music' may on closer examination turn out not to constitute music in the generally understood sense of the term. It was a conviction he was never to compromise.

> Listening to *Pli Selon Pli*, I could not relate the varied succession of aural phenomena to music as my musical intelligence and senses recognise music. . . . Boulez has, I agree, invented or rather opened up a new tonal territory. He has broken up the thickening congestion of the harmonic palate of

the German–Austrian schools. But I . . . await a convincing verbal argument or demonstration revealing to the ordinary experienced intelligence exactly where and how *Pli Selon Pli* takes its place as a masterpiece of organised music, unambiguously to be classified as such.[14]

[IV]

As the years passed Neville found himself settling into a routine as comfortable and broadly satisfying as the one he'd enjoyed before the war. True, there were moments when he regretted not having more to do. 1957 and 1958 were particularly lean years, so lean in fact that he was reduced to writing articles in praise of Ernest Newman. For the most part, however, he found little difficulty in occupying himself. When the joys of music stilled and conversation temporarily faded, there was always cricket. The legacy of 'Cricketer' lived on in the form of hundreds of invitations to speak at cricket functions of one kind or another. Most of these Neville politely but firmly declined, but sometimes, as on the occasion of a dinner in Birmingham to celebrate Warwickshire's winning of the County Championship in 1951, he was persuaded to accept. A day or two later he jotted down a few memories of the evening in a notebook:

24 Oct.: Back from Birmingham. The dinner was immense and Lord Iliffe a perfect host. There were more than 350 of us in the large hall of the Grand Hotel. I'm told that Joe Chamberlain spoke in this room many times. There are alcoves and balconies high above and at Lord Iliffe's invitation the wives of the Warwickshire cricketers were sitting there, also guests at dinner, but apart from the males. I have never before seen or heard of women at a cricketers' dinner. The usual boring speeches with the exception of one from Tom Dollery, the Warwickshire skipper, and Lord Iliffe, who late in the evening reminded us of a fact that none of us had kept in mind – that today was the anniversary of W. G. Grace's death in 1915. He added, 'I saw him only once and then I was a small boy and I immediately decided to become a first-class cricketer. Hitherto I had concentrated on becoming an engine-driver. I need hardly say that neither ambition was realised.' The charm of

these old men; the white-haired courtesy. God grant these things to me in advanced years. I got a few laughs in a short speech. Sydney Barnes, greatest of bowlers now aged 77 at least, was at one of the tables, so I thought some reference should be made to his presence and I told how on one of the few occasions when he played with Ranjitsinhji, he bowled against him at Brighton on a 'green wicket' which suited Barnes perfectly. Barnes was unplayable; he quickly got rid of Fry and Vine. Then Ranji came in and took charge. Barnes scarcely had a chance of bowling at anyone else but Ranji for the rest of the Sussex innings. His analysis at the end was 2 for 80 or roundabout. Ranji scored a century. After he had been batting for a quarter of an hour he came down the wicket and paid Barnes the greatest compliment paid to any bowler. 'Barnes,' said Ranji, 'you are bowling magnificently. You are, in fact, bowling better than I ever imagined it was possible to bowl. So I want to practise against you.'

I was told by somebody sitting next to Barnes that he was vastly pleased by the story and generally approved as to its accuracy. I made it up myself, more or less as my speech went on.

The last sentence doubtless contains the secret of much of Neville's success and fame. Problems only arose when his 'ad-libbing' became a shade repetitive. On the way back to London after this event, Neville shared a carriage with E. W. Swanton of the *Daily Telegraph*. As Swanton has written about Cardus on several occasions, it is only fair to let Neville have a few words, albeit posthumously, about his fellow cricket-writer.

Travelling back from Birmingham, Jim Swanton was in the carriage and at once he had the window opened, then talked to and held up a ticket collector about some question of a return to Oxford, then opened his three or four newspapers one after the other, and on the whole was as restless and disturbing as ever. He is a most likeable man when you come to know him; but he can't expect people who *don't* know him not to get the impression of self-importance and unnecessary resonance of speech and a certain pompousness – which last is, I'm sure, not part of his nature. There is some sense of inferiority somewhere. He probably never got over not having been to Oxford and Eton.[15]

There were times too when despite his protestations to the contrary, Neville couldn't resist the temptation to return to the Press Box. Well aware of this weakness, the *Guardian* managed to lure him out of retirement to cover the great events of 1953 – or at least the cricketing ones! Throughout that memorable summer, 'Neville Cardus' – like 'N.C.', 'Cricketer' was never to be resurrected – brought the details of the Ashes struggle to *Guardian* readers. It was almost like old times again, except that the matches attracted so much interest that Neville found himself occupying pride of place on the front page. There, on Wednesday 1 July, under the headline 'MIRACLE OF FAITH AT LORD'S', he recounted over fully two columns the great stand between Watson and Bailey that saved the match for England. Paragraph by paragraph the years were rolled back to reveal 'Cricketer' in all but name:

> Panic gibbered around the ground when Evans was nearly stumped. . . . It was a stand of noble martyrdom; and in the end it was the martyrs who each had been crowned with a laurel wreath . . . compared with Lindwall of Monday he could be likened to a volcano which having erupted was content to sleep awhile. And just as the villagers dwelling on the mountain sides settle down again as soon as the lava has subsided, so did the England innings begin building itself up again. . . . In little more than an hour 53 runs had rippled over the field, like background music at a funeral service. . . . Oxygen was in the shape of the new ball, was administered at three o'clock.

The language, the metaphor, the phraseology, all are of unmistakable ancestry but, lest any lingering doubts remain, the columns also contained abundant examples of 'Cricketer's' distinctive brand of digression:

> The cricket before lunch was rather limp and indecisive and the quiet, attenuated crowd sat and waited for the end. Even the Australians seemed to be waiting with all the rest of us. I was reminded of Jowett at Balliol on his death-bed. In the ante-room, a distinguished company was silently gathered together, resigned yet hoping. And towards midnight Jowett, who had

been comatose – like this match this morning – wearily raised himself from his pillow and, turning to his nurse, said: 'Please tell those dear, kind people outside that I don't think I'm going to do anything tonight.' He lived several hours longer and the dear, kind people were at liberty to rest, as today we were free not necessarily to agitate ourselves.

'Ah,' the reader might say, 'here surely we have the finest flowering of a unique literary talent. The writer of prose of this quality must be a man entirely at one with himself, secure and happy in the knowledge that he has a mastery of talent and style that few will equal, but that many will enjoy.' Neville, for he was not given to modesty, would probably have agreed with this sentiment, and yet in the very next breath he might make a confession of uncertainty which served only to re-emphasise the fascinating unpredictability of his character. The same man who wrote the above article at Lord's in 1953 had only shortly before told of his 'ridiculous diffidence'. 'In the Press Box at cricket,' he explained,

> where I am the doyen, the only survivor from the 1921 Test matches, the most celebrated writer on the game in the world, I can never bring myself to call out in a loud voice 'Messenger', if I need to send my copy away. Others of my colleagues boom out their commands like men; I crawl from my seat and go to the Messenger in abject person, and give him my copy almost surreptitiously. I am always astonished when I see anybody in a hotel examining and challenging a bill. Yet I would not at my time of life call myself shy.[16]

In less charged times back in the sanctuary of 1, Whitehall Place, Neville liked to begin his daily round with a period of writing – or at least of thinking about writing. It was rare for him to set foot outside before eleven o'clock. As long as the *Guardian*'s publication schedules permitted, he preferred to write his notices in the morning; after this facility had been withdrawn he sought to minimise the night's work by writing most of his copy before a performance, leaving himself only to add references to the exceptional or the unexpected. He rarely discussed the contents of his criticisms with anyone, not even Else Mayer-Lismann who accompanied him to many concerts and operas.

Extra detail and a final polish was added in the Cafeteria of the Festival Hall, or a similar venue close to Covent Garden. Unlikely though this may seem, it was a case of Neville remaining true to his conviction that the act of writing could be undertaken virtually anywhere. Bars, cafés, restaurants – even the counter in a post-office – could be drummed into service if necessary. In his view, surroundings were much less important than discipline. 'Sit down in front of a blank piece of paper for a couple of hours every day and something will happen,' was his advice to aspiring writers. 'Even if the effort produces only twenty words, it will have been worth it.' (Guidance which, as my publisher will confirm, is not necessarily foolproof.)

Before the *Guardian* came to London in 1960, Neville's notices had to be phoned through to sub-editors in Manchester, but from then on he delighted in arranging for them to be transported to the Grays Inn Road office in a chauffeur-driven hire-car. It was one of the rare occasions on which he would have anything to do with cars. Normally he treated them with a suspicion which often bordered on contempt. They were noisy, claustrophobic and, as he got older, impossible to get in and out of. Except in the direst of emergencies, he preferred to walk or catch a bus.

By eleven o'clock it was time to start thinking about the order of the day, but before preparing for lunch he would phone Edith at Bickenhall Mansions. It was a daily ritual; they talked about anything and everyone, the precise detail being much less important than the simple act of communicating. As had been the case in Manchester and Sydney, it had not taken Edith long to settle down in London. Bickenhall Mansions suited her down to the ground; there was (just) enough room to spread herself and her always growing belongings, and to paint. It was also very conveniently located. Three years older than her husband, Edith was immensely enthusiastic and energetic. Every new day held out the prospect of another visit, preview or meeting. Like Neville she was a creature of habit, one of her regular pleasures being the five-shilling tea at the Ritz – usually followed by a trip to Harrods.

Much of Neville's social life revolved around that venerable institution, the gentleman's club; not the seamier versions in side streets off Piccadilly, but revered, respectable organisations like the Savage and the Saville (to which Neville belonged during the '50s), where men reviewed the world or read the papers or simply slept.

Clubs like these provided the ideal ambience for Neville. At first sight one could have been mistaken for believing that he belonged to that instantly recognisable and eminently avoidable species, the club bore; but closer acquaintance would emphasise the dangers of relying on first impressions. There was no denying that Neville's entry was usually the signal for an animated monologue, but at this stage in his life few begrudged him centre stage.

The Cardus style was not that of the story-teller, though much of what he said was fiction. His conversation consisted more of re-collections, comments and opinions (both his own and others'). In some ways he could be very self-centred. 'If he had been a painter,' one of his friends observed, 'three-quarters of his output would have been self-portraits. He found himself very interesting.' But at the same time there was generally so much to enjoy about a conversation with Neville that few seemed to object to his idiosyncracies. There was an earthiness to his character which manifested itself in an intense dislike of pretension, particularly amongst theatre- and concert-goers. 'Snobs are the curse of music,' he used to proclaim, dismissing the offending objects from his mind as if he was swatting mosquitoes. His monologues were full of physical gestures. Lips, arms and hands moved in subconscious harmony, as if to orchestrate the verbal line.

When he spoke of women, which was frequently, lips would pucker in imaginary (or perhaps real) remembrance of a bygone embrace. Unlike the archetypal 'clubman', Neville was never a supporter of the male preserve. As well as loving to talk about women he delighted in their presence and always took the opportunity to indulge in such old-fashioned gestures as opening the door for a lady. By the same token, he often hated those moments when the ladies departed to another room, leaving the men to cigars, port, dirty stories and, worse still, party politics. A very liberal gentleman, he nevertheless hated Liberals who touted for membership of their party.

At lunches and at dinners, impersonations were Neville's stock-in-trade. Even those of his friends who took little interest in cricket were forced to admit that his imitations of the Lancashire players of the 1920s were 'terribly good'. Many were the occasions on which the voices of Tyldesley, Brearley, MacLaren and Makepeace echoed around the dinner tables of Westminster, Kensington and Chelsea. Whatever the company, Neville had a way of making everyone feel at ease and important. Going to Lord's with him was a great experience; walking round the ground and through the Pavilion, according to one friend, 'you felt as though the Red Sea was opening up before you.'

No matter how much he may have enjoyed the National Liberal, the Savage and the Saville, there was one club above all that Neville wished to belong to. The opportunity arose in 1959, but in his enthusiasm to be admitted Neville came perilously close to breaking one of the golden rules of the institution in question; viz. that there should be no canvassing for 'signatures'. In a letter to Ruper Hart-Davis written on 10 May 1959, he explained his concern: 'I have been "proposed" for the Garrick by Sargent and seconded. The main thing now, I am told, is the Club "book" and the names of members who are my friends. Would you help me here and sign for me and mention the matter to Hamish Hamilton, Ivor Brown or any other Garrick members you think might support me.'

Had word of this illicit lobbying got out, Neville and his unwitting accessories could have found themselves 'blackballed' for life, but happily his infraction was kept a secret and he was duly elected. Admittance to the Garrick marked the summit of his career in the genteel world of London's clubs, an achievement which predictably prompted him to leave both the Savage and the Saville. The famous club was to be the scene of many memorable meetings, though after a while he came to suspect that some members might have been trying to avoid his monologues. What made matters worse was that on first joining the club, he himself had been advised to avoid sharing a table with a certain theatrical knight who, it was said, 'never stopped talking about his Lear'. Nevertheless, Neville usually managed to find someone to dine with.

One of his favourite conversational adversaries was John Barbirolli. As well as being close friends, they were both great actors and each enjoyed upstaging the other 'for the greater glory of God'. At one of their lunchtime meetings, true to form both spent the first hour talking sixteen to the dozen without taking the slightest notice of what the other might have been saying. The occupant of a nearby table recalled that to his surprise and admiration at one point in this exchange Sir John took out his false teeth but still kept talking. By this time Neville was of course a master of the art of masticating and conversing simultaneously.

Although most of the restaurants he frequented offered an

excellent cuisine, Neville rarely showed any interest in what he termed 'fancy foods'. He was by nature a 'nibbler' who spent much of the meal playing with his food. Walter Legge used to say to him, 'Neville, when you have finished eating, there seems to be more on your plate than when you started,' which perhaps explains why Neville always had reservations about Legge. Rich sauces, he always complained, gave him a 'bad tummy'. Given a free choice, he would usually opt for simple unadorned dishes like liver and bacon, fried sole, chicken and shepherds pie, followed by figs and cream or rice pudding. He adored creamed potatoes; and sausages were another favourite but had to be cooked correctly. Else Mayer-Lismann, whose schnitzel he (and I) adored, never managed to get them brown enough, whereas Margaret Hughes used to find that the ones she took to Lord's disappeared surprisingly quickly.

Manchester saw relatively little of Neville after his return from Australia. Northern music was covered for the *Guardian* by J. H. Eliot, Colin Mason or Gerald Larner, and it was only really major events which drew him back to his old haunts. In 1951 he attended the opening of the new Free Trade Hall, an emotional evening which was climaxed by Kathleen Ferrier's singing of 'Land of Hope and Glory'. From the audience Neville was moved to write: 'Imagine the case of a Manchester man, returning from exile after many years to the place where he first heard music, where he learned all that a man need know of music, returning to the place he thought lost for ever and not only returning by an incredible swing of the wheel to any sort of Hallé Concert, but to the Hallé Orchestra on the night of resurrection in the desired paradise.'[17]

Three years later he came back for a concert devoted to a performance of one work – Mahler's Ninth Symphony – to which Barbirolli had devoted an amazing fifty hours of rehearsal time. On that occasion Neville gave the audience a short, pre-concert introduction to the work, an innovation which Michael Kennedy described as 'a kind of Hallé canonisation for a great critic and supporter of the orchestra'. But as he was now based in London, it was only when Barbirolli brought his orchestra south that Neville really had a chance to judge their well-being. Such was the praise he lavished on the Hallé on these visits that some began to wonder whether nostalgia hadn't affected his critical faculties. In February 1961 he wrote that 'it is hard to complain or find fault with Sir John', and in 1963, on the occasion of the twentieth anniversary of Barbirolli's arrival in Manchester, he advanced the view that 'none since Richter has shared his influence, not only over performance but over musical policy'. Two years later, however, as if anticipating the charge of favouritism, he offered a far more balanced appraisal of the orchestra and its conductor.

It was good last night at the concert of the Royal Philharmonic Society to welcome to the Royal Festival Hall the Hallé Orchestra, with the maestro Sir John Barbirolli (that is the only word for him in charge). True, the Hallé could not ravish our senses as the Vienna players did the other evening. Now we are hearing an orchestra as English and British as Manchester and the North of England, direct of speech, honest-to-God, with recurrent evidence that these instrumentalists are free mortals, and, being so, occasionally prone to slight error. There was no nylon in the music made for us at their concert, and no lacquer.

Of all the journeys Neville undertook on behalf of the *Guardian* after 1950, it was the annual pilgrimage to Edinburgh that gave him the greatest pleasure. Ever since Salzburg he had liked the idea of festivals and, even though public opinion was now moving strongly in the opposite direction, he never compromised his belief in excellence *per se*; in his eyes there was no virtue in popularising the arts simply on egalitarian grounds. As often as not, he believed, the result was counter-productive. Besides, excellence was itself contagious; the higher the quality of a performance, the greater its likely impact on the audience. In his own words, 'I don't believe in the contemporary idea of taking the arts to the people. Let them seek and work for them.' It was a creed that clearly owed much to his own experience.

Like Salzburg, Edinburgh offered everything he valued – artistic excellence, variety, a degree of informality and atmosphere. Ever a creature of habit, he also came to value the routine and ritual associated with his visit. After the frantic, noisy world of London, he found Edinburgh both relaxing and stimulating. It was not a case of having less to do; on the contrary, during the four weeks of the Festival he wrote as many as ten and never less than five substantial notices. These would generally begin with a scene-setting piece in which he sought to catch the mood of the Festival, before moving on to those items on the programme that caught his eye. One of the main attractions of a Festival like Edinburgh's was that there was always something to do. It was nothing for him to attend a piano recital in the morning, a lunch-time or early afternoon lecture and a concert or opera in the evening. The rest of the day was spent either in solitude – reading, writing or thinking – or with friends, artists or admirers taking tea at the Caledonian or a late dinner at one of the city's restaurants. Again, these gatherings provided the perfect setting for Neville's monologues; the atmosphere was sympathetic, the company interested and usually admiring, and the Festival programme a more than adequate source of discussion, argument or plain gossip. And even he was willing to admit that many of the performances he attended were worthy of comparison with the best.

In a rash moment, one of his companions ventured to suggest that all this concentration of activity might somehow blunt his critical edge. But nothing could have been further from the truth, as the New York Philharmonic were to find to their cost in September 1955. 'Insensitive, unsubtle; no light or shade; rhythmical as a steelyard' was how he summed up a concert they gave under the young Guido Cantelli. It was a roasting that Neville had reason to remember just over a year later after the conductor had been killed in an air crash. In his tribute, Neville recalled how he had 'protested against the superficiality of his [Cantelli's] conducting at Edinburgh', but then went on to reveal how subsequently he had come to appreciate Cantelli's promise: 'Every conductor, except Bruno Walter, who has visited and lived in America has in some degree failed to keep free of American influences affecting tempo and easeful, mature relaxation. Cantelli was growing out of them.'

The informality of the Festival made it an ideal setting for Neville to indulge his sense of fun. There is no better example of this side of his nature than the following notice which appeared in the *Guardian* after a performance in 1960 of Rossini's *Stabat Mater*:

A LETTER FROM ROSSINI

Caro Signor Cardus,

I have recently been taking a holiday in my beloved city of Rome, but have been compelled to leave owing to the distractions caused by the Olympic Games, which have already arrived at a crescendo of noise and bustle entirely foreign to my habits and temperament. Hearing that my *Stabat Mater* was about to be performed in Edinburgh, conducted by my old friend Vittorio Gui, I decided to fly on the tail of the latest Comet to the once native city of my friend David Hume, who, by the way, now lives near me in a beautiful villa in the most select part of the Vale of Hades.

I arrived in Edinburgh just in time to hear my *Stabat Mater* most excellently played and sung. I at once fell in love with the enchanting voice and personality of Senorita Victoria de Los Angeles, so much so that I have already decided to compose, especially for her, a comic opera entitled 'The Barbarina of Seville'. . . . But this same sense of humour, which has frequently been my undoing, urged me to play, by means of my *Stabat Mater*, another wicked little joke. So I composed for it some of my most comic music. The *Cujus Animam* is, as I fondly believe, the funniest piece in the whole of my output. . . . Imagine my surprise and disappointment, Caro Signor, when at this performance in Edinburgh, nearly everybody in the large audience received the work with a solemnity which was proof that they had missed the whole humorous point. . . . I can understand, on reconsideration, the long-faced demeanour of the audience in general. After all, the performance was taking place on the evening of a Scottish Sabbath. But while partly comprehending the audience's unsmiling attention to and throughout my *Stabat Mater*, I was quite taken aback that the music critics obviously were sharing the same respectful and ponderous view of my work. . . . What is worrying me now after being present at this performance . . . is that all my works may come in time to be regarded with the same pious devotion which is given to the B-minor Mass of John Sebastian Bach, whom I am sorry to say, I have not seen for many years, as he lives rather a long distance from me. . . .

Please, Signor Cardus, may I ask you to do your best to perpetuate my brief portion of posterity in the right flippant way? I am encouraged to make this request because, on several occasions on this very austere Scottish Sabbath, I noticed that you were unashamedly smiling during the performance of my

Stabat Mater. The indignant 'shushes' you heard were not directed at you by —

> Yours in profanity,
> Gioacchino Rossini

Vittorio Gui happened to be staying in the same hotel, and the next day Neville received the following reply:

Dear Mr Cardus,

Thank you for your present under my door! Reading with care and with the utmost attention the letter of *our friend* Rossini from the Hades, I found it really delicious and much more serious and profound than it appears. . . . I would like to discuss with you about your interpretation of the intentions which did lead Rossini to write the *Cujus Animam.* I think that he was not so cynical to do it deliberately in that sense of humour; rather I think to his epoch [*sic*] when all the musicians, even the greatest composers, were under the dictatorship of singers – and obviously *Cujus Animam* is a piece for a celebrated tenor, Rubin or someone else. . . . Rossini was perhaps too much interested in money and success – This is my idea. . . .

I am so happy to have with me someone who has understood me.

> Your affectionate,
> Vittorio Gui

It was at the first Edinburgh Festival that Neville had heard the singing of Kathleen Ferrier. Her famous concert with Bruno Walter marked for him the beginning of an intense professional and emotional admiration which her tragically early death in 1953 did nothing to interrupt. Thereafter Edinburgh was always associated with her memory. He was utterly captivated by her art and her personality; he enjoyed being in her presence almost as much as hearing her voice. No sacrifice was too great if it enabled him to be present at one of her performances. Even his greatest favourites could not withstand her magnetic challenge. In one of his Edinburgh notices in 1952, Neville wrote: 'On Thursday night I was obliged to fly from *Der Rosenkavalier* to hear Kathleen Ferrier in *Das*

Lied von der Erde; for no other singer could I have been torn away from the Strauss–Hofmannsthal comedy with music.'

Neville's feelings for Kathleen Ferrier were genuine and heartfelt, and it was typical of the man that he never foresaw the possibility of their being regarded in any other light. Nor, at first sight, did there appear to have been any reason why he should have done so. In her short career, Ferrier achieved a popularity which extended far beyond the narrow confines of those who knew her or who had seen her perform. When she died in October 1953 at the age of forty-one, less than six months after her last performances in *Orfeo* at Covent Garden, the entire musical community shared the grief of family and friends. Neville felt her loss as deeply as anyone. His response was to set about collecting and editing a set of tributes from those who had played an important part in her musical life, including John Barbirolli, Gerald Moore, Roy Henderson and Bruno Walter. The result, *Kathleen Ferrier: A Memoir*, was published in 1954.

On closer examination, however, Neville's intense admiration for Kathleen Ferrier did raise a serious problem. As well as being a music-lover, he was a much respected, internationally famous critic, and in this latter guise he was the custodian of artistic standards and an immeasurable influence on the attitudes and judgements of his readers. Influence of this order necessarily entails responsibilities; and in retrospect it was probably only a matter of time before someone asked whether Neville had properly discharged these responsibilities. Is it not possible, the charge might have read, that an admiration which at times seemed to border on adulation could, indeed must, at some point compromise the critic's professional integrity? Put simply, did Neville's affection for Kathleen Ferrier blind him to her faults? Though this is not the place to pursue the argument, it is worth noting that whereas other critics noted a certain rigidity and distance in some of her performances, Neville's notices rarely contained even the most passing admonitory phrase. In the *Memoir*, he openly acknowledged the agonies he went through before including in one of his notices a critical reference to Ferrier's gestures of hand and head and facial expression. The recital in question took place in 1952. It is difficult to square Neville's inability or reluctance to criticise her singing with his reply to one of Robin Daniels's questions: 'Technically she wasn't the best singer in the world.'

[V]

But Neville's travels during the 1950s and early 1960s weren't confined to Glyndebourne, Edinburgh and Manchester. Provided there were not too many car journeys involved, he was happy to journey far and wide in search of the sights and sounds he loved. As his notices confirm, November 1954 found him setting off for Vienna to cover the opening of the State Opera. The Austrian capital had always been one of his favourite haunts. As well as being the source of much of the cultural tradition he most admired, it was a city whose charms he found irresistible, though expensive. After one visit, he wrote of Viennese coffee-houses – 'the waiters are as solicitous as ever; the lower the bow, the larger the tip'. In November 1963, he made a similar voyage of rediscovery to Munich for the opening of the new Opera House, and a year later he went to Bayreuth, the city which had awarded him its Wagner Medal.

Despite his previous complaints, Neville also found the will and energy to return to Australia to cover the M.C.C. tours of 1950–51 and 1954–55. On both occasions, it was his own idea. On 5 May 1950, Angus McLachlan received a telegram from Neville which contained one simple question:

WHAT OFFER EXCLUSIVE AUSTRALIAN TEST COVER.

McLachlan's reply was equally brief and to the point:

WITHIN REASON REPEAT ANYTHING YOU SUGGEST.

By the end of the month negotiations had reached the point at which McLachlan could cable the following offer:

SUGGEST ONE HUNDRED GUINEAS STERLING FOR EACH OF FIVE TESTS AUSTRALIAN RIGHTS STOP PLEASE LET ME HAVE YOUR COMMENTS.

Neville's answer, despatched on 7 June, was encouraging:

FAVOURABLY CONSIDERING STOP WILL WRITE CHEERIO.

True to his word, Neville sent the following message from Whitehall Place on 12 June:

I think the offer of one hundred guineas sterling for each of the five Tests is one that I can afford to accept, though I'm sure you'll agree that it isn't exactly generous. Would you allow me air-travel expenses? Is it your limit? I'm coming out more or less as a free-lance and only after much cogitation. Another book is brewing in my interior and I've a feeling that I'll write it best in Australia. London is grand to *live* in, but it is distracting.

Angus McLachlan's reply was polite but firm – no more money but the *Herald* were prepared to pay his travel expenses. Later Neville dropped the idea of flying and decided instead to sail with the M.C.C. party on 10 September.

The letter he wrote on 10 August telling the *Herald* of this change of plan also set out his understanding of the kind of material he was expecting to provide: 'I take it that Tom Goodman and Bill O'Reilly will be covering the news and purely technical side of the Tests for you and that from me you'll want a sketch of general as well as of particular cricket interest. I don't want to sit all day with my eyes glued to every ball.' The same letter contained two dire warnings, the first of which was distinctly reminiscent of *Autobiography* – 'I have arrived at my THIRD period, and am now very objective, ironical and economical' – while the second suggested a change of habit of far-reaching significance: 'I have abjured the semi-colon altogether.'

McLachlan's reply confirmed Neville's impressions of what the *Herald* were anticipating by way of coverage, and at the same time demonstrated a mastery of the deft ironic touch which its recipient would have been proud of.

There will be no need for you to sit all day with your eyes glued to every ball. Personally I should much prefer you to stay away from the matches altogether, because I have always felt that your reports were more exact and much more colourful when you kept your eyes glued to the bottles on the shelves of the bar and your back resolutely turned to the green field throughout the day.

I am interested to hear that you have arrived at your third period. You describe it as ironical and economical. I prefer to think of my Cardus in his third period as Hamletish, introspective, tragic. Soon, I suppose, we may expect your fourth period with a *Tempest*. But the transition will hardly be noticeable. Your writing was always 'such stuff as dreams are made of'. We shall bear your weakness when your old brain is troubled. We shall not be disturbed with your infirmity.

Though Freddie Brown's team failed in their bid to regain the Ashes, the series never lacked for incident and interest and ended in the best possible way from England's point of view with their first victory since 1938. Any disappointments Neville may have felt at the loss of the series were more than offset by the pleasure he gained from revisiting old friends. Before he left, the *Herald* had suggested that he prepare a piece for them on the Festival of Britain and, more in hope than certainty, had proposed a regular 'Cardus' survey of current events and personalities in British music. The Festival article duly arrived in mid-May 1951, and in his letter of thanks McLachlan reminded Neville of his second commitment. As he went on to explain, the activities of a rival had lent a greater urgency to the original idea:

> I wish you would write for us more often and preferably on a fairly regular basis. We should like to have for the *Sunday Herald* one article a month from you, rounding up musical events in Britain and letting us know something about trends and prominent articles. The *Telegraph* have suddenly developed an interest in music, and that is a field in which we will not allow them to establish themselves. At the moment they have a Miss Eunice Gardner in England, and she is sending a good deal about the Festival concerts. . . .
>
> Please don't ignore this letter as is your wont. I do not ask for a reply; I merely ask you for the first of your monthly articles.

The reminder could not have been better timed. To McLachlan's surprise but great pleasure, Neville immediately produced another article on London, and in the accompanying letter he wrote: 'Summer has come in – for the time being anyhow. I have never loved and revelled in London so much as now.' McLachlan continued with his subtle mixture of fulsome compliment and delicate chiding, and on 13 July received the following missive from Neville which confirmed the wisdom of this tactic. 'Bless you for those kind words. I'll send you an article every month.'

The closeness of his relationship with the *Herald* made it inevitable that when the time for the next M.C.C. tour came round,

Neville would give Angus McLachlan first option on his services. And so it proved. On 18 May 1954, he wrote once again to his old friend:

> My dear Angus,
>
> What do you propose to do about the next England v. Australia series? I have been sounded by a personage of your beauteous country to come out with the English team next September and write. I am not keen on the trip at the moment; but perhaps in the end I'll be tempted to see one more, and definitely my 'farewell', rubber; (semi-colon you'll observe) but I would never dream of writing for any Australian paper until I have given the *Herald* (meaning yourself) the first refusal of my services. So please let me know. . . .

Again the *Herald* jumped at the chance of more front-page Cardus, and McLachlan suggested a similar arrangement to that which had worked so successfully four years earlier. At this point communications between England and Australia seem to have broken down, for it was not until September that Neville wrote to confirm arrangements. In his letter, he referred (rather sheepishly) to certain medical problems he had been having of late.

> I forget if I've told you that the main reason I'm coming this time is in the hope of curing a frightful sinus trouble. (And of course I want to see you and all my Australian friends again.) My doctor warns me against anything like overwork in a stuffy atmosphere. I'm wondering if you really want a day-to-day article from me – at least you won't want a detailed report. Rather a 'Cardus' impression.

It is difficult to imagine a better occasion for an English cricket correspondent to make his final trip to Australia than the winter of 1954–55. The English team under Len Hutton became only the second this century to mount a successful defence of the Ashes in Australia. The series was full of drama. After being comprehensively thrashed at Brisbane, Hutton's team found matchwinners in the shape of Tyson, Statham, May and Cowdrey and recovered to win three successive Test matches. For Neville these victories provided abundant compensation for all the defeats he had been obliged to report on previous tours. The second Test at Sydney proved to be the turning-point of the tour. From his favourite seat in the fourth row on the left in the Bradman stand, Neville hardly missed a ball as Tyson pulled England back from seemingly inevitable defeat to a famous victory at twelve minutes past three on the fifth day. After the match, Neville was walking away from the ground with Margaret Hughes when a somewhat wild-looking gentleman approached and asked if he was Neville Cardus. On receiving confirmation that this was indeed the case, he offered his assessment of Neville: 'F.....g English bastard.' At this Neville removed his glasses, slowly, and replied. 'English – yes. Bastard – yes. But f.....g – not at the moment.'

Thanks to the latitude afforded by his arrangement with the *Herald*, Neville found that he had plenty of time for 'joyous' reunions with old friends. He also found time to take in some of Sydney's music programme, though here he experienced perhaps his only disappointment of the visit. Despite the presence of many of the performers he had so much enjoyed on earlier trips, and the rise of new artists of the stature of Joan Sutherland, Neville sensed a decline in aesthetic standards. As he explained to *Guardian* readers on 8 January 1955:

It is unwise perhaps to return after a long absence to a place where one has lived usefully and happily. . . . The main atmosphere of an Australian concert hall is one of 'provincial' social self-consciousness. . . . The main need in Australia of artists of all sorts is a qualified, experienced critic to establish and maintain reasonable standards of aim and conception as well as of performance. There are no nuances of consciousness in the Australian way of life. . . . Noise is taken for vitality.

The criticism may have sounded harsh, and doubtless to some ears it must have read as an exercise in self-promotion. But at the age of sixty-six, Neville never returned to take up the challenge he had identified. Nor was it at all clear that his presence would have been welcome.

6

Passing Years

'What is the worst of woes that wait on age?
What stamps the wrinkle deeper on the brow?
To view each loved one blotted from life's page,
And be alone on earth, as I am now.'[1]

[I]

At the beginning of the 1950s, Neville's letters to various old friends
reveal that he felt himself to be on the verge of another major literary
undertaking. The precise form of this work had still to be settled, but
for some time he had been mulling over various possibilities. The
one that most appealed to him involved combining a study of a major
musical figure – Gustav Mahler, for example – with a definitive
statement of his own approach to musical appreciation and criticism.
In this way, he would both realise a lifetime's ambition and secure
the survival of the critical tradition he represented. Just as Ernest
Newman would always be remembered for *Wagner Nights*, not to
mention his authoritative study of Gluck, so now Neville would
produce the work which would set the seal on his own illustrious
career.

If this was Neville's ambition, a quick glance at J. H. St J.
McIlwaine's admirable bibliography of his works shows that it was
never fully realised. The decade started promisingly enough with
the appearance of *Second Innings*, but thereafter, though he contributed articles by the dozen to journals as diverse as the *Bedside
Guardian*, *World Sports*, *Hallé*, the *Spectator*, *Wisden*, the *Saturday
Review of Literature*, the *Playfair Cricket Monthly*, *Records and Recording* and the *Gramophone Record Review*, the *magnus opus* never
appeared.

Instead his readers found themselves presented with a seemingly
inexhaustible series of collections and reprints. Starting in 1951

with Rupert Hart-Davis's *Cardus on Cricket*, the decade saw the publication of *Cricket All The Year Round* (1952), *Close of Play* (1954), *Talking of Music* (1957) and *A Composer's Eleven* (1958), the latter, to be fair, containing a new chapter on Anton Bruckner in addition to revisions of the material previously published in *Ten Composers*. Neville himself edited, and contributed an article to, *Kathleen Ferrier; A Memoir* (1954), and in 1961 he was responsible for the production of a similar posthumous tribute to his old friend, Sir Thomas Beecham.[2] The emphasis in all these pieces was on the past, the mood reflective and autumnal. Even much of his 'new' work was based on reminiscences of bygone heroes.

By the beginning of the 1960s even Neville's most ardent admirers began to suspect that they would never see the final, conclusive statement of his musical creed. It was no longer a question of his not being able to find the time as by now his *Guardian* contributions were more regular than frequent, rarely numbering more than forty in any one year, and many of the requests he received from other periodicals could have been politely, but firmly, rejected. The major problem, as Neville himself privately acknowledged, was that at the age of seventy he could no longer summon up the energy and inspiration necessary for a full-scale assault on a massive musical subject. Three- or four-page reflections were one thing; detailed comprehensive analysis another matter altogether. Yet 1965 saw the publication of *Gustav Mahler: His Mind and his Music*, the first of a projected two-volume analysis of the composer whose music Neville had done so much to popularise. Many felt this last piece of original Cardus to be unworthy of him and some wished that it had never been published; the critics, including many of his old colleagues, were generally unimpressed and one or two of their reviews said so.

Away from writing, Neville began to find himself faced with problems of another kind. As old age crept up on him, memories of the poverty he had seen as a child in Manchester crowded in and no amount of reassurance could entirely rid him of the fear of ending his days in destitution. It was a lingering concern that expressed itself in a variety of ways; some of his less devoted friends began to notice and resent his liking for being taken out to dinner, while publishers found that the author who had once found all talk of contracts and royalties to be unutterably tedious and tiresome was now taking a keen interest in his financial affairs. On 3 October

1955, Rupert Hart-Davis received a letter from Neville on the subject of royalties: 'In your royalty lists to me, details are given of *Good Days, Australian Summer* and *The Summer Game*; but for long I haven't had any information about *Days in the Sun*. Is it defunct?' Only three days later, he received a similar enquiry: 'I can't remember receiving royalties on *Days in the Sun* for some time. Could you look into your payments to me to find when, if ever, royalties on *Days in the Sun* have been paid to me by you.'

Responding immediately to Neville's enquiries, Hart-Davis discovered that royalties were indeed owing, but to Richards Press rather than to Neville. A cheque was quickly despatched, together with suitably profuse apologies, and there, it seemed, the matter would end. But not so. On his return from a visit to Vienna, Neville let Hart-Davis know that, as far as he was concerned, there were one or two loose ends still to be tied up!

National Liberal Club
Whitehall Place SW1
24 November 1955

My dear Rupert,

Back from Vienna I have now had time to consider your letter to me of October 10, telling me that an amount of £285.10.8 has been paid to the Richards Press, royalties on *Days in the Sun*: I had no idea that the Richards Press was still in existence!

I am not a man of business and I can't remember if I had a contract with you concerning the reprint of *Days in the Sun*. But I had taken it for granted that all your reprints of the Cardus cricket books had been under one and the same royalty arrangement. What am I now supposed to do to get my *Days in the Sun* royalties from the Richards Press? I have no arrangement with them; I imagined the books were now entirely between you and me.

Love,
Neville

The problem was soon resolved to everyone's satisfaction, but thereafter Hart-Davis made certain that Neville was kept fully supplied with royalty statements. Their professional relationship continued until 1961, at which point an offer from Collins prompted Neville to write to his old friend once again:

> National Liberal Club
> Whitehall Place SW1
> 27 January

My dear Rupert,

  I seem to remember your telling me that you had decided more-or-less to scrap my cricket books, and I agreed; for goodness knows you have given them a good, generous run.

  But now Collins want to bring out a sort of omnibus of all my cricket books. Would you give me permission to let them go ahead. The Edition might keep me financially when I am in my old age.

'Seem to remember' and 'a sort of omnibus' are excellent examples of the cultured vagueness that typified Neville's attitude to business affairs. It was only when things went wrong (or at least seemed to him to have done so) that he could be bothered to look beneath the surface, and even then the moment soon passed. When Hart-Davis indicated that he would not object to the 'omnibus' project suggested by Collins, Neville wrote to thank him not only for giving his permission but also for pointing out that Richards Press held the rights to *Days in the Sun*.

> National Liberal Club
> Whitehall Place SW1
> 1 February 1961

My dear Rupert,

  My blessings and thanks for allowing me to tell Collins to go ahead with a collected edition of my cricket books. . . . And thanks also for reminding me that Richards Press still have the rights of *Days in the Sun*. I can't remember that they have paid me anything for years!

> Always,
> Neville

This inability or unwillingness to manage his own business affairs didn't deter Neville from seeking to help other budding authors get their manuscripts accepted. On more than one occasion, he took advantage of his friendship with Rupert Hart-Davis to get a first reading for neglected masterpieces. But here, as elsewhere, he fell victim to his own good nature; all too often, generosity outweighed business acumen in his assessment of 'publishability'. In 1954, for example, he wrote to Hart-Davis about a friend of his: 'Meanwhile, my friend Kathleen Watkins is sending her MS again, entirely rewritten. I haven't read it but Naomi Lewis has a high opinion of it. *Anyhow*, it *has* to be published – it will mean so much to her. I think you will find it good enough, and if it is a risk I'm prepared to guarantee an amount.'

When the manuscript was turned down, Neville found himself not only disappointed but highly embarrassed. As he confessed to Hart-Davis a few weeks later: "I am very sad about Kathleen Watkins's book. I haven't read it myself, but I was made confident by Naomi Lewis's commendation; and I'm afraid I have foolishly or rather impetuously given Kathleen reason for considerable optimism. Don't write to her yet, and let us meet soon. Could you manage a lunch towards the end of this coming week?'

Throughout the second half of the 1950s Neville awaited the appearance of a collection of his music writings being compiled and edited (as he thought) by a fellow critic, Ernest Bradbury. The idea had been in the air ever since Neville's return from Australia, but it was not until 1954 that the project was finally launched. What followed makes sad reading even today, particularly for those who still await the publication of an 'omnibus' collection of Neville's music notices. At first, the omens were encouraging. The two men soon reached agreement over the material to be included, and it was left to Bradbury to order, present and edit it as he wished. To be fair to Bradbury, the fact that Neville was still very much 'alive and kicking', with plans of his own, did not make his task any easier. By the beginning of 1955, the first signs of friction began to emerge. Hart-Davis, the would-be publisher, received the following ominous letter from Neville, then in Australia covering the M.C.C. tour for the *Herald*:

I really don't think that Bradbury can reasonably complain if I wish to use my own *Surveys* for book publication. Still, if he

insists on some claim to four of them, I don't mind relenting.
But I am trying to imagine my reactions if, when I was
Bradbury's age, Newman (say) had allowed me to help myself
to all his newspaper criticism. Would I have felt hurt . . .
however!

But he mustn't use any character sketch – Toscanini or
Beecham. Or any of the *Surveys* dealing with a specific composer – because in my collection, I shall bind essays dealing
with a composer into a section. He will find ample character
sketches of Toscanini, Beecham in the *M.G.* notices. I also
wish to retain the *Survey's* entitled: 'Relative Values', 'Period
Music', 'Contemporary Music'.

This gives him ample *Survey* material from which to draw.
Indeed, if he is planning the book in the way I think it should
go, the sequence will be interrupted by too many abstract
essays.

I am still not enjoying Australia. The injury to Compton is
tragic.

Much love,
Neville

No doubt his disillusionment with Australia contributed to
Neville's growing irritation with Bradbury, but the key to the
problem lay elsewhere. A few months later, now safely back in
Whitehall Place, Neville returned to the attack, this time revealing
his own intentions to Hart-Davis: 'I am rather tired of waiting for
Bradbury. I gave him a generous chance – all royalties to him – and I
am pressing ahead with my own selections. I wish I could give the
book to you – but Collins is adamant.'

At the beginning of 1956, his hapless friend received another
letter from Neville, this time written in a very sardonic style which
clearly signalled Neville's growing frustration and foreshadowed
more trouble:

Thank you for your Spring catalogue. Bradbury's book, I see,
has gone up in price to 21 shillings but the date of publication is
still not revealed. Why not continue to keep the public in
suspense? Announce it every year at an increased cost; but
don't publish until the 'psychological moment'.

Thus: 'Any advance on *Cardus on Music?* In good condition.

Any advance on 21 shillings – thirty? – forty? – going, going, gone!!

By the way, I asked Bradbury some time ago to let me see the proofs. I can't very well let everything pass without some personal scrutiny. I go hot and cold when I think of some of my earlier excesses. My own collection won't appear until the autumn.

How much of Neville's animosity towards Bradbury stemmed from this concern to protect his professional reputation is difficult to gauge, not least because he never seemed to be able to make up his own mind about the merits of the young 'N.C.'. Sometimes, as on this occasion, he was clearly very apprehensive about reminding his public of his youthful phase with its flowery, romantic indulgence; yet elsewhere, he recalls this period with pride and satisfaction. In 1960, for example, Rupert Hart-Davis was left in no doubt about the valuation Neville placed on much of his earlier work: 'Frankly I have been envious of the ease and, on the whole, reliability of the writing and opinions. After the first performance, in 1930, of Mahler's Ninth Symphony, I wrote a column which I am sure I could not equal today – nor any other living music critic, if it comes to that.'

The Bradbury saga dragged on until 1960 by which time Neville saw himself – with more than a hint of self-pity – as the innocent victim of a grave breach of faith. On 10 May, he again voiced his sense of grievance to Hart-Davis:

It's a sad business – I think Bradbury has treated both of us with unbelievable discourtesy and contempt. Five years ago I gave him full freedom – and all the royalties (you yourself chided me for my generosity).

Desmond Shawe-Taylor would gladly have sponsored and edited the book – also Andrew Porter. I suppose the best thing would be to abandon the idea altogether.

Hart-Davis thought likewise, and shortly afterwards the project disappeared from his lists. Neville's response to this decision makes interesting reading; at this moment of greatest disappointment, he went out of his way to sympathise not only with Hart-Davis, but also with Bradbury.

National Liberal Club
Whitehall Place SW1
10 June 1960

My dear Rupert,

Heaven knows that you have been wonderfully patient
with Ernest. I certainly feel for you when you say 'I really don't
think I can bear to have any more dealings with Ernest.' . . . For
all his exasperating dalliance I feel rather sorry for Ernest. He
was in a dreadful state when I saw him the other day. Are you
sure you won't reconsider?

Love,
Neville

Let's lunch at the Garrick soon.

Bearing in mind all that had gone before, Neville's plea for a last-
minute reprieve may come as a surprise, but then it has to be realised
that the musical notices were his pride and joy. Though he made
light of it at the time, Bradbury's failure and the fact that no one else
came forward to take up the challenge hurt Neville deeply. Though
there was undoubtedly an element of injured pride in his attitude –
no one who knew Neville would claim otherwise – it was not just the
reaction of an old man intent on milking one last curtain call from his
audience before they finally dispersed. What was at stake was more
than distinguished prose; in his eyes, the music writings contained
the apotheosis of a lifetime devoted to musical appreciation. They
were to stand as a testament to the enduring impact of the critical
tradition he represented, and a legacy to all those who come to music
in search of beauty, art and a deeper understanding of humanity.

Despite these disappointments, the last fifteen years of Neville's
life were to provide him with many moments of satisfaction and
genuine happiness. He was by nature too vibrant a character to allow
circumstances to get the better of him for long. As long as he could
talk, write and listen life would retain its meaning and charm.
Moreover, it was Neville's great good fortune to have at hand a small
circle of devoted friends; some, like Else Mayer-Lismann, Margaret
Hughes and Lilli Williams, had known him for many years, while
others – John Arlott, for example – were more recent, but no less

admiring, acquaintances. In Arlott's case, the relationship was to embrace not only mutual affection but also collaboration in the writing of *The Noblest Game*.

Mercifully free from serious illness, Neville was able to maintain a presence at concerts, recitals and operas in London throughout the 1960s. The Garrick saw a lot of him, and radio and television provided another outlet for his talents, sometimes talking about bygone heroes, sometimes about himself. Though he managed to visit Manchester several times a year, normally to attend one of Sir John Barbirolli's concerts or a Test match, the margins of his world were inevitably starting to shrink. The Festivals at Glyndebourne and Edinburgh could still be assured of his support, but cricket – particularly the new species of one-day match – had largely lost its appeal. It was simply not the game he had once played and loved. Along with skill and style, what Neville sought most in a cricketer was character; yet in the late 1960s the game seemed to be falling into the hands of a new breed which he dubbed 'pedestrian cricketers'. Devoid of character and colour, these players were but pale shadows of the generation he grew up with – though in fairness, it would have been very difficult to compare them with bygone heroes whose reputation, in some cases, owed as much to 'Cricketer's' vivid and fluent imagination as to their own abilities!

As Neville passed through his seventies, he dwelt more and more in the past. Even his closest friends could not have failed to notice that much of his conversation consisted of recollections, nor that they had heard many of these more than once. Yet it was a mark of the man, and of the esteem and affection in which he was held, that few seemed to care. Part of his secret lay in the way he told these stories. Jack Fingleton, who 'adored' Neville, recalled in *Batting From Memory*, how he (Neville) 'would ape all the characters he spoke about. People around him never bothered Neville: he had his stories to tell and demonstrate, and bystanders might have been in another country. He would fall into their dialect when speaking of the men from his original north.' Later in the same passage, Fingleton pinpointed another of Neville's hallmarks as a raconteur: 'Nobody,' he wrote, 'enjoyed his stories more than Cardus himself. He would cup a hand to his mouth and laugh behind it, his eyes sparkling behind his glasses, while his shoulders shook with merriment. Indeed his whole frame would enter into the joke.'

[II]

In 1959 several of Neville's friends decided that his approaching seventieth birthday should be marked by a celebration a little out of the ordinary. After a lot of discussion, they hit upon the idea of a lunch at the Royal Festival Hall, and the arrangements were duly made. By all accounts, it turned out to be an enjoyable, if not especially memorable occasion. Some of the guests afterwards wondered whether the R.F.H. had been such a good idea after all; the musical association was appreciated, but the sheer size of the place had deprived the event of a little of the warmth and intimacy they had hoped for. One of Neville's oldest friends confessed later that all he could remember of the occasion was the moment when a very senior, female member of the acting profession leaned over the table and, in a manner so secretive that at the very least he expected to be privy to a state secret, confided that the clock on the Shell Building opposite was known by the locals as 'Big Benzine'.

Amongst the many gifts and tributes he received, one that particularly pleased Neville was a 'tribute' book in which many of the guests and other friends and colleagues had recorded their appreciation of his life and work. There were contributions from Otto Klemperer, Lord Birkett, Sir John Gielgud, Jack Hobbs, Len Hutton, Kirsten Flagstadt, Gerald Moore, Wilfred Rhodes, Elizabeth Schwarzkopf, Ernest Tyldesley, Bruno Walter and the ubiquitous Emmott Robinson. Dietrich Fischer-Dieskau caught the mood of the book when he wrote: 'There is only one Neville Cardus. To one of the outstanding representatives of the English spirit, I make my reverence on his great day.'

The seventieth birthday luncheon was to be the first of a series of occasions at which Neville's achievements were recognised. Foremost amongst these, though for different reasons, were two visits to Buckingham Palace and a concert at the Free Trade Hall given in his honour by the Hallé Orchestra. On 10 November 1964, Neville received the C.B.E., an event he recalled a day later:

> National Liberal Club
> Whitehall Place SW1
> 11 November 1964

Dearest Marjorie,

   You may be interested (and amused) to hear of my

experience yesterday at Buckingham Palace, where I was given my C.B.E. ribbon and medal by the Queen. I drove to the Palace (in a car hired from Harrods, complete with a chauffeur) and was held up in the Mall for a quarter of an hour – there were 172 other 'candidates'. At last I was in the Palace, up a flight of wide stairs and ushered, or ordered, by men in uniform, through miles of long rooms like the National Gallery (but the pictures weren't as good), finally into an apartment, very cold, while I waited with the first batch to go into the hall. After half an hour of zero temperature, we went in, waiting at the door, in the wings of a stage. We each walked in singly. There was a large audience of relatives (Edith was one of them), and a string orchestra played softly in the music gallery – Franz Lehár, Johann Strauss and Sousa. The Queen stood on a small platform, looking very tiny, dressed in a sleeveless orange affair. She might have been any nice shy young lady in D. H. Evans or Kendall Milnes.

The procedure is to bow before her and bend your head, so she can put the ribbon round your neck. She didn't say a word, but moved her mouth as though about to say something. Obviously she can't be expected to remember everybody – especially as I had never been on television!

Edith, who went with a lady friend, fell asleep. You are not allowed to leave until the investiture is entirely over. So I was sent back to sit in the audience, watching over a hundred anonymities pass by. I calculated that it took the Queen five seconds to 'do' each candidate. Most times, I must admit, she had a smile. But, alas, not for me!

Dearest Marjorie, I am still glowing over my rememberance of the lovely stay with you and your darling mother. You must ask me again, in the spring. And remember me to Peter.

My love to you,
Always,
Neville

As well as bestowing great honour upon him, the investiture provided Neville with a fresh stock of anecdotes. From the relative objectivity of his letter to Marjorie Robinson, it was but a short step to a host of off-the-cuff, oft-repeated 'one-liners'. 'Investitures are all right,' he would begin, 'but they are terribly uncomfortable. You stand in a long queue, frozen cold and very nervous; you can't joke, can't sit down and can't pee.' The last of these complaints caused Neville such discomfort that in the end he was forced to ask a footman where he might find a toilet. 'Second door on the right, sir,' were the instructions which Neville followed to the letter and found himself in a broom cupboard. Distressing though this experience may have been at the time, it didn't prevent him from being immensely gratified when a knighthood was conferred upon him in the 1967 New Years Honours' List. On the way to the Palace for a second time, he might well have recalled the advice Sir Thomas Beecham had once given him: 'In the unlikely event of you being offered a knighthood, Neville, take it. It makes tables at the Savoy so much easier to come by.'

Neville was and remains the only music critic to have been knighted this century. That his chosen profession could have been so consistently ignored was to his way of thinking an affront to both the most outstanding of his colleagues (Newman, he said more than once, should have been made a C.H., if not a member of the Order of Merit) and the profession itself. Yet for all the pleasure it brought him, Neville was later to tell Robin Daniels and others that it was neither his knighthood, nor the various international awards conferred upon him (nor even an invitation from the BBC to feature on 'Desert Island Discs'*) that gave him most satisfaction. That accolade was reserved for the tributes paid by the two organisations that had meant so much to him in his early days, the Lancashire County Cricket Club and the Hallé orchestra. 'In both cases,' he recalled, 'I was reminded of my childhood in Manchester. I first went to Old Trafford at the turn of the century when I was eleven or twelve, and I went to my first Hallé concert around 1907 when I was eighteen.'[3] The wheel had now come full circle.

The man who had gone to such lengths to ornament his autobiographical description of childhood, who had virtually ignored his mother and 'killed off' his favourite Aunt Beatrice, and who had not lived in the city for over twenty-five years, had now found in

* The records he selected were: Schumann's *Fantasia* in C; Prelude and Liebestod from Wagner's *Tristan und Isolde*; Mozart's Clarinet Concerto; Beethoven's Fourth Symphony; Mahler's *Das Lied von der Erde*; Schubert's Unfinished Symphony; Prokoviev's Classical Symphony; Richard Strauss's 'The Four Last Songs'.

Manchester associations and memories of greater personal meaning
than the tributes of nations. It was a striking example of the way in
which, at the end of his life, Neville revalued and in some cases
rediscovered many of the simpler pleasures of his earliest days, and
in so doing acquired a sense of contentment that had once seemed
beyond his grasp.

In 1971, the man who as a young boy had watched in awe and
excitement as the likes of MacLaren, Trumper and Tyldesley had
bruised the boundary fence at Old Trafford was invited to become
President of the Lancashire Cricket Club. In all but name, it was
'Cricketer' who accepted the invitation with genuine gratitude and
affection, and thereafter presided with energy and enthusiasm over
the affairs of the Club. For its part, the Hallé chose another
landmark in Neville's career to honour his contribution to musical
life. In 1966 Neville celebrated his fiftieth year with the *Guardian*.
To mark the occasion, two concerts were arranged in his honour –
one in Manchester on Thursday 14 April and one in London two
days later. With Barbirolli conducting, the concerts would have been
an unquestioned success but for one terrible, jarring moment. In his
speech after the concert at the Free Trade Hall, Sir John naturally
referred to Neville's long association with the *Guardian* and revealed
that he had been asked by the paper's management to make a
presentation on their behalf. He then handed a small envelope to
Neville who opened it in full view of the audience and found himself
the proud possessor of a cheque for £100 – '£2 for every year I
worked for them', as he commented later, a little darkly. Barbirolli,
who was hurt, embarrassed and reportedly furious, was all for
revealing the contents of the envelope before the assembled throng,
but Neville chose to maintain his silence.

It is difficult to appreciate how insensitive a gesture it was. Neville
had long since resigned himself to being ignored by the civic
authorities in his home town. After receiving the Wagner Medal for
the City of Bayreuth, he had told an old friend in Manchester,
'Many thanks for your congratulations about the Bayreuth award. It
came as a complete surprise. But if it had come from Manchester I
might have suffered a severe shock.' And now it was the *Guardian*'s
turn to deepen the wound. How ironical those lines from *Autobio-
braphy* must have seemed at this moment:

A dear tyrant, the *M.G.* I have never been able to break free from it. Others have made the wrench and have prospered in the accumulation of earthly goods. I doubt if they have ever afterwards known the happiness and pride that comes from membership of the staff of the *M.G.*[4]

This seemingly trivial episode confirmed all his worst suspicions that all was not well with the *Guardian*: first there had been a change of design, then a change of name and finally the move to London. Now he knew that these moves amounted to more than a mild attack of rationalisation; what was happening involved nothing less than betrayal – not of himself (though money was an ever-present worry) but of the legacy handed down by C. P. Scott.

There is little doubt that Neville's attitude towards the *Guardian* at this later stage in his life was prompted in part by his growing uneasiness about a pensionless retirement. Among the congratulations he received on the announcement of his knighthood was one from his old friend in Sydney, Angus McLachan, which read: 'CONGRATULATIONS WE HAVE NOT FORGOTTEN YOU AND AM GLAD THE QUEEN HASN'T EITHER.' In his reply, Neville thanked McLachlan for the the telegram and then went on, 'Incidentally, while on the *Sydney Morning Herald* I was the lowest paid music critic in the world – and I still am on the *Guardian*. Talk about a 'Freeze'; it has operated in my case for years!'

But there was more to Neville's reaction than simply financial worries. Looking at the modern *Guardian*, he felt more and more that he was a hapless bystander witnessing the final moments of an uneven contest. In his heart of hearts, he recognised that all the fundamental changes made to his *M.G.* since the war were unavoidable, that without them it would have reverted to the status of a provincial rag, or else disappeared completely; but he also knew that each change took the paper one step closer to renouncing its heritage. He had been brought up to cherish and revere the ideals and integrity that Scott had stood for. What made the desecration of this heritage harder to bear was that it was being undertaken in the name of a savage god by men who had no right to be mentioned in the same breath as its creator.

In a world of glossy tabloids and gossip columnists, it is easy to forget the enormity of the transformation which had overtaken Neville and his like since the war. Today they appear as the 'old school' of journalism, a phrase which, as Dickens once noted, 'generally means any school that seems never to have been young'. But in the 1920s and '30s, any music critic worth his salt would have expected to be allowed (and required) to devote a full broad-sheet column to reviewing a concert. In his talks with Robin Daniels, Neville recalled how, after a Schnabel recital,

> I wrote almost a whole column – 1,200 words – about Opus 111 because to hear it had been a profoundly moving experience. Suddenly I realised I was coming to the end of my alloted space, and I hadn't even mentioned Schnabel. So, in the last paragraph, I had only 20 words to say he had played with extreme insight. When I saw my column the next morning in the *Manchester Guardian* – an enormous column about Op. 111 and a little paragraph, a six-line footnote, stitched on at the end about Schnabel – I thought to myself 'Good God, what will Schnabel think of this'?[5]

Thirty years later, he would have had no cause to worry; the same notice would never have extended beyond 500 words, much less for a second-rate performer.

Signs of the trouble to come were to be found in the *Surveys*. At least twice he went out of his way to contrast the freedom enjoyed by pre-war critics (and the consequent sense of ease and flow in their notices) with the strangulating constraints applied to their modern counterparts. Whatever might have been said about the old days, Neville concluded, the one unassailable fact was that both critic and reader enjoyed the notices. But in the 1960s he and many of his fellow critics felt that they were being obliged to perform a wretched juggling act just to ensure that the most important facts (even names, places and works performed) were not omitted from their tiny paragraphs. The result, as one of Neville's colleagues has summed it up, is that 'our faculties, insofar as we have any, have become simply atrophied'.

Neville's profound resentment at the injury and indignity being inflicted on music critics in the name of financial salvation was a recurrent theme in a series of letters to Harold Priestley, an old Mancunian acquaintance who was to play an important role in collecting the material for *The Delights of Music*, the last collection of Neville's music writings. 'I hope I shall be able to write a notice satisfying to you,' he told Priestley in May 1964, 'but what can a critic do of any value between 10.15 and 11.15. . . . Oh, for the old days when we could go on writing until the early hours.' The same correspondence also illustrated Neville's rapidly dwindling regard for the new masters of the *Guardian*, and for the sort of journalism they seemed to be intent on encouraging. In 1963, for example, he complained to Priestley of the paper's declining standards:

> It is good to know that *Guardian* (*Manchester Guardian*) readers of vintage still persist. I often wish that these old and qualified *M.G.* readers would write to the present Editor asking why his critics are not given more space – and why so many obscure names are allowed to appear on the 'Arts Page'. Goodness me, in Scott's, Crozier's and Wadsworth's time, a contributor to the *M.G.* had to be pretty good even to get his initials printed.

As if to emphasise his growing disillusionment with his own paper, Neville went on to compliment the work of Michael Kennedy, the Northern music critic of the *Daily Telegraph*. Not only were Kennedy's notices in his view worthy of the national press – which by implication was more than could be said about much that appeared in the *Guardian* – but they also stamped him, in Neville's own words, as 'a man after my own heart'. It was an important consideration at a time when Neville felt himself to be very much out of fashion. As he confessed to Harold Priestley in February 1966, 'You are very generous to write to me so warmly about my *Guardian* article the other day. As a fact, I was almost shy about sending it in – they are so timid in the paper nowadays of personal "subjective" stuff.'

Priestley was one of the first to congratulate Neville on his knighthood; in his reply Neville expressed his thanks but added in ominous fashion, 'I've received telegrams and letters from editors everywhere – Brisbane to Berlin, USA and South Africa; but nothing from Hetherington.' The 'Hetherington' in question was none other than H. A. Hetherington, then the *Guardian*'s editor, and a man for whom Neville latterly had little regard and less liking. It was Hetherington whom he held to be largely responsible for the debasement of C. P. Scott's bequest. But by the end of 1967, a year in which Neville succumbed to a bout of laryngitis so severe that his specialist was obliged to order him to remain silent for a week (a sentence of unimaginable severity), it was not only Hetherington who was coming under fire.

A visit to Lord's caused him to lambast Yorkshire for an 'unbelievably spineless' display of batting that would have been 'enough to make Maurice Leyland revolve in his grave'; and later that year it was Barbirolli's turn to have his competence called in to question. Partly because of his personal abilities and partly because of his contribution to the Hallé cause, Sir John had always been one of Neville's special favourites, but on 13 December Harold Priestley received a letter from the National Liberal Club which included the following less-than-adulatory paragraph:

> Sir John conducting Elgar's second symphony last night was rather too self-indulgent. Slow caressing tempo in the middle section of the first movement almost brought proceedings to a standstill. A 50-minutes duration work was made to last 70 minutes. I was hard put to it to write a notice diplomatic enough not to offend the Maestro.

Clearly, in private if not always in public, the famous pen had retained much of its edge and energy. In prose as in conversation the best lines and stories were used more than once, but at least the presence of the written word seemed to alert him to the worst dangers of repetition. 'Cardus' articles kept appearing throughout the 1960s, usually in the more familiar cricket or music periodicals, but occasionally he would break new ground by contributing pieces to journals like *Wine Mine* and *About The House*. In one respect, however, Neville remained a model of consistency; wherever the article, whatever its subject, it was always a safe bet that the name of Beecham would crop up sooner or later.

In the piece entitled 'Candles By Day' which appeared in *Wine Mine* at the end of 1971, Neville began with a familiar assertion: 'For me, wine is not the main theme of a meal; it is the orchestration which blends food and conversation into harmony.' A paragraph later, Beecham made his entrance – 'I support Sir Thomas Beecham's conviction that champagne is a flamboyant intrusion at a dinner table' – and later returns for an encore: 'I remember that, at a dinner party, a guest of Sir Thomas Beecham slushed through a vanilla ice-cream after the port was served. Beecham merely

murmured, *sotto voce*, 'Good God', which by Beecham's standards
let the fellow off very lightly.'

If by the end of his life Neville's imagination had lost a little of its
originality and variety, he could still be counted on to produce the
evocative image, the vivid phrase and the telling line.

[III]

Edith Cardus died of a heart attack on 26 March 1968. She was
eighty-one. The following morning the *Guardian* carried a simple
notice:

> CARDUS – On 26 March 1968 LADY EDITH CARDUS came to the
> end of a full happy life. No flowers or mourning.

In a letter to Harold Priestley written shortly after her funeral,
Neville described his late wife as 'a great and loyal companion'. Her
death left him terribly alone. Theirs may have been an unconventional partnership, but for all his occasional indiscretions Neville
always recognised his debt to his wife. He had several close,
affectionate and utterly devoted friends, but there was only one
Edith. 'There will never be another Lady Cardus,' he always
insisted, and there never was.

Loyalty and companionship were qualities Neville was now to
find himself desperately in need of. On the surface, Edith's passing
seemed to make little difference to his way of life. He still loved
music, writing, conversation and, at a pinch, cricket. On 29 May
1968, he wrote to Harold Priestley:

> Thanks for your appreciation of the Rubinstein piece. It is not
> often one gets the chance to expand. The arts page in the
> *Guardian* nowadays seems to want quickly written (or typed)
> snippets. . . . I was tremendously impressed last week at Lord's
> by the bowling and presence of Brian Statham. How he will be
> missed in the Lancashire team of tomorrow!

A month later he was again at Lord's, but this time the elements
were against him: 'It was terribly frustrating at Lord's,' he complained. 'What a climate. I really am thinking of going back to
Australia.' The idea never came to anything, but he did move – from

the National Liberal Club to Edith's old home: 112, Bickenhall Mansions. The change of scene obviously helped to revive his spirits for on 9 October 1968 he wrote to his old friend again: 'I have given up the club as a residence. I have had this flat redecorated – and the music room is one of the loveliest in London. Come and see it. . . . I've written a piece once or twice a week since Edinburgh – including a special last week about the book on "Sir Malcolm".'

But beneath this buoyant exterior Neville was languishing. Personal bereavement and a sense of professional betrayal had left him vulnerable and disillusioned. Worst of all, he felt obsolete; there seemed to be no place for him in a world dominated by considerations of cost and convenience. Much of 1969 was passed in this mood of embattled fatalism. Even some of his best friends and colleagues seemed to be drifting away. Barbirolli, in particular, was latterly very remote and introspective. On 2 September 1969, Neville mentioned this tendency in a letter to Priestley. 'John never gets in touch with me when he comes to London,' he lamented; 'he is also a darling, but entirely absorbed in himself, bless him.' Later in the same letter, Neville offered his views of two of the younger generation of English musicians: 'He [Michael Kennedy] wrote to me saying "what about Janet Baker", when I said that Jacqueline was the richest asset to English music since Kathleen. But a cellist of Jacqueline's gift is rare – unique – while Janet, at her best, can't be described as a "better" or a greater enrichment than Kathleen.'

A criticism frequently levelled at Neville is that his emotional affinity with certain types of music and musicians made for a partial assessment of their merits. While no one could doubt that Neville had his favourites, and that Jacqueline du Pré was certainly one of them, he was rarely, if ever, so besotted with an artist that he lost sight of their failings. So it was with Jacqueline du Pré. In another letter to Priestley written nearly eight months later, the mood of his assessment of her talents was more critical (and perhaps tragically prophetic):

Thank you for letting me see Michael's notices about the Barenboim performance of the Elgar cello concerto. It is pretty tough – the trouble with critics in general is that they can't or won't, lighten their death sentences with some wit. Jacqueline has for some time been losing her touch in the Elgar concerto, which she could play beautifully a year or two ago. I doubt if she was wise to take lessons from Rostropovitch, a very different cellist.

The second half of 1968 was one of the most depressing periods of Neville's life. After smiling on him for so long (as he would have it), the gods now seemed to have taken umbrage and withdrawn their favours. A hitherto richly satisfying life now seemed beset with problems. Without falling seriously ill, he was nevertheless afflicted by a series of minor ailments; first he had trouble with his eye, then his voice and finally his foot, which eventually required minor surgery. The editors of the *Guardian* seemed intent on destroying a great institution, while the sub-editors took a perverse pleasure in mutilating his copy. The Inspector of Taxes, so he believed, was about to swoop and his bank balance would not stand the challenge. And beneath it all lay a lurking sense of irrelevance, of having no place or role in the modern world, of being, in a word, redundant.

In his disenchantment and depression, Neville turned for comfort to the past. If the present was difficult to bear and the future unimaginable, at least his memories – selective and embellished though they sometimes were – gave pleasure, solace and a reason for hope. In public he remained loyal to friends, but in private his views were often less charitable. Many of the artists he had once admired now seemed fallible in comparison with their predecessors. Thus, in December 1968 he wrote:

Michael has already sent me his article about the Hallé. I agree with him entirely – for a long time the orchestra has been only so-so whenever it has played in London. And John himself seems to get more and more self-conscious. He is so much in love with his own fondling of a line of melody that the music in general has no continuous flow, no embracing shape.

And returning to one of his favourite themes, Neville placed much of the responsibility squarely on the shoulders of modern music critics:

It is dangerous for any artist to do his work in an environment where he gets little or no criticism. Does Michael ever really take John to task? I was constantly in trouble, in my Manchester period with the Hallé Orchestra, with the Committee, with Harty – and with Beecham.

Ungenerous though these remarks may sound today, they were not intended to be so. At heart Neville was desperately concerned for the future of the institution which first introduced him to music, with which he had enjoyed a long association and with which his reputation was, and still is, most intimately linked. As he explained to Harold Priestley: 'The question is what will happen to the Hallé when John definitely vacates his post.'

His fears were well founded, as those who regularly attended Hallé concerts in the post-Barbirolli era may confirm. But at this moment it was not the orchestra but its conductor who most concerned Neville. It was Barbirolli's company he most missed; again and again, his letters referred to John's absence. From Edinburgh he wrote, 'John arrives here this morning to conduct the Scottish Orchestra, Arrau the soloist; but I don't suppose for a moment that I'll see him, except on the rostrum. He never gives me a ring.' And later in London, 'J.B. stays in London, but never gives me a ring. . . . He is naughty – much too self-centred.' In his own despair, Neville perhaps forgot that Barbirolli, who was by this time visibly ageing and weary, had little energy or time to meet all the demands made of him.

Be that as it may, the fact remains that the less Neville saw of Sir John, the more privately critical he became of his old friend's conducting. Towards the end of 1969 he told Priestley: 'For some time I've been aware of a certain rhythmical weakness in John's conducting . . . he seems so much to love a single phrase that he lingers over it, caressing it; meanwhile the general momentum is lost.' Six months later, it was the same story: '. . . I have for some time found John's phrasing an embarrassment. I'm quite apprehensive about his conducting here next week of Bruckner's Eighth Symphony – Bruckner himself dallies enough!'

Evidently similar fears were being expressed in Manchester for in his next letter to Priestley, Neville was moved to post the following complaint:

I seem never to get a communication from Manchester that isn't about John! . . . I don't often agree with Gerald Larner, but he is right about John's present inability to go through a movement without making a dozen tempo changes. John has lived too long in a place where he has not been submitted to some frank criticism. After all, as a critic you can't seem to be an artist's publicity agent! The trouble in Manchester for years is that you have heard none of the truly top conductors – though there aren't too many on view nowadays.

Neville's strictures on the weakness of contemporary music criticism was more than just a rejection of different tastes, irritating and incomprehensible though he undoubtedly found many of them. In his view, too many of the current generation of critics suffered from an inability to write (his old 'bête noire', Ernest Bradbury, was specifically exempted from this category) and, worse still, their approach to music criticism smacked of an unhealthy infatuation with the 'objective' approach he disliked so intensely. In reply to a request for advice from a would-be critic, he once wrote:

> I agree entirely with your views on musicology and all the rest of the 'scientific' jargon. You could develop your ideas much farther. What is the 'objective' score? What is this fixed 'science' (changing in every age!)? Today the fashion is for the material organisation. Wagner argued that – 'It is sometimes necessary that we musicians should talk about technique. But the public should never hear of it.'

Though Neville's private opinions of the Manchester-based *Guardian* critics, particularly Colin Mason and Gerald Larner, were often less than complimentary, it was their counterparts on the *Daily Telegraph* – 'the Stadlens and the Coopers of this world' – who attracted his most scathing observations. Sometimes it was the quality of their notices that prompted him to comment, 'Isn't Stadlen a conceited ass? – pitting his views of Mahler against Schoenberg's' or 'Stadlen the Incomprehensible. A charming man but – as a writer !!??!!' Elsewhere it was their critical method that upset him; 'I agree with you about these score-reading critics,' he told Priestley in 1969, 'The *Telegraph* lot are my special aversion, especially Cooper and Stadlen. Cooper is sour; he was yawning (over his score) during the performance of the Elgar symphony.'* By

* It may not have been entirely coincidental that these views were expressed after the gentleman in question had given a very critical reception to Neville's book on Mahler.

the end of his life, the only critics Neville really admired and respected were Andrew Porter and William Mann – though even the latter was suspected of secretly reading Ernest Newman's notices.

Throughout these difficult years, Neville and Michael Kennedy had shared a warm personal regard for each other. Not only was Kennedy one of the few critics Neville had any time for, but he and his wife also provided much enjoyed and appreciated company. Thus it was particularly unfortunate when the two men suddenly fell out in 1971. The cause of their feud was Neville's review of two biographies of Sir John Barbirolli (who died in 1970), one by Kennedy and the other by Charles Reid. Thinking that Gerald Larner was to cover Kennedy's book in a separate review, Neville dealt with both books in a single article. Unfortunately, for reasons that were never fully explained, Larner's piece never appeared, leaving Neville's diplomatic but not particularly searching assessment to stand as the *Guardian*'s final opinion.

There is no doubt that Neville was greatly embarrassed by the whole episode, not least because both Kennedy and Hamish Hamilton, Reid's publisher, were personal friends. On 9 November 1971, he wrote to Kennedy to try to explain what had happened:

> I'm not sure if you would have approved of my review of Reid's book. I didn't slate it but rather damned it with palsied praise – no not exactly praise. It is a fair journeyman's work. In my view, I said that you looked at John from the inside, Reid from the outside. . . . I praised your book highly; it is really top-class. It even inspired Martin (Cooper) to good humane English. . . .

But it was too late. As well as feeling that Neville had never fully understood Barbirolli either as a man or a conductor and having little regard for Reid's authorship, Kennedy suspected that the joint review was the outcome of a spot of behind-the-scenes chicanery to which his old friend had knowingly been a party. Deeply hurt, he made no attempt to hide his feelings. At first Neville failed to appreciate the extent of Kennedy's anger and tried to play down the issue:

> So the eccentric Bill Webb has used my review of the Barbirolli books – and I am sure you are disappointed in me. Of course the review was cut . . . it's always difficult to review a book

written by somebody you are close to, admire, and love. I think you are hard on Reid; he is a good working-journeyman. Inaccuracies? We all make them – which goes for Shakespeare himself.

These bland assurances only made matters worse. Where insensitivity unwittingly collides with oversensitivity, the damage is usually extensive and hard to repair. Kennedy responded with a letter which hurt Neville's pride and stung him into a response which he too would later regret. On 12 November, he wrote again to Kennedy: 'Your letter astonishes me. Heaven help you if you ever get a review like the review Cooper wrote of my Mahler book. But we remained – and remain – friends. I didn't write a protesting "hurt" letter to him. Why are critics so touchy?'

That the row left both men severely shaken and upset emerges from other letters they wrote at the time. At first both reacted by forcefully decrying the motives and behaviour of the other. Cardus told a friend, 'Obviously he [Kennedy] is annoyed because I linked his book with Reid's which is a very competent piece of work,' while Kennedy wrote, 'When someone like Cardus can find no difference between my attempts at writing something a bit special and different and Charles Reid's inaccurate work, then I despair. I shall never forgive N.C. . . .'

At this point all communication between the two men ceased and it was some time before Neville learned the full reason for Kennedy's anger. It transpired that in the course of a conversation with Lady Barbirolli Neville had been heard to say that Kennedy's book 'ought to have been done by a real writer'. On learning, or being reminded, of his indiscretion Neville quickly sought to make amends:

If I *did* say to Evelyn . . . I am ashamed and shocked. I think she must have misunderstood; perhaps I suggested that there was room for a more detached, realistic estimate of John. Anyhow, if I actually expressed myself so crudely to Evelyn, I am *profoundly* sorry. . . . Try to forget it all, please, Michael. . . . Consider this correspondence closed, and come soon to London and I'll try to clear my character over a vintage Mouton Cadet.

It had been an upsetting episode for both men; Neville because 'at my time of life I cannot afford to lose precious kindred spirits', and Kennedy because although he was never entirely convinced by Neville's explanation of events, he nevertheless soon regretted having reacted so emotionally. In his own words, 'One should never stand on one's dignity. . . . I'd reviewed enough books and been a journalist and a critic long enough not to have been so upset, and after all Neville was over eighty.' Both were thus greatly relieved when their friendship was restored in June 1972. After Kennedy had agreed to let bygones be bygones, Neville wrote to him on 12 June: 'Your letter has made me very happy, not only because you are generous about my talk the other day. More important is that you have broken a silence. As I told you in a letter months ago, I can't afford at my time of life to lose dear friends.' And then again on 23 July: 'Warm thanks for sending me a copy of your most generous tribute to me. You have always been a great encouragement. I am sorry that, unwittingly, I hurt you by my notice of your book on John.'

[IV]

Now well into his eighties, Neville was at last beginning to show signs of physical infirmity. Friends noticed that his handwriting looked shaky; aches and pains were more frequent and took longer to shake off – though, as he told Harold Priestley, even ill-health had its compensations: 'I'm fairly free of muscular pain now, after a crippling period. The sciatica has responded to massage (by a very pretty girl).' Latterly, too, his enthusiasm for live performances had begun to wane, and with it inevitably his journalistic output. Though in part this was simply a reflection of old age, unhappily there was another reason.

It was common knowledge that Neville's relationship with the management of the *Guardian* had been deteriorating for years. During the Edinburgh Festival in 1969, he had complained bitterly about the way the sub-editors treated his copy. 'The *Guardian*,' he wrote, 'cuts and misprints me so much that after reading every notice, I want to resign. I call the "subs" room at Gray's Inn Road the Abattoir!' Three weeks later, these same 'subs' caused more offence; 'Last week,' he fumed, 'they cut my notice of the Hallé, in the Festival Hall, in half with no attempt to see what might be taken out here and there. No; the notice was chopped into two, like a butcher cutting a weekend joint.'

Time after time, his letters harked back to the same theme – the treatment meted out in the 'subs' room. In 1970, he wrote:

I write 'special' articles on cricket for the *Guardian* but they usually print them after the topical point has been dulled. I wrote one last week, referring to the 'Test' at Headingley; it hasn't appeared in print yet. Really I'd like to throw it in with the *Guardian*.

Early in 1972, it was the same grievance:

It [a piece on Karajan] was the only notice I have written for weeks *not* butchered by the *Guardian*. The notice I wrote for Thursday about Menuhin and Sibelius was terribly mauled ... if I could afford it, I'd send in my resignation tomorrow.

And later that same year:

I'm not writing much for the *Guardian*. They have turned down three specials – including a long piece on Chaliapin!! So I am 'on strike' ...

Finally, in October 1973:

I haven't covered a concert for the *Guardian* since April! I can't cope with the sub-editors. And though I have sent in two or three 'specials' lately, the brisk boys who run the Arts Page tell me they can't print them yet, because (believe it or not) they are not 'topical'. Delius, Mahler, Sibelius etc., are not topical! God help us.

These paragraphs need no commentary; their pathos is self-evident. Yet the unkindest cut of all was still to come. In April 1974, Neville reached the ripe old age of eighty-five. Congratulations came in from all over the world. On the 27th, he wrote his last letter to Harold Priestley. In it, he noted: 'I have heard from Michael. He sent me a copy of a very generous tribute he wrote for me. I received telegrams and calls from many newspaper editors, even as far distant as Sydney and Vienna. NOTHING from Hetherington or the *Guardian*.

7
Farewell

'Die Sonne scheidet hinter dem Gebirge.
In alle Täler steight der Abend neider
Mit sein Schatter, die Voll Kühling sind. . . .
Die liebe Erde allüberall
Blüht auf im Lenz und grünt aufs neu!
Allüberall und ewig blauen licht die Fernen!
Ewig . . . Ewig . . .'[1]

[I]

Despite the widening rift with the *Guardian*, Edith's death and the insidious loneliness which followed, Neville's last years weren't all gloom and despondency. Though he may have wearied of the hurly-burly of journalism and despaired of many of his successors, his primal love of late eighteenth- and nineteenth-century music remained. When concert-going became too disruptive and uncomfortable, sustenance was at hand in the form of a 'baby grand' and an extensive collection of records. As important as the music itself were the memories it evoked. Many of his records featured artists who had been and sometimes still were his personal friends. (In Muriel Cohen's case, Neville had gone to great lengths to persuade her to have records made from tapes of her Australian recitals.)

Though advancing years may have taken the edge off his energies, Neville's enthusiasm for 'pet' projects remained undiminished. Despite the criticism directed at his book on Mahler, he still half-believed that a major literary project was within his compass. For several years he had cherished the idea of writing a study of Lotte Lehmann. They had first met in the 1930s and had remained friends ever since. The fact that Lehmann was now an American citizen living in California, and had already written an autobiography, did not deter Neville from suggesting that she should allow him to write her memoirs. About a couple of months later, he received a letter from Lotte Lehmann, the contents of which are as intriguing now as they were disappointing then:

4656 Via Huerte
Hope Ranch Park
Santa Barbara
California 93110
28 July 1973

Dearest Neville,

I have not forgotten what you asked me to consider: to write my Memoirs. But the more I think about it, the less I see the possibilities of doing so. I think it was in 1939 that Routledge in London published my Memoirs under the title of *On the Wings of Song* . . . In rereading it, it sounds to me commonplace and obsolete.

Some time ago, I wrote some chapters which are quite unconnected and I showed them to Cassells and Praeger. Both said the same: That it would be a lovely book if I would be able to make it interconnected. But, dear Neville, I would not know how to find explanations: It is easier to say 'I do not like so-and-so' . . . instead of saying 'I like him too much. . . .' Dear Neville, I think you overestimate my writing abilities. And if you, as you so kindly suggested, helped me, it would no longer be my book. I think you want to talk about my artistic experiences – but I have a very poor memory and honestly could not tell you what it meant to me to sing with all the great conductors of my time. My singing has always been my expression of myself. What you want is to give a general impression of the time of my career – but there are so many things that cannot be discussed! In general I was known as a 'Lady' – I really was not! I was a primitive human being and your 'My Lady'* reminds me very much of myself!

So please do understand when I say I cannot write my Memoirs – and I neither could accept your assistance. Because – if I write something it has to be absolutely mine.

Please forgive me and take much love from your old friend.

Lotte

All his life Neville had tended to compartmentalise his world.

* Barbe Ede.

Very few of his friends transcended the margins of the specific contexts in which they knew him. As one left the stage, so another made an entrance; while Neville moved from set to set, enjoying each and helping others to do the same, but never resting long enough to become a permanent fixture. There was undoubtedly something in his nature that left him wary of revealing too much of himself to any single audience; hence the feeling expressed by many of his friends that they never knew more than a part of Neville. At his prime this was a happy arrangement, but later on, particularly after many of his closest friends had died, Neville found that there weren't so many people that he could rely on for company. Like many public figures Neville had attracted his share of fair-weather friends; many who had once been only too pleased to bask in his glory, were now less willing to devote an evening to a garrulous, sometime infuriatingly self-centred, octogenarian. Their defection coincided with his greatest vulnerability. He had always liked and needed solitude, but now all too often the prospect of being alone was more than he could stand.

At the start of 1969, yet another publishing house approached Neville. This time it was Cassells and their idea was an 80,000 word book 'about Things, People and Places of a lifetime'. The outcome was *Full Score*, published in 1970. Neville was apprehensive about the venture. 'I have my doubts about it,' he told Harold Priestley, 'but Cassells are very enthusiastic. My swan song!' *Full Score* was indeed to be his last book, and while no one would claim that it could stand comparison with *Autobiography* or even *Second Innings*, as always with Neville it proved to be an entertaining read which also, and almost incidentally, helped place a few more pieces in his autobiographical jigsaw puzzle. But the real importance of the book lay not in its literary merits or its factual content. *Full Score* was probably unique amongst Neville's literary output to the extent that it meant more to him than to its readers. Prompted and encouraged by David Ascoli, Neville found that the act of planning and writing the manuscript not only occupied his time but also gave a meaning and a purpose to his life in the empty days that followed Edith's death.

The name of Cardus is so indelibly linked with the *Manchester Guardian* that it comes as something of a surprise to discover that his last pieces of journalism were the result of requests from a different paper. In asking Neville to contribute a few articles to the *Sunday*

Times, Harold Evans helped dispel some of his (largely misplaced) financial worries as well as providing another much needed morale-booster. As far as Neville was concerned, the invitation was evidence that he was not entirely obselete; that the standards he had set were still respected; that he could still command an audience; and that he still had a place in the modern world.

The interviews with Robin Daniels which were to be the basis of *Conversations With Cardus* had a similarly reviving effect. Daniels's visits to Bickenhall Mansions occupied many a Sunday afternoon in the two years before Neville's death; and if there were times when Neville found the business of being interviewed a trifle tedious, nevertheless he still much enjoyed reflecting on his own life and times. And from the comments of friends and some of the statements found in the final pages of the book itself, it seems that the self-enquiry involved in *Conversations* helped Neville reach, crystallise and articulate a deeper understanding of himself. He found that in the course of talking to Robin Daniels many of the essential strands of his life came together in a way that was for him coherent, if not profound. As he came to view his life on a broader canvas, so much of the disenchantment of the last few years became tolerable. By the end of his life he found that he could talk with regret but not bitterness of 'feeling out of touch', of not 'being sure who my readers are', and of not knowing the 'instrument I'm playing: the *Guardian* is still a great newspaper but it too has changed'. He had glimpsed that 'unity inherent in life itself', not as a precise, detailed vision but, like Wordsworth, as an intimation of 'something far more deeply interfused'; and in so doing had found a sustaining faith in the ineluctable mystery of life. As he told Robin Daniels,

> I feel like quoting George Meredith, from *Modern Love*, which few people read nowadays and yet it contains some of the most marvellous sonnets since Shakespeare. One of them has this couplet:
>
> > Ah what a dusty answer gets the soul,
> > When hot for certainties in this our life.
>
> I don't want certainties; I want mystery.[2]

Mystery may have been the order of the day on Sunday afternoons, but a good deal of this new-found tranquillity and contentment was a product of 'certainty' – the certainty which came from reliable, trusted friends and sympathetic company. During his last years when not too many people were willing to spend their evenings listening to an old man reliving (often more than once) events from his past, it was Neville's final and perhaps greatest stroke of good fortune to have at hand a small circle of devoted friends – people like Eileen Ralph and her husband, Livia Gollancz, John Arlott, Nicholas de Jongh – all of whom still delighted in his company. Most important of all he could always turn to Else Mayer-Lismann, Margaret Hughes and, until her death in 1971, Lilli Williams. Each was in her own way utterly devoted to him, each more than happy to cook for him or eat with him at the London Steak House round the corner from Bickenhall Mansions; each in daily contact by phone if not in person. They rarely met each other, but together they secured a peaceful end to his life.

[II]

Neville died peacefully in his sleep on 28 February 1975, only a few weeks away from his eighty-sixth birthday. A week before he had been found semi-conscious on the floor of his bedroom at Bickenhall Mansions. His last few days were spent in a nearby clinic.

A private cremation service was held at Golders Green where his ashes were also scattered. It had been suggested that Lord's might have been a more appropriate last resting place, but the authorities there thought otherwise. St Paul's Church, Covent Garden, was the setting for his memorial service. Here, on 4 April 1975, a congregation of over two hundred, including two former captains of England and many representatives from the worlds of journalism and music, came together to share in what Father John Hester called 'a celebration' to honour the memory of Sir Neville Cardus. It was a service of thanksgiving organised by his closest friends around the music and words he had loved. Clifford Curzon played the second movement of the Mozart Piano Concerto in A Major (K 488); Dame Flora Robson read one of Shakespeare's sonnets and Wendy Hiller some verses by Francis Thompson, suitably entitled 'At Lord's'; and the Royal Philharmonic Orchestra played. After more Mozart, this time the second movement of his Clarinet Concerto, David Gray brought the occasion to a close with a reading of selected passages from *Second Innings*:

The years flashed by like a kaleidoscope, with one's experiences exquisitely related, each a separate 'shot' in the continuous film of full imaginative living. . . . I confess I cannot, and would not, deny the age of everything that is in me. Only the very young should be new-fashioned; they can grow out of it. . . . Only the material, the rare stuff for imagination's manufacture, is given to us, whether by Bach or the Matterhorn, or by César Franck or by the stillness of snow at Christmas, or by Dickens or Harry Dean. We must ourselves fashion it into spirit and sensibility and weave it into the texture of our being.

Whether the shape or symbol be sonnet or sunset, curve of fiddle-bow or curve of cricket bat, only with our own vision may we see the light and be free to say:

> 'I was for that time lifted
> above the earth,
> And possessed joys not
> promised in my birth.'

NOTES

Prologue
1   N. Cardus, *Autobiography* (London, 1947), p. 123.

1   Origins
1   *Hamlet*, Act 1, Scene 3.
2   W. Dodd, *The Factory System Illustrated* (London, 1968), p. 194.
3   R. Daniels, *Conversations with Cardus* (London, 1976), p. 223.
4   ibid., pp. 249–50.
5   Unpublished MS loaned to the author by Margaret Hughes.
6   F. Engels, *The Condition of the Working Class in England* (trans. W. Henderson and W. Chaloner, Oxford, 1958), p. 54.
7   ibid., p. 46.
8   J. P. Kay, *The Moral and Physical Condition of the Working Classes Employed in the Cotton Manufacture in Manchester* (London, 1832), p. 73.
9   S. D. Simon, *A Century of City Government: Manchester 1838–1938* (London, 1938), p. 112.
10 N. Cardus, *Second Innings* (London, 1950), pp. 8–9.
11 D. K. Royle, *William Royle of Rusholme* (Manchester 1924), p. 34.
12 See M. Kennedy, *The Hallé Tradition* (London, 1960), chapter III.
13 L. Faucher, *Manchester in 1844* (Manchester, 1844), p. 21.
14 C. Aspin, *The First Industrial Civilisation* (Helmshore Local History Society, 1969), p. 81.
15 Faucher, *Manchester in 1844*, p. 21.
16 Cardus, *Autobiography*, p. 48.
17 Simon, *A Century of City Government*, p. 63.

2   *Discovery*
  1   Matthew Arnold, 'The Wanderer'.
  2   Daniel, *Conversations*, p. 254.
  3   Cardus, *Autobiography*, pp. 182–3.
  4   Daniels, *Conversations*, p. 218.
  5   Cardus, *Autobiography*, p. 30.
  6   ibid., pp. 36–7.
  7   Cardus, *Second Innings*, p. 84.
  8   ibid., pp. 148–9.
  9   Cardus, *Autobiography*, pp. 30–1.
 10   ibid., p. 143.
 11   N. Cardus, *Full Score* (London, 1970), p. 97.
 12   Cardus, *Autobiography*, p. 37.
 13   Cardus, *Second Innings*, p. 87.
 14   D. Birley, *The Willow Wand* (London, 1979), p. 165.
 15   Cardus, *Autobiography*, p. 140.
 16   Cardus, *Second Innings*, p. 46.
 17   ibid., p. 51.
 18   ibid., p. 121.
 19   Cardus, *Autobiography*, p. 54.
 20   Cardus, *Second Innings*, p. 132.
 21   ibid., p. 133.
 22   L. Woodward, *Great Britain and the War of 1914–1918*, quoted in R.
       Roberts, *The Classic Slum* (Manchester, 1971), p. 156.

3   *High Summer*
  1   Goethe, *Faust*, 1, 'Studierzimmer'.
  2   Cardus, *Autobiography*, pp. 166–7.
  3   Daniels, *Conversations*, p. 258.
  4   Cardus, *Autobiography*, pp. 105–6.
  5   ibid., pp. 32–3.
  6   Daniels, *Conversations*, p. 212.
  7   Cardus, *Autobiography*, p. 115.
  8   ibid., pp. 128–9.
  9   R. Hart-Davis, *Cardus on Cricket* (London, 1977), pp. 40–1.
 10   Quoted in J. Agate, *Saturday Review*, 7 June 1924.
 11   Cardus, *Autobiography*, pp. 151–2.
 12   *Manchester Guardian*, April 1920.
 13   Grant Richards, *Author Hunting* (London, 1934), pp. 282–3.
 14   Daniels, *Conversations*, p. 62.
 15   R. Hart-Davis, *The Essential Neville Cardus* (London, 1949).
 16   Cardus, 'One Hundred Years of Lancashire', *Guardian*, 6 May 1964.
 17   Quoted in Kennedy, *The Hallé Tradition*, p. 159. I gratefully acknow-

ledge that much of the detailed information about the Hallé Orchestra
contained in the following pages is drawn from this source.
18 ibid., p. 158.
19 Quoted in Cardus, *Full Score*, p. 10.
20 Cardus, *Autobiography*, p. 67.
21 N. Cardus (ed.), *Samuel Langford: Music Criticisms* (Oxford, 1929).
22 Quoted in Kennedy, *The Hallé Tradition*, p. 214.
23 ibid., p. 216.
24 ibid., p. 237 (quoted in).
25 Letter to the author.
26 Cardus, 'Bradman 1930', quoted in Hart-Davis, *Cardus on Cricket*, pp.
    117–18.
27 Hart-Davis, *Cardus on Cricket*, pp. 156–7.
28 Letter to author.
29 Hart-Davis, *Cardus on Cricket*, p. 154.
30 N. Cardus, *Australian Summer – The Test Matches of 1936–7* (London,
    1937), p. 85.
31 M. Hughes (ed.), *Play Resumed with Cardus* (London, 1982), p. 128.
32 Cardus, *Autobiography*, p. 200.
33 N. Cardus, *Ten Composers* (London, 1945), pp. 140–52.
34 Cardus, *Autobiography*, p. 273.

4 *Australia*
1 *Macbeth*, Act 3, Scene 3.
2 Cardus, *Full Score*, p. 163.
3 ibid., p. 173.
4 Cardus, *Second Innings*, p. 225.

5 *Rediscovery*
1 Hermann Hesse, 'September'; lines used by Richard Strauss in his
   'Four Last Songs'.
2 Cardus, *Full Score*, p. 194.
3 Kennedy, *The Hallé Tradition*, p. 291.
4 ibid., p. 289.
5 ibid., p. 303.
6 ibid., p. 305.
7 Cardus, *Autobiography*, p. 244.
8 'Sir Thomas Beecham', *Manchester Guardian*, 24 April 1954.
9 'Klemperer at Eighty', *Guardian*, 20 April 1965.
10 Daniels, *Conversations*, p. 124.
11 Daniels, *Conversations*, p. 88.
12 'Turangalila', *Manchester Guardian*, 14 April 1954.
13 'A New Tonal Concoction', *Guardian*, 10 February 1965.

14 'Pli Selon Pli', *Guardian*, 2 September 1965.
15 Unpublished MS.
16 Unpublished MS.
17 Quoted in Kennedy, *The Hallé Tradition*, p. 349.

6 Passing Years
1 Byron, *Childe Harold's Progress*, II.
2 N. Cardus, *Sir Thomas Beecham: A Memoir* (London, 1961).
3 Daniels, *Conversations*, p. 253.
4 Cardus, *Autobiography*, p. 117.
5 Daniels, *Conversations*, p. 140.

7 Farewell
1 Eighth-century Chinese poems, 'Mong-Kao-Jen' and 'Wang Wei', used by Gustav Mahler as the basis of 'Der Abschied' – the final part of *Das Lied von der Erde*.
2 Daniels, *Conversations*, p. 258.

SELECT BIBLIOGRAPHY

Ayerst, David, *Guardian: Biography of a Newspaper* (Collins, London, 1971)
Cardus, Neville, *A Cricketer's Book* (Grant Richards, London, 1922)
    Days in the Sun: A Cricketer's Journal (Grant Richards, London, 1924)
    The Summer Game: A Cricketer's Journal (Cayme Press, London, 1929)
    Cricket (Longman Green, London, 1930)
    Good Days: A Book of Cricket (Jonathan Cape, London, 1934)
    Australian Summer: The Test Matches of 1936–37 (Jonathan Cape, London, 1937)
    English Cricket (Collins, London, 1945)
    Ten Composers (Jonathan Cape, London, 1945)
    Autobiography (Collins, London, 1947)
    Second Innings (Collins, London, 1950)
    Cricket All The Year (Collins, London, 1952)
    Kathleen Ferrier: A Memoir, ed. Cardus (Hamish Hamilton, London, 1954)
    Close of Play (Collins, London, 1956)
    Talking of Music (Collins, London, 1957)
    A Composer's Eleven (Jonathan Cape, London, 1958)
    Sir Thomas Beecham: A Memoir (Collins, London, 1961)
    The Playfair Cardus (Dickens Press, London, 1963)
    Gustav Mahler: His Mind and His Music (Gollancz, London, 1965)
    The Noblest Game, with John Arlott (Harrap, London, 1969)
    Full Score (Cassell, London, 1970)
Daniels, Robin, *Conversations with Cardus* (Gollancz, London, 1976)
Hart-Davis, Rupert, ed., *The Essential Neville Cardus* (Jonathan Cape, London, 1949)
Kennedy, Michael, *The Hallé Tradition: A Century of Music* (University of Manchester Press, 1960)

INDEX